I0749892

T. B. LARIMORE.

Smiles and Tears

or
Larimore and His Boys

by

F.D. Srygley

ISBN 1-58427-164-7

Guardian of Truth Foundation
P.O. Box 9670
Bowling Green, Kentucky 42102
1-800-428-0121
www.truthbooks.net

PREFACE.

Let it be distinctly understood, once for all, that this book was not written at the request or suggestion of T. B. Larimore. The author alone is responsible for the book, as well as for all it contains. As to T. B. Larimore, his well-known modesty and reticence about himself, and especially about everything connected with his childhood and early youth, rendered the idea of such a book as this exceedingly distasteful to him when his attention was first called to it. He finally consented for it to be published, after much misgiving and serious protest, because the author, as well as many others in whose judgment he had confidence, assured him it would do good. With this explanation, the author asks attention to some of the leading motives which prompted him to bring out this book.

Something may be modestly claimed for the book on the ground of harmless, and, indeed, profitable amusement. It is thought that some of the historic and descriptive passages will provoke a smile as well as point a lesson.

No care has been spared to make the book interesting and profitable to boys. Few boys have ever suffered harder lots or gloomier prospects than the boy Larimore. His trials and triumphs can not, therefore, fail to encourage others. The style and matter of the book, it is hoped, will attract the attention and awaken the interest of the boys, while the story, as a whole, will encourage them to attempt and accomplish great things.

Why should not something be asked for the book on the ground of encouragement for young preachers? Is there nothing in the story of Larimore and his boys to encourage others in a similar work?

Every Christian feels that the work of preaching the gospel, establishing churches and converting sinners is, of all things, the most important; but brethren seem to differ as to the best plan of doing such work. Some favor general co-operation in organized missionary societies, while others stand for personal efforts, aided and directed by the churches, without any general organization apart from the churches. While the author inclines to the opinion that a general organization, properly managed and universally approved, is permissible, according to the Bible, and more efficient than personal efforts as to permanent results, he is not disposed to scoff at the arguments or ignore the work of those who do not agree with him. May not something be claimed for this book on account of its bearing upon this important question? As a sample of work done by personal efforts, without the aid of general organization of any kind, Larimore and his boys at and around Mars' Hill are entitled to more than a passing notice. There were no churches and but few Disciples in all that country when Larimore went there. The country was poor by nature and impoverished by war. Religious prejudice was bitter, and general education sadly deficient. Larimore was young, green and awkward. It is doubtful whether any wisely managed general organization would have trusted him to lead in such an important enterprise. And yet, the work was self-supporting and the workers were all self-reliant from the very first. No aid was ever given by any general organization. It is doubtful whether any general organization could have brought out one-fourth the local support which he rallied to his help. It is also exceedingly problematical whether four-times the amount he spent, if gathered in other fields by a general organization, would have accomplished as much in his field as he accomplished. It is often very helpful to a man to let him help himself. But, while all these things may be said, and not without force, in favor of personal efforts, directed and aided by churches without a general organization, as against a general missionary society apart from the churches, it is still an unsettled question whether a general organization might not have made the work more permanent in nature, and more efficient in perpetuating itself after the man who gave it tone and vigor as a personal work, shall have passed to his reward. While a general organization might not have succeeded as well as this personal effort in immediate results in the beginning, the author inclines to the opinion that what was accomplished would have been more stable, and the churches established would now be more active and efficient if the work had been more systematic and the co-operation of all the forces and resources had been wisely secured and directed by a general organization. The brethren will hardly agree as to this; but whatever the reader's convictions may be touching this question, it is hoped he will find food for reflection and inspiration for renewed efforts in behalf of our common Christianity in a careful examination of the book.

Nothing is claimed for the literary merits of the work. In that line the author has no reputation to maintain and no ambition to gratify. Still, it may be a perfect literary gem for aught he knows to the contrary. As he holds himself incompetent to form a reliable opinion of his own on that point, it seems proper to refer that question to the critics.

Very truly,

F. D. SRYGLEY,

Coal Hill, Ark., May 23, 1889.

SMILES AND TEARS,

OR

LARIMORE AND HIS BOYS.

CHAPTER I.

T. B. Larimore is now in his forty-sixth year, and for more than twenty years he has labored entensively and successfully in the Southern States as a general evangelist. He has probably baptized more people than any other man of his age now living, and possibly he has established more churches of Disciples in the South than any other man of any age, living or dead. He is personally more widely known than any other preacher among the Disciples in the South, and probably more universally popular with all churches and the world as a man and preacher, than any one else wherever he is known. He is a representative Christian in the broadest sense. People differ in opinion as to his gifts of oratory, profundity of thought, thoroughness of scholarship, breadth of intellect and orthodoxy of faith; but all who know him believe implicitly in his depth of piety, honesty of purpose, sincerity of convictions and godliness of life. Everybody calls him *Brother* Larimore, not in a restricted or denominational sense; but in a feeling of broad and Catholic brotherhood in Christ without regard to denominational limitations or the dogmas of church creeds.

As an evangelist, he is free from the sensational methods, low slang and vulgar catch-phrases usually employed by clerical mountebanks who have sustained personal notoriety as traveling evangelists at the sacrifice of all dignity and propriety in the pulpit. During a meeting he never patrols the streets to capture proselytes; he never seeks to popularize his sermons by passages of wit or humor; he never resorts to frivolous anecdotes to illustrate an argument or catch the attention of an audience. He evidently implicity believes the doctrine he preaches, and he delivers it from the pulpit with a solemnity and earnestness which powerfully emphasize the importance he attaches to it.

As a scholar, he is an expert in the use of the English language and thoroughly conversant with the common English version of the Bible. Beyond this, his preaching gives no indication at all as to the extent of his attainments in books. No one can hear one of his sermons without being impressed, yea *charmed*, by the accuracy and nice discrimination he manifests in the use of the English language. In the selection of words, formation of sentences and distinct enunciation of each word in a sentence, every syllable in a word, and even each letter in the syllable, his delivery has the fascination of music to the attentive listener. Every sermon bears abundant evidence of his perfect familiarity with the common version of the Bible. He has not only read the Bible much; but he has evidently studied it carefully sentence by sentence. But from his preaching one would be puzzled to determine whether his education extends any further than this. The fact that he never stumbles into absurd or superficial interpretations of Scripture in the face of scholarly exegesis, would indicate that he is not ignorant of the trend of modern criticism; and the fact that he never manifests want of information touching the established facts of history and the recognized principles of science, would argue that he is a man of general reading and liberal education. But these are only inferences. His sermons are replete with Bible information and expressed in faultless English—whatever may be his attainments as a scholar beyond this does not appear from his preaching, except by inference of the hearer as before explained. Like Paul, he relies upon the revelation of God, rather than the wisdom of man, in his preaching.

Socially, he is very congenial and never disagreeable. He is a good listener in the social circle and a skillful director of conversation. He never compromises his convictions nor engages in a controversy in the social circle. He will listen patiently to any amount of conversation against his most cherished convictions without returning a word in reply or contradiction. If fairly cornered in a way that he must accept or reject a position touching some controverted point in conversation, he never fails to state his convictions plainly and courteously, at the same time waiving all arguments in support of them.

He is reticent, emotional, noncombative and thoroughly devotional by nature. Except in the pulpit he never commits himself on any subject save in strictest confidence to a few close friends. In the pulpit, he never even incidentally expresses an opinion concerning any subject not essentially connected with the theme of his sermon. If he ever has an opinion or preference in politics or on any other subject of absorbing public interest outside of the Scripture themes he discusses in his sermons, the world never learns it. In neighborhood difficulties and church troubles where he labors, all factions love him and have implicit confidence in him; but no body seems to think it the proper thing for him to take sides with one party as against others. In such things he never commits himself, and the people have come to consider his course as a matter of fact and eminently proper. With a large heart, a clear head and a fervent spirit, he preaches the gospel to all. Factionists are not unfrequently drawn away from their petty disagreements and united in love in the great common salvation he so earnestly sets before them. His emotional nature is variable in its moods. His feelings never "pursue the even tenor of their way" for long at a time. He is either on the mountain of transfiguration or leaning over the bridge of sighs. One day he gushes with David, "Bless the Lord, oh my soul, and all that is within me bless his holy name;" the next, he laments with Paul, "If in this life only we have hope in Christ we are of all men most miserable." It is difficult to determine which of those moods is the most favorable for effective speaking with him. When he speaks from the top of the mountains his sermons encourage, elevate, inspire and electrify an audience; when he preaches from the bridge of sighs his hearers are subdued, deeply moved with sympathy, impressed with the worthlessness of this world and its joys and sobered down to a deeper piety and a firmer faith. He never stirs up strife nor provokes antagonisms. He is not combative in nature, and his sermons never arouse a war-like feeling where he goes. He is a religious man by nature, and pious by life-long training. He lives near to his God every hour in his faith and feelings. He believes God is always present with him. In fact, it is something more than believing—he makes it a matter of *consciousness*, of knowledge. There is a very plain and literal meaning, to him, in the text "I *know* that my Redeemer liveth."

His power in the pulpit consists mainly in the plainness

with which he states his propositions, and the pathos and persuasiveness with which he appeals to the hearts of the people in exhortation. The intellect readily approves the correctness of his doctrine, and the heart warmly responds to the tenderness of his appeal. If we add to these two powerful elements of strength as a preacher, his splendid ability as an orator and universal popularity as a man, his wonderful natural gifts and almost perfect educational accomplishments in the use of the English language, his strong faith in what he preaches and his deep piety touching what he believes, years of experience and observation in evangelistic work and a ready and accurate judgment touching human nature, and above all a keen sympathy for all mankind and a perfect familiarity with the teaching of the Bible—if we put all these things together, we have fairly summed up the elements of power in this distinguished evangelist.

The venerable and talented T. W. Caskey, after hearing T. B. Larimore during a protracted meeting in Sherman, Texas, in 1888, said in a private letter:

"For more than half a century I have been mingling with poets and preachers, philosophers and pettifoggers, politicians and philanthropists, statesmen and scientists. I have listened to the eloquence that fell from lips half inspired in congressional halls during our nation's great crisis. I think I know a great man when I see and hear him. I have known T. B. Larimore from boyhood days of sunny youth. I have enjoyed his friendship for years, and have seen him often in his own home in the bosom of his family. At home he is a model man in a model family. To estimate him as a preacher is my present purpose. There are, with me, three elements of mind in which true greatness abides and in which power dwells to move mankind—logic for the thinker, word-painting for the poet, pathos for the sympathetic. Brother Larimore has not the logic of A. Campbell, nor the word-painting of J. B. Furguson, nor the pathos of J. T. Johnson; but he has a happy blending of the three. He reasons well and never violates the laws of logic. At times his descriptive powers rise to the sublime. Often his pathos calls forth tears; but he rarely cries himself. He is not a driveling,crying preacher. He is never sensational in the pulpit; he resorts to no clerical claptrap for effect. He is always deeply in earnest. In social life he never falls below the dignity of a Christian gentleman; in the pulpit he never falls below the dignity of his sublime theme. His style is simple, dignified and prepossessing; his gestures are easy, graceful and natural. His pronunciation, enunciation and emphasis are perfect. In eight lengthy sermons close critics detected but one word erroneously pronounced. In all the sermons I heard, I could not see a single place where I would a word omit, or add a single thought—just enough and not too much at every point. Even in phraseology I could not suggest a change which in my judgment would make it better. This I can not say of any other speaker I have ever heard. He gives no offense to Jew or Gentile, nor to the church of God, nor any other church; and this not from a time-serving policy, for he shuns not to declare the whole counsel of God; but from the nature of the man; his gentleness, meekness, kindness and tenderness make it impossible that any should be offended at him. He is the most universally acceptable preacher in our ranks. We have greater preachers in many particulars; but none better balanced, and few as well balanced. To sum up the man in one sentence, he has the mind of a philosopher, the heart of a woman and the innocence and guilelessness of a little child."

J. T. Spaulding, of Nashville, Tenn., a business man of wide experience and extensive observation of men, and now filling an important position in a large railroad corporation, says, in a private letter:

"I have known T. B. Larimore several years, and I regard him as one of the greatest men I have ever known. He is a pure, earnest Christian man who loves God and his fellow men. He would consider no sacrifice too great to make for the cause of Christ and for his fellow men. His powers as a preacher of the gospel are second to none. He has absolute command of the English language, and can clothe his thoughts in more beautiful expressions than any man I have ever seen. Everybody who comes in contact with him loves him."

Mrs. E. Cooper, of Nashville, Tenn., a woman distinguished by many natural talents and varied accomplishments, and withal an excellent judge of human nature, gives the following interesting description of him:

"One of the most noticeable things about Mr. Larimore, in the pulpit, is a remarkably youthful look. A gleam of pleasure lightens his countenance, and almost a smile touches his lips as he recognizes, here and there, a familiar face in the congregation, and he seems to feel the 'blessed influence' of the 'faithful friends' about him. It is easy to see the earnest purpose of the steadfast soul in the luminous depth of his expressive eyes. He seems ever conscious of the sacredness of his place and calling, and brings to his work a quiet, gentle dignity which impresses his hearers at once and imparts to them a portion of his own humility and prepares them to listen attentively to what he has to say.

"To an almost unrivaled gift of language is added, in him, a vivid imagination, and his mind and heart are religiously cultured and attuned to the highest and noblest aspirations. There is no looking back with him; he feels and says that 'things without remedy should be without care.' He goes ever onward in patient simplicity and purity of character, doing his work for God's and Christ's sake. With him, 'That only is important which is eternal.' To the aid of other talents he has brought the genius of hard work. As Buffon says, he has 'an infinite capacity for taking pains.' He shows this in the careful placing of verb, adjective and preposition; in the nicely rounded periods; in profound, tried thoughts; in the almost inspired harmony of gesture, voice and language. He has a pure, magnetic voice, clear, resonant and penetrative, and his enunciation is so distinct that every word he utters is easily understood in the furthest corner of a crowded auditorium. Occasionally there comes to his voice, when raised in invocation or in earnest pleading with sinners, a sudden pathetic tremor or drooping of tone which adds greatly to the power of his pathos. Very deaf persons have heard, understood and enjoyed his sermons, when the sermons of louder, shriller, harsher-voiced preachers were unintelligible to them. After listening to one of the latter a few times, it is a positive luxury to the tired ear and brain to come within the sound of the rythmn and pure cadences of his voice. In his speaking there is no straining after effect. The modulations are pure, correct and under perfect control, the voice rises grandly to a climax and the changing, deepening intonations produce an electrical effect upon his hearers. The dull, heavy prose of doctrinal points is turned into the purest poetry, and the soul of the hearer, too weary, perhaps, to lift itself, is raised to his own high plane of thought and feeling. If he but touches the mountain tops of thought, he makes clear some difficult or obscure passages and pierces with rays of light the mists veiling some doubt-tortured heart.

"He never rants, and his sermons are not marred by slang phrases, coarse vulgarisms, or theatrical starts, pauses or poses. There is nothing of the clerical mountebank in him. He does not pretend at any time that he feels more righteous than the God he serves, or more liberal than Jesus Christ. He understands that divine and human wisdom are allies only when the 'human is subservient to the divine.' He leaves no crooked furrows in the minds or souls of his hearers; but sows patiently the seeds of humility, gratitude and the desire to promote all good and no evil. He is so remarkably free from the pulpit errors of the day that there is but little in his work as a preacher to criticise, and certainly nothing to ridicule. His language is concise and simple, a dignified self-possession characterizes him, and his gestures are easy and natural, therefore graceful. There is no unseemly haste or groping about for ideas or words. He does not dull the Sword of the Spirit by apologies. He has a story to tell and he tells it so plainly that the children on the platform at his feet—he never denies the children room in the pulpit when the house is crowded—understand and believe it. He has a message for saints and sinners, and he delivers it without fear or partiality. There is no obtrusion of his own determinations or personal feelings into his sermons. One does not become acquainted with the number and names of the members of his family or friends from hearing his preaching. The listener could not tell he had such ties save that in the deeper tones of his voice and the yearning tenderness of his language, he reveals such sacred secrets of his heart when he speaks of 'the blessed home,' the 'blessed mother,' the 'blessed wife,' the 'blessed children,' or the 'blessed friends.' When you hear him use such expressions you intuitively know he not only has all such ties, but that he appreciates them as only a sensitive, loving nature can.

"That Mr. Larimore does not lack spirituality or ability, and that his pleading is not in vain, the numbers added to the churches where he labors attest. 'What do you think of the preacher?' one lady asked another at the close of one of his sermons. 'I think he believes what he preaches' was the prompt answer. That was a high compliment, and it touched the secret of his power in the pulpit.

"He has the virtue of punctuality, as well as executive tact and ability. He readily adapts himself to his surroundings in the many and varied conditions of life through which his work leads him without losing, for a moment, the Christian dignity and humility which always clothe him as a garment. He is equally at home with the rich and the poor, and he knows how to be 'all things to all men' in the Scriptural sense.

"A quiet vein of humor shows in him occasionally, and he sometimes uses it to good effect. He was once preaching for a congregation whose members were in the habit of rushing out of the house as soon as the benediction was pronounced. This did not suit his warm-hearted nature; he believes in the power of friendliness expressed in hearty handshaking. He gave them a short lecture about their haste to leave the house, and closed by saying that when he pronounced the benediction he did not mean to say '*scat.*' The effect may be imagined. The congregation at once developed a staying capacity, and a gratifying habit of general handshaking after the benediction.

"One of the pleasantest features of the man in social life is his appreciableness. That may not be exactly the right word; but it seems to convey the idea. No one can feel cramped or embarrassed in his company, or at a loss for a moment for something to talk to him about. The common things of life interest him in conversation, though his work for Christ is ever the subject of chief concern with him. The 'blessed Savior' is the burden of all his sermons, and a burning anxiety to save souls the subject of all his thoughts and prayers. A few lines from Jean Ingelow will express the sentiments of many hearts concerning his preaching:

"'I have heard many speak;
But this one man,
So anxious not to go to heaven alone,
This one man I remember,
And his look.'"

Similar estimates of him as a man and preacher might be added to the foregoing indefinitely from men and women of every station in life and of every vocation and degree of intelligence. Everybody loves him and compliments him; nobody ever criticises him. It remains to notice a phase of his character which is known to but few, but which is none the less lovable on that account. As a confidential friend, the few who know him in that relationship are unstinted in his praise. His most secret motives are as pure and lovely when revealed to his closest friends, as his public life. He is not a man of the whited-sepulcher kind. He is careful to make clean the *inside* of the cup and platter as well as the *outside.* One who has enjoyed the closest and most confidential relationship with him for years, gives the following account of his innocent, rolicking nature when in the freedom and privacy of his small confidential circle:

"In 1878 I met him at his home toward the close of his evangelistic labors in the vacation of Mars' Hill College. He was completely worked down, and I urged him to take a rest and have some fun before beginning another session. He is a very discreet man, and never suffers a feeling of relaxation or spirit of levity to break the force of his preaching in potracted meetings, and hence I advised him to leave off all preaching for a week and take a horseback trip for fun and recreation through the country and among the mountains. I agreed to go with him on such a trip, and he was to write me at a certain place by a certain day if he could make his arrangements for the trip. At the appointed time and place I received a card without date or signature in his well-known writing, with one word heavily underscored and designedly misspelled, '*Kum.*' I answered by card with one word, without date or signature, spelled after like manner, '*Kumming.*' I went on to his house, and he laughed heartily over our novel correspondence, saying it had the merits of military brevity and orthographical originality. Our journey was to be through a very rough, hilly country, inhabited by very poor and illiterate people. He decided to ride a young horse he called Napoleon, a large, lazy, awkward animal without a single trait of a saddle horse. He greatly admired the animal and insisted on riding him because, he said, Napoleon was too brave to scare and too lazy to run away. Those who have seen Larimore on horseback will agree that cautiousness in holding on, and not gracefulness of attitude, is his strong point as an equestrian. Before mounting, he carefully examined every part of saddle and bridle to see that everything was strong and properly adjusted. Then he mounted, doubled his long legs up till his knees were in his lap and his big feet firmly planted in the stirrups, grasped the bridle firmly with one hand and the horn of the saddle with the other, and with eyes rivited on Napoleon's head, gave the word and we started. While Napoleon would neither scare nor run, he

2

seemed to be an expert in falling down. This was a great hinderance to us, as it necessitated a dismount at every rough place in the road. I shall never forget that trip. A whole week were we together among the poor inhabitants of that mountain country. He was at home wherever we went; he talked freely of himself and his work; his spirits were always bouyant, and he showed an appreciation of the ridiculous I had not before suspected him capable of. He revealed his inner life to me on that trip as he had never done before, and the revelation made me love him more than ever before."

Such is the man, now in his forty-sixth year. It is the design of the following chapters to give an account of his development from childhood to manhood. Every boy should feel especially interested in such an account. The road he has traveled is the royal road of life. It is the path of the good and the great, and boys who will walk in it can not fail to attain a measure of the success he now enjoys in life.

CHAPTER II.

I first met Theophilus Brown Larimore at Rock Creek, Ala., in July, 1868. Any effort to describe what manner of man he then was would be incomplete without a few words descriptive of that country and its inhabitants. Rock Creek is a small stream in the hill country of North Alabama, and in those days was understood to extend from Reuben Yarbrough's Spring, in Colbert County, to Bear Creek, in Franklin County, a distance of perhaps twelve miles as the crow flieth. It was crowded in between rugged mountains for the greater part of the distance, and hence offered but little inducement to farmers in the way of bottom lands for agricultural purposes. The largest body of bottom land on any one farm along that creek near the point now under consideration was estimated at sixteen acres by a liberal count. The country for many miles around in every direction was rough, hilly, rocky, and by no means productive. Here and there patches of hill-side lands, with an occasional level spot on the hill-tops, were utilized for agricultural purposes, but the great bulk of the country was uncultivated and lay wild in native forests, barren rocks and rugged mountains. It was a country of springs. No purer water ever blessed the earth than gushed from the innumerable springs among those mountains. And the water from those many springs glided merily down the hill-sides, filling the land with picturesque waterfalls which rippled cheerily all the year round.

The people were healthy, but poor. They were simple in customs, but honest of heart. They were not highly educated as the world counts education, but they were strong in practical sense and trained by experience and observation in the matter of drawing conclusions from what they saw and heard.

That was a great country for dogs. It was said that in olden times game of various kinds abounded there. In those early days dogs were appreciated for their value in hunting the game. The game had long since departed, but the dogs remained. And being entirely useless, they were simply carried about whithersoever their masters listed, and not unfrequently found their way to church whether anybody listed or not. To a stranger, so many dogs at church might have seemed out of place; but to those accustomed to their presence they seemed appropriate enough. A stranger might even have suggested that so many dogs in church would disturb public worship; but those good people could hardly have seen how that could be possible. Who that appreciates preaching and really wants to hear a good sermon, they thought, could be disturbed by a living pyramid of fighting dogs in the open space about the pulpit? Such a thing might attract the attention of frivolous girls and fun-loving boys; but what does a real worshiper care for a dog fight so long as there is no disposition among the owners of the dogs to take up the quarrel? A stuck-up preacher might have felt it necessay to suggest that the dogs be put out of the church, but those people would have wanted to know very promptly what the preacher had to do with their dogs. Was he not there to preach the gospel? What right had he to take any part in a dog-fight anyhow?

There were many things along and about Rock Creek worthy of special note, not the least interesting of which, to my childish mind, was Bill Sanderson's mill. It was about half a mile below the spring where the creek had its source, and was wedged in between two large hills, adown the steep sides of which the waters rushed, while it was raining, with immense volume. The mill-dam extended from hill to hill, so that a dashing rain would accumulate a considerable pond of water in a very short time. And the way that mill would rattle around and spirt out meal while that water was running off, opened my childish eyes with astonishment and caused me to regard the miller as possessed of valuable property and lacking only sufficient capital to push it to make a great fortune. The lack of capital finally caused the downfall of the enterprise. The people could rarely get their corn to the mill till the water would be all gone. If the miller had only had capital enough to keep corn of his own to grind while he had water, he might have exchanged meal for corn at a good profit when the people came in with their corn and found the water all out. He did drive a fair trade of that kind as far as he was able; but he never could get corn enough on hands to make the thing a success. So the water power, what little there was of it, was abandoned, and a horse power substituted for it. This was not so fast, but it was far more regular in its methods of business. One day father sent me with a large, but not very reliable, mule, to grind at the mill. The mule took a fright and dashed off at break-neck speed, and I skipped out and left him to spin around the circle in his own original style. When I got into the mill-house the top stone had jumped out of socket and was whirling around over the floor like mad, seeking what it might devour.

Another thing of neighborhood importance was the meeting-house known as Rock Creek Church. It was built for all denominations to preach in, and was also used as a school-house. At first it was a log house, perhaps about twenty-four feet square, but as it proved to be entirely too small for the audiences that assembled there, an addition of about the same dimensions was made to it. This made the house about forty-eight feet long, by twenty-four feet wide. The pulpit was set in the side of the house, and right where the old and the new parts of the building joined. This pulpit was a sort of box, about ten feet long by probably six feet wide, one side and one end of which were open. This box-like concern was set on posts about two feet high, the open side up and the open end constituting an entrance for the preacher. The book board extended the full length of the side of the box which fronted towards the audience. In depth this box-like pulpit was about four feet, so that a very short preacher, when standing, was only visible to the audience from his shoulders and upward, while all preachers, of whatever size, were alike invisible when seated. In those days it was thought to be a good thing for preachers to take a little wine for their stomach's sake and for their often infirmities, and most of the preachers in that country seemed to have stomach troubles and infirmities of one sort and another. They had discovered, too, that other spirits acted more effectually than wine upon their peculiar maladies, so that there seems to have been a sort of fitness in the box-like pulpit which concealed them, when seated, from the scrutinizing gaze of the vulgar audience. Thus concealed they did not receive, indiscriminately, every kind of spirit; but they tried the spirits while the congregation engaged in singing. Do not think this a thing incredible. While such a thing now seems unreasonable, it was then no unusual occurrence for preachers to try the spirits. Thanks to temperance workers for this great change in public sentiment.

A hole about three feet wide by four feet long, called a window, but without glass or shutter, immediately behind the pulpit, afforded light and ventilation for the preacher; while a similar arrangement on the opposite side of the house immediately in front of the pulpit provided an outlet for the rousing exhortations and ear-splitting yells of strong-lunged brethren and soul-happy sisters. There were other windows of the same general description scattered along the side of the house, and a large hole, called a door, in each end of it. That part of the house which was built of logs had other and more abundant ventilation through the large cracks between the logs, and such a thing as ceiling any part of the building, overhead or around the walls, was an idea that perhaps had never occurred to any one who worshiped there. The only means to warm the audience were log fires, built in a stick and dirt chimney, and the preachers' exhortations, each of which usually contained more smoke than fire. One end of the house, with its door, was set apart for women, while the other was given to men. On this point public opinion drew the line with rigid exactness. A man "on the women's side of the house" would have created a sensation indeed. Dogs could cross the line with impunity and mingle with the women at pleasure; but a man? never! The seats were logs split in halves and supported upon pegs driven into augur holes underneath. Such things as rests for feet or supports for backs were strangers to those seats.

The addition to Rock Creek Church was built of boards, or perhaps I ought to say slabs, from Sam Kennedy's saw-mill—another enterprise of which the neighborhood felt justly proud. It was run by horse power, and four horses could pull it fairly well. The saw was a piece of steel about three or four feet long, perhaps six inches wide and about one-fourth of an inch thick, with two teeth—one tooth in each end. When running it revolved rapidly, and each tooth took a whack at the saw-log every revolution. It was called a peck saw, and in the course of a day it would peck through several logs turning off a dozen or more nice, new boards, besides slabs and sawdust in great abundance. One day old Tag, the miller's dog, came nose-ing around while the saw was in motion, and, in less time than it takes to tell it, he was pecked into mince meat, and his disfigured carcass spattered all over a lot of nice new lumber.

There was a post-office at Rock Creek, and the mail came out once a week from Cherokee, a small town on the Memphis & Charleston Railroad. When the office was established after the war no pouch was provided in which to carry the mail. But that was of no consequence. The contract for carrying the mail was awarded to Uncle Jeff Smith, and his overcoat pocket was large enough to hold all the mail on that route with room enough left for his gloves and lunch. And in his over-coat pocket he carried that mail regularly once a week for months. What need for lock and key? Did not everybody know uncle Jeff? Perish the thought of ever locking anything from *him!*

In early days they had many preachers in that country. My father was one of the first settlers, and he remembers that there were thirteen preachers in the sparsely settled neighborhood of perhaps twenty families. Every body preached who believed himself called of God to the ministry, and the crude religion of that day recognized a mysterious "call to preach" in almost every thing that happened out of the usual course of things. To one man the fact that he could not sleep well at night was evidence that God wanted him to preach, while to another the death of a favorite child was God's clear call to the ministry. One incident of those days, often related and generally believed to be true, will serve to illustrate how so many men were called to preach. A man named Walker heard a powerful voice in the distance which seemed to say very distinctly—"Walker—go preach—go preach—go preach!" Now Walker had been greatly troubled in spirit many days to decide whether God had really called him to preach, and was just discussing the evidences of his call with Jesse Stanford, a notorious sinner, when that voice, clear and distinct, awakened the echoes in the stillness of the night. Jesse said, "Do you hear that? God is calling you now." No longer doubting his call, good Bro. Walker began at once to preach, and continued in the ministry to the day of his death. The value of such calls to the ministry may be inferred from the fact that Jesse Stanford always contended that Walker's call was simply the braying of John Taylor's donkey!

They had camp meetings in those days, and such revivals as modern times have never witnessed. The way they could preach and pray and exhort may be inferred from a few facts and incidents, gathered from those who were eye witnesses of the glory of those good times of old.

One of the preachers, being requested to pray for the mourners during a great revival, earnestly, solemnly and seriously besought the Lord "to come down and take one of the mourners by the hair of the head, jump across hell and drop him in as a warning to the others."

One of the preachers who heard experiences before admitting persons into his church, received a young lady upon the statement that she dreamed she was a chicken and saw a hawk high up in the heavens above her. The hawk swooped down to catch her, but she darted through the fence and escaped. The interpretation was clear to the preacher and satisfactory to the church. Evidently the hawk was the devil. The young sister had escaped him by darting into the fold of grace, but the escape was a narrow one.

Once the question was gravely discussed in the neighborhood as to whether a man could possibly learn, by reading the Bible, how to get to heaven. The question was finally referred to the preachers of the neighborhood, who, after long and careful consideration and investigation, decided that a man might possibly learn how to get to heaven by reading the Bible provided he could live long enough to read it through carefully; but they did not believe any man ever lived long enough to read every thing in as large a book as the Bible! This incident dates back in the forties when the best scholars among the preachers in that country could only read the familiar texts they had carefully practiced passibly well, while many of them did not pretend to try to read at all.

Once when a great revival was in progress at Rock Creek church, my father bought a new wagon in Frankfort, and, leaving one of his men behind to bring the wagon, he rode on to the church and there stopped, partly to be at night meeting and partly to wait for his man to come up with the wagon and team. The wagon had never been oiled, and, being of the old style wooden axle kind, it made a most hideons screeching. The preaching was over, and the meeting was wholly given over to shouting and praying for the mourners. It was one of those times of refreshing when everybody seemed anxious to hear Gabriel's trumpet calling the world to judgment. They were all ready to go and anxious to be off. Then the wagon drew near, making night hideous with its unearthly sounds. One of the mourners was the first to hear it. He waited not for an investigation, but made for the door, saying, as he went—"Tarnation ef Gabriel aint a blowin' right now!" Then they all began to hear it, and in a moment the greatest confusion prevailed. My father was not a member of any church, but he was a great lover of a practical joke. As they asked no questions, he volunteered no information, so the people all dispersed in confusion without thinking to leave another appointment, and that revival closed prematurely in the midst of great interest.

Several years after the State had inaugurated its free-school system, my father was elected county superintendent of public schools. In that neighborhood lived a man who often boasted that he had thirteen children and had never sent to school but thirteen days. So fixed was he in his prejudice against the extravagance of "book larnin'," he had not even learned there was such a thing as *a free-school.* One day he said to my father—"Jim, they tell me you have got up some sort of a 'cahoot' to get money frum some furin country to pay school teachers to teach our children 'book larnin' free." When he was assured that the State had been supporting free-schools for many years, he said: "Well, hanged if ever I hearn tell of such a thing till yesterday. I started my thirteen chaps this morning, and bust me if I don't make 'em keep the path hot as long as this thing lasts!"

I have not drawn upon my imagination for anything in this chapter. I have not even exhausted the list of commonly received facts. These things are not written for the idle purpose of holding that country up to ridicule. It was my home, and is still dearer to me than any other spot on the globe. I am not ashamed of the place, nor of the people. Railroads and other modern improvements, along with a portion of what we call the enlightenment of the nineteenth century, have changed all those things. Some of the changes are for the better; but who shall say not one of them is for the worse? If I smile at the queer ways of those dear folks about the old home in the sweet long ago, it is not because I think we have gained everything and lost nothing in the changes that have come over the spirit of our dreams. How many times, in the dark and dreary trials of life since I left those blessed scenes of my childhood, would I have given worlds, if I had possessed them, to exchange scholarly words of consolation and encouragement, spoken in rounded periods and well modulated voices, for the homely language of sympathy and love fresh from the guileless hearts of those old-time folks. How many times, in trouble and disappointment, have I thought with gloomy heart and weary soul, of that dear old place and its associations, as I drearily sang:

"Some day I'll wander back again
To where the old home stands
Beneath the old tree down the lane
Afar in other lands!"

But I have written this chapter to give the reader an idea of the sort of country in which that now great and always good man—Theophilus Brown Larimore began his ministerial labors.

The incidents related in this chapter refer to a comparatively small territory in the hill country of North Alabama. In point of time, they cover a period from about 1840 to the beginning of Larimore's preaching there in 1868.

CHAPTER III.

Such a congregation as might be expected at such a place as is described in the preceding chapters, had assembled to hear the new preacher. Old brother John Taylor, had announced beforehand, that the stranger was a young man just out of College, an eloquent speaker, a learned man and a mighty preacher. Now it was something unusual for a college preacher to visit Rock Creek, and many of the congregation had perhaps never seen a genuine graduate from college. It is possible that many people in that audience felt no other interest in the occasion than a mere idle curiosity to see and hear a man who had really been to college. The irrepressible small boy was there as usual and as a matter of course, and seems to have been sufficiently numerous and inquisitive to attract the special attention of the new preacher. In a private letter, referring to that occasion years afterwards, he wrote:

"A little black-eyed boy had taken his stand a few feet from the narrow path leading to the door of the meeting house, and was standing there barefooted, hands in pockets, eyes and mouth open, to get a glimpse of the big preacher he had 'hearn tell of.' The preacher turned aside to speak to the little fellow, and to take him by the hand, and thus began a friendship that nothing but death can ever destroy."

The first impression of the entire congregation after "sizing him up" was unconcealed disappointment. There was nothing in his dress or outward appearance to distinguish him from common preachers of that country. I shall not attempt any further description of him than to say he looked both green and awkward. Doubtless he took in the situation at once, and felt that he was received under protest and at a heavy discount. Of this, his first appearance at Rock Creek, he wrote good humoredly in a private letter, years afterwards:

"One striking point of analogy between my appearance then and the beginning—at birth—I was bald headed. A barber at Tuscumbia, taking me for a tramp and encouraged by some dudes, shaved my head, *en route* to Rock Creek, as a sort of practical joke. That was when hair was fashionable all the year round. The bigness of the preacher, he thought, consisted much in the baldness of his pate; but Rock Creek evidently did not think so."

He did not stop to discuss the best plan of *sending* the gospel to destitute places. While others were arguing that question, *he went and took it.* Nor does it seem that he troubled himself much about the best plan of going; but availed himself of the only plan in his reach, of which he said, in a private letter, years afterward, in his characteristic off-hand and good humored style: "I made that missionary tour by private conveyance—*on foot.*" It seems that he had money enough to pay his way by railroad to Tuscumbia. Leaving the railroad at that point, he was fortunate enough to fall in with a gentleman traveling in a buggy in the direction he wished to go whose kind invitation to a seat in the buggy he thankfully accepted. About night fall, however, their ways parted, and he was set out of the buggy at the forks of the road alone in a strange country. It was a desolate spot, no signs of human habitation in sight; but towering mountains, rugged cliffs and dark deep ravines all around him. Fortunately his baggage was not cumbersome, consisting only of a plain cheap Bible, an extra shirt and a paper collar! He walked on till he came to the humble home of good old brother Taylor, who received him with joy and gave him genuine Christian entertainment for the night in the very best style his poor home could afford. The next day he met the anxious and curious congregation at Rock Creek and began his first meeting of much importance.

Everything about him was expressive of Christian humility, deep piety and intense earnestness, and, from the first, every body felt that he was a good man, actuated only by a sincere desire to do good. His dress was plain and cheap, but neat and becoming a Christian, and such as that entire congregation of very poor people could well afford to imitate. In manner he was unassuming, frank, cheerful, dignified and courteous to all. His voice was the wonder and delight of all who heard him. It was strong and sonorous, but well modulated and so full of tenderness, love and persuasive pathos, that it gave a new beauty and power to the plain commandments of God and the touching story of the cross. In exhortation, he melted an audience to tears as if by magic, and the love of God, the death of Christ and the hope of the saints were the only themes he chose during all that meeting for the exhortations that followed every sermon with such good effects. He preached to us so earnestly and spoke to us so kindly, that we all began to love him from the very first. Even before he preached, we were in love with him. He did not seem to think he was very smart, and certainly there was nothing in his appearance to indicate that he underestimated himself. So great was our love for him, and so intense our anxiety to see him succeed, that we all began to be afraid he could not preach very well, and each one seemed anxious to help him all he could. We loved him so much that we could not bear the thought of his making a failure.

Before he preached, an incident occurred among the small boys which illustrates the strong hold he had upon the ruder element of that class of society. Some boys having indulged in a few uncomplimentary remarks concerning his green appearance and awkward movements, wound up by expressing the opinion that he was not much of a preacher any how. Instantly two dirty-faced urchins championed his cause and proposed to lick any body who said he was not the best preacher that had ever been to Rock Creek.

When he began to preach we all felt relieved. He could preach and no mistake. His command of language was simply wonderful. He never hesitated for a word, and seemed always to express himself in the most choice way without premeditation. Plainness of speech and simplicity of illustrations were marked features of his sermons. We could all understand him, and, what is better, we remembered his sermons. I heard him preach sermons then which I have not heard since, and yet I remember them distinctly and could easily repeat from memory the leading thoughts in them.

Of course he knew he was in the backwoods. He could see that the people were very poor and very ignorant. Yet not a word, nor a look, nor a gesture ever indicated that he considered them unworthy of his very best efforts to present the gospel in its strongest light. In later years I have seen him before select audiences of the rich, refined, and educated, in fashionable city churches; but I have never known him to try harder to win souls to Christ than during that meeting. I have seen him the favored and flattered guest of wealth and refinement; but I have never seen him more appreciative of acts of hospitality than when he shared the humble fare of the poor in their log huts during that meeting. I have seen him in the presence of great sorrow, in high life, in richly upholstered parlors and surrounded by every comfort and luxury refined taste could suggest and money could buy; but I have never seen him more deeply moved by sympathy or more successful in speaking words of consolation, than when seated beside a heart-broken widow on a rough bench in a log hut surrounded by tokens of poverty, wretchedness and despair. I have heard many mothers appeal to him to make special efforts to save their wayward sons; but I have never seen him more deeply moved by those who came in silk and dazzling jewels than by those who came in homespun garb and honest poverty. He does his best for all.

As we knew him to be a college preacher, we naturally expected him to talk much about Latin, Greek, Hebrew and all that sort of thing. But we were disappointed. He not only did not advert to those languages at all; but he even studied to select the very plainest words of the English language. And in his illustrations he used only such things as were perfectly familiar to every body in that country. The meeting was less than a week in duration; but it resulted in about twenty conversions, most of whom were leaders in neighborhood affairs. It also made a deep and lasting impression upon the community for many miles around. Another result of the meeting was the establishment of Rock Creek church, from the membership of which in later years came some good preachers and valuable church workers who are now scattered over the country doing valuable service for the Lord in several different states. It was his first meeting of special importance, and it gave abundant promise and assurance of the great power he was destined to wield over the people as an evangelist. From Rock Creek he went to Hopewell, in Lauderdale

3

county by such conveyance as the brethren were able to provide for him. That conveyance was probably the good old Jerusalem kind, *viz:* riding a donkey, or mule, which was the nearest possible approach to the Lord's plan. Of his reception at Hopewell, he wrote at length in his own peculiar style in a private letter in 1888.

"I came to Hopewell to hold a protracted meeting. They let me try to preach once, and they were so well pleased with that 'sarmint' that they let me off—suddenly! The meeting closed with a jerk and a bang. It was not wound up much, hence required but little time to run down; or, perhaps it ran down so very fast is why it struck bottom so quick. It was wound up for eight days and it ran down in an hour. An Irishman once said: 'They thuck me into the church for six months on trial; but I did so well they let me off in three months.' Hopewell did better by me than that—they took me for eight days and let me off in sixty minutes. Well, they did exactly right. They reasoned thus: 'We have had none but good preachers here; we are few and weak; our enemies hold the fort and camp on the field. Now, if we let *him* try to preach here, it is good bye to our prospects. Better have no preaching than his sort.' Then they said: "What shall we do with him? This will we do—Brother and sister Young live a way back—good preachers rarely go there; they will appreciate any kind of preaching; to them will we send him.' They said to me: 'We will take you to Bro. Young's; he and sister Young and Frank and another one or two are the church there; they are good people and will treat you well.' They sent me—I believe Bro. Andrew Gresham took me in a buggy. I could have walked though if I had known the way, in three or four hours. It was only fourteen miles, and twenty miles before dinner was not unusual walking for me then; but I am getting old now. They treated me well, that they did, and we had a glorious meeting in an old log meeting house then occupied by what were called Hard Shell Baptists in that country. I remember how the weather *did not* stop us, though it rained almost incessantly. The motto of that meeting was the old negro's saying 'nebber mine de wedder so de win' doan blow.' Well do I remember baptizing some young ladies when it was raining—Oh! it fell in torrents. I thought the crowds on the bank of the little stream in which we were baptizing must hear the ceremony; so I pronounced it at the top of my voice, but could scarcely hear it myself. It was all right; no body grumbled; no body took cold; no body said, 'Too bad weather for a meeting.' What teachers and preachers came out of that meeting. That was a wet nest, and the house was a 'Hard Shell' house; but some wonderful birds were hatched then and there. Hopewell sent me to the right place. Had I been a big preacher I might have stayed at Hopewell. What then of the noble hearts and brilliant minds that were won for Jesus in that meeting? I am drifting, simply drifting, ever drifting, have always been drifting—before the breath of Providence. Mattie, George, Bennett—these are some of the converts made at that meeting."

The George of the last sentence is George P. Young, President of Orange College, Stark, Florida, and well known as an able preacher; Bennett is W. B. Young, an able Christian minister now of St. Louis, Mo., and well known throughout the Christian church as an accomplished scholar and gifted preacher; and Mattie is Mrs. Mattie Y. Murdock, for several years teacher in the city school of Ennis, Texas, and recognized wherever she is known as a thorough scholar and highly talented lady of many literary accomplishments. The confident declaration of faith in Providential guidance is characteristic of the man. With him it is always "God's own hand that leadeth me." He never for a moment doubts but that God is leading and helping him in every thing he undertakes to do. In this one thing his faith is simply sublime.

CHAPTER IV.

T. B. Larimore made his first missionary tour through North Alabama on foot in company, for the most part, with John Taylor. The latter was one of the first preachers of the doctrine of that church in that country, and his ministerial labors dated back to the very beginning of the reformation. His life, and the condition of the churches throughout that country soon after the close of the war, as well as their establishment and history, therefore, constitute a part of our story. A queer old man was John Taylor. In early life he was a Baptist; but he always had a way of thinking out conclusions for himself which constantly brought him no little trouble in that church. He never could understand from reading the New Testament that God had promised to pardon his sins before baptism, and hence caused trouble at the very beginning of his religious life by requesting to be baptized "for the remission of sins." However, he was received into the church by a special and very liberal interpretation of what then prevailed as "Baptist usage" in that country, and soon he began to preach. Then came the tug of war. Those people were not the sort of folks to quietly sit and hear John Taylor or any body else say their religious ideas were not correct, and John Taylor was not the sort of man to fail to declare his honest convictions from the pulpit. Enough has been said in a former chapter about the preachers and preaching of that day and country to show how vulnerable their crude ideas of religion were from a Bible stand point, and John Taylor was just the sort of a man to improve every opportunity to expose and correct errors. He had long tolerated errors and excesses in the guise of religion, because he neither wished to be an agitator against time-honored traditions, nor saw any definite way to correct them; but once the issue was fairly made and the conflict openly begun, he gave himself wholly and unreservedly to the support of his cause. The first move was to exclude him from the Baptist church for preaching Campbellism. "And before God, brethren," the old man would say in his earnest manner in after years, "I had never heard of Campbellism nor of Alexander Campbell before in all my life." That was way back when Campbell first began to preach. The truth is, he learned Campbellism from the New Testament and was excluded from the Baptist church for preaching it in North Alabama before he ever heard of Alexander Campbell or his teaching. John Taylor was a brave man and an honest one too, whatever else may be said about him, and as such he preached his convictions. From the time he was excluded from the Baptist church for preaching Campbellism, it is impossible for any one who knows nothing about those times to form any idea as to the fierceness and bitterness of the war of words and clash of arguments which agitated the people of every neighborhood. It was literally a hand-to-hand conflict, unceasing and without quarters. There were no reserve forces on either side; all the available forces of both sides were called into action. The moral courage and self-sacrificing zeal and devotion to convictions exhibited by the grand old man and his few co-laborers in North Alabama in the early days of the reformation, beggar all powers of description. Shoulder-to-shoulder with him in those days which tried men's souls, stood John McKaleb, of Fayette county, Jerry Randolph and his brother Dow, Mat Hackworth and a few others. These were all men of courage and convictions, and each the equal of John Taylor in every respect. It is to be regretted that no connected history of those men and their labors has been preserved. I knew John Taylor from my earliest recollection, and many an hour have I listened to him tell of the trials and triumphs of his teaching in North Alabama in the beginning of the reformation. But as I have no chronological order of events, I can only give the account of certain incidents which impressed themselves upon my mind as I heard them related by good old brother Taylor on more than one occasion. From such broken fragments of history as these, the reader is left to infer the general character of those times.

John Taylor was a smith and carpenter by trade, and so constant was the discussion of religious themes among all classes of people, that he never went to his shop without his Bible. He had a way of carrying a small leather bound Testament in his hat, and, from constant rubbing against the top of his head, both backs of the book were worn in holes and as he always believed, the hair smoothed off the top of his head leaving him prematurely as bald as an onion. He was so familiar with the New Testament, when in the prime of life that if any verse of it were read to him he would readily name the book and chapter and repeat the succeeding verse from memory. He delighted in this exercise, and often entertained a circle of friends around the fireside in this way for hours at a time. Such a man, in such a country, was, of course, as a city set on a hill which could not be hidden. Unable to put him down by fair means, men of small minds and bitter prejudice soon began to try to suppress his teaching by intimidation. But John Taylor was one of those men whom intimidation will not intimidate. One night, while he was preaching, some bad men shaved the mane and tail of his horse close, and cut off the stirrups from his saddle. Some, and perhaps all, of the men before mentioned as his co-laborers were present on that occasion, and each one shared the same fate. A nice spectacle they made as they rode off from the church that night, each one swinging his long legs from a stirrupless saddle to the horn of which he was compelled to cling for support. The good old man received such treatment in perfectly good humor, and laughingly remarked that Jesus rode into Jerusalem on a shaved-tail donkey and without stirrups, therefore he thought it no great hardship to ride through the country in that style. Once when he entered the pulpit at night in a country church to preach, he found several bags of stones under the seat in the pulpit. He was handed a written notice to the effect that he would be stoned through the window by unknown persons from the dark if he persisted in preaching that night. He gave no attention to the bags of stones, or to the warning; but proceeded to preach in his strongest and most convincing style. In the midst of his sermon a perfect shower of stones fell upon the roof of the house, causing such noise and confusion for a few seconds that he could not be heard. He waited quietly till the noise ceased, and then proceeded with his sermon without saying a word concerning the interruption. He was not further molested that night; but when it is remembered that he stood thoughout that sermon with his back to one of those large open windows described in a preceding chapter, some idea may be formed as to the nerve he displayed in preaching that sermon. Once when he was preaching a great bully stood up in the audience and several times interrupted him by speaking out in a loud voice and saying: "That is all a pack of old Taylor's lies." He continued his sermon without any notice at all of the ruffian. Once a lady confessed Christ and asked to be baptized. A man who was known to be a dangerous fellow wrote him a note stating that if he baptized that woman he would be shot before he came out of the water. Disregarding the threat, he baptized the woman; afterwards he baptized the man who made the threat and always retained his friendship to the day of his death. Once he saw some desperate characters fighting in a small town; it was an unequal conflict of several against one; he saw they were using knives and literally carving the lone combatant to pieces; the poor fellow had called pitifully for help, but the infuriated men were waving their knives defiantly towards all who came near and shouting to those who sought to give relief not to interfere. It was like courting death and ugly wounds to come near; but John Taylor heard the man call for help and he cooly went through the circle of gleaming knives and brought the poor wounded man, bleeding from a score of ugly knife-wounds and more dead than living, out from that infuriated crowd. While that was a time of intense and bitter religious prejudice as well as sharp and continual religious discussion, John Taylor's preaching was not altogether dry disputation without emotional piety. The old man often grew pathetic in exhortation, and appealed to sinners with tears in both eyes and voice to "ground your puny arms of rebellion and close in with the offers of mercy before it is ever-lastingly too late." That was one of his favorite sayings. He did not hope to argue his way into Heaven without penitence or prayer. He prayed often, long and earnestly. Blessed old man, I can see him now, down beside some little stream where the people had collected to witness a baptism, deliberately *kneeling* for prayer. Yes, he *would* kneel to pray, no matter how much mud or dust might be in his way—kneel deliberately, carefully set his hat before him on the ground, reflectively stroke his bald-head with his hand and then set about praying in his characteristic earnestness. One day as I was riding with him, he pointed to a large stump by the road-side and said: "On that stump I rested my book and set my glass of water one day while I gave the congregation scattered around here a two-hour's sermon. The sun came down on my bald-head till it was all blistered and sore; but I gave them God's truth for one spell." He was not responsible for unreasonable prejudice exhibited in the treatment he received, any more than Jesus was responsible for the still worse treatment *he* received. John Taylor was not always spoiling for a dispute. He could preach on other than controverted subjects. He was a strong believer in special Providence, and often spoke tenderly of the love of God and communion of the Spirit. But he had a hard set to deal with, and they gave him no little trouble. But, while the narrow minded religious bigots were his bitter enemies, he had some good friends among the big hearted sinners who were always ready to stand up for him, and unsparing in their denunciation of any unfairness shown him in religious matters. When "the boys" enlisted in the war, a "union meeting" was appointed to pray for divine protection to accompany them on the eve of their departure. The preachers were all at the "union meeting," John Taylor with the others. Many and earnest were the prayers offered by the preachers of all churches, and loud and deep were the "Amens" and "Lord Grants" chorused by the brethren. But, while John Taylor was invited to lead in prayer once or twice, his prayers were not backed up by any heavenly groans from the brethren as were the prayers of the other preachers. At this one of the boys—noble hearted man, he was; but a wretched sinner—became indignant, and swore right out in meeting that he could lick any church member who wouldn't "grunt for John Taylor's prayers." After that, John Taylor had all the "grunting" he could wish to hear when he prayed. By patient and unremitting labors under such difficulties as we have tried to describe up to the beginning of the war, John Taylor succeeded in establishing a few small churches in that rough country, and he also had scattering members in almost every neighborhood for several counties round. But during the four years of the war, every thing was lost. That far-back mountain country became an excellent hiding place for bad men, and a band of robbers established headquarters there from which they carried on shameful depredations against both persons and property in the country for miles around. All law was set at defiance, and all religion put to open shame. Dark and bloody crimes were committed almost openly in every neighborhood, and wide-spread demoralization destroyed all social and religious organizations. When the war closed, the country had neither society, schools nor churches. Many of the best men of the country were either killed or maimed in the war, helpless widows and orphans filled the land with want and sorrow, and thriftless negroes, erroneously supposing that their newly found freedom guaranteed them a living without labor, added their support to the burdens of the impoverished country. Good old brother Taylor found himself with only a few scattering members, and they were utterly discouraged as well as wholly unable to do any thing financially towards setting the cause on foot again. But John Taylor never faltered. His wife was now dead and all his children large enough to provide for themselves, so he had nothing to do but go about his Father's business. His first work was to collect from the brethren in Tennessee, Kentucky and other states north, some material help to relieve the actual suffering among helpless women and children in the bounds of his labors. This work finished, he began preaching in earnest. He had not even a horse, so he had a small pouch made in which to carry his hymn-book and Bible, and with this little pouch on his arm and a stout stick, for support, in his hand, he went out, on foot, into the dreary, war-swept land to carry glad tidings of great joy to the sorrow-burdened hearts of a people in despair.

I have purposely omitted any mention of the fact that before the war good churches were established at Moulton, in Lawrence county, Alabama and at Russellville, in Franklin county, Alabama, through the labors of the talented and lamented Fanning. Those churches consisted, in the main, of families of wealth. John Taylor preached but little in that class of society, and T. B. Larimore began life as a preacher with John Taylor.

It is difficult to make any one not familiar with the social customs of that country before the war, understand how completely the poor people who lived in the mountains were isolated from the wealthy planters and slaveholders who inhabited the more fertile valleys or populated the towns. In the valleys broad plantations in the highest possible state of cultivation spread out to the utmost limit of vision in every direction, and on each plantation the home of the owner was a palace in which living was a studied round of luxuries. Private governesses and tutors looked after the education of the young children at home, while the grown up young ladies and gentlemen finished their education in distant colleges. The religious interests of those old plantation people were looked after by talented and highly educated preachers under whose ministry elegant churches were built here and there along the valley at appropriate places. Each of those churches accommodated the select circle of dozy worshipers from three or four plantations, and those well paid pastors measured out the spiritual food each week to their fleecy flocks with a grace of gesture and elegance of diction charming to behold. When the young ladies and gentlemen from "the big house" finished their education in college, and a dash of dissipation and general profligacy not unfrequently constituted the most notable part of the finishing touches with the young men, they usually took a trip abroad and, returning, settled down to spend life on the plantation as others before them had done.

The narrow fields of the poor among the mountains were scarcely more than an hour's ride on horseback from those magnificent valley plantations, yet how different! Homes in the mountains were but rude log huts, and life in them was one continual burden of hardships, want and toil. The fertile valleys, well cultivated by slave labor, produced an over-supply of every thing demanded in the markets, and the poor mountaineers found every thing they carried to market dull sale at starvation low prices. They had neither time nor facilities for education; their social advantages were just nothing, and many of their religious ideas and teachers scarcely ranked above the lowest grade of civilization. They were as completely isolated from the rich planters socially, religiously and educationally, as the untutored Indians of our western Territory from the citizens of the populous states and towns contiguous. The two peoples had no dealings with each other. The line was drawn with rigid exactness on both sides. The wealthy planters did not encourage their preachers to waste precious time and talents trying to save the illiterate poor who dwelt among the mountains; and the poor mountaineers felt that no amount of gospel preaching could save the "stuck up" rich folks who lived in towns and owned the big plantations in the valley. Such was the condition of things before the war.

Words are but feeble things to express the condition of affairs a few years after the war. Changes were manifest on every hand. The time of the poor mountaineers seemed to have come at last. The valley plantations were all in ruins, and their once prosperous owners in abject want. Mules all destroyed in the war, barns burned, palatial residences fallen into decay, fences laid waste, and negroes all freed, this once glorious country was now one vast neglected, abandoned and ruined cemetery of buried magnificence. The times dealt far more kindly with the poor mountaineers. Produce of all kinds commanded high prices, and those mountaineers knew how to work and economize. The mountain boys found more time for self-improvement, and a readier market at higher prices for all kinds of produce provided the means to improve the grade of homes, schools and churches. The young ladies and gentlemen among the mountains began to count their hard earned savings to see whether they could not go to college, and a feeling of hope and general prosperity irradiated all faces with smiles joyful to see. Those boys and girls went to college by scores, and when their education was finished they returned to their homes and started out in the various professions and vocations of life with an earnestness that insured success. But we have to do only with John Taylor and the religion of those days at present.

John Taylor bought a horse, and with the general feeling of prosperity in that country came also an increase of religious zeal and faith and hope. Successful meetings blessed almost every neighborhood, and churches sprang up as if by magic all over that country. The old man spent his last days in the supreme happiness of living as a father among his children in all that country, and of preaching to his heart's content among the many churches he had so long and earnestly labored and prayed to see established. But he never, to the day of his death, rode on a train. The brethren tried hard to get him to take just one trip on the train, and offered to pay all expenses; but the old man would lean on his staff and gaze after it meditatively as it rushed by him, and then, hobbling off, he would gravely shake his head and say: "No, brethren; it runs too fast. Why, God bless you, I might faint. If I had to go to New York I would rather walk than get on that thing." Such were John Taylor and the hill country of North Alabama when T. B. Larimore made his first preaching tour through there on foot in 1868.

As a preacher John Taylor was never rated high; as a man, he was not widely known. In every sense his genuine merits went far beyond his reputation. The portion of God's moral vineyard assigned to him for keeping by a far-seeing Providence was small and apparently barren; but long, and faithfully did he cultivate it. Much of his toil and self-sacrifice seemed "Love's labor lost;" but here and there the old man would find in unexpected times and at strange out-of-the-way places, harvests both rich and rare from his patient sowing and persisent cultivation. There are those now living in important positions of honor and usefulness in more than one state who will remember, as they read this, how the good old man's simple faith, abiding hope and constant cheerfulness, exercised a strong influence to keep their young lives in virtue's ways and to lay in their childish minds many of the indispensible, inflexible, elementary principles of true greatness.

In those early years the good old man formed an opinion that one of the lads in a certain part of his field of labor possessed a peculiar preaching talent especially adapted to another part of his field of labor more than seventy miles away. How to get the lad to the preaching point, was, with the old man, a problem; with the lad it was something more than a problem, it was an obstacle we will say. As I was the lad, and only twenty, I was in favor, young man like, of laying the whole question "on the table." Not so, good old brother Taylor. He had a good horse, we could ride and walk alternately by half-hour spells, and on good smooth roads we could double on the animal and both ride. I considered the plan inexpedient if not unlawful. I had been to college two sessions already, and it was against every principle of my education and life-long training to consent to ride while such an old man walked. It also seemed too great a burden on the horse to double on him; and I doubted my ability to make seventy miles and more on foot under a July sun on time with a well-kept horse and I but a few weeks out of college. While the matter was under advisement, the old man came to me one day with that glad triumphant smile on his face which I learned to reverence and appreciate so highly in after years, and said: "Now my brother, the Lord has fixed every thing for us." Though I dared not intimate as much to him just then, I must confess that just at the time I could not think of any thing of mutual interest that I had been expecting the Lord to fix. But that blessed old man had gone humbly to his God in prayer about that preaching trip, and he had found a solution of the difficulty. Had not the Lord fixed it? Whom else had he bothered about it? He had asked God to fix it, and it was fixed. To his mind the conclusion was irresistible—I must confess I did not fully share his faith in this—I wished then, and I have wished a thousand times since, I could. "Why brother, let me tell you," the old man continued. "Bro. William Taylor has a young horse he does not need at all, he really wants him broken to the saddle, and yesterday sent me word that he would be glad for us to take him on that trip of ours." So every thing was arranged to start on the morrow. Bro. William Taylor lived five miles away; but in the direction we were to go. So I walked that distance, and then began my career as a horse tamer and gospel preacher. If I have not succeeded very well in either calling, it is certainly not for lack of encouragement and assistance from some as good people as ever lived. The settlements in that country were on small creeks in narrow valleys between which were long stretches of barren, uninhabited mountain country. From each lodging place when we started on the morrow, we provided against want at the noon hour in case we should be caught between settlements, by taking a sizable lunch for man and beast. Thus provided, and with a mug to drink from the many springs at frequent intervals along our mountain route, we made the journey in about four days. In every neighborhood, the old man would have riders sent out and call the people to-gether for preaching at night. At noon we would stop beside some specially refreshing spring, remove saddles and carefully bathe the backs of our horses, eat our lunches, feed our horses, give them "grazing liberty" and then take a rest of one hour. With him this noon rest was simply a nap of refreshing sleep which at his age, he greatly needed. Under the spreading boughs of some stately oak, his head pillowed on his saddle and his heart divested of every care and filled with strong and abiding faith in God, the old man slept as sweetly as an infant in the Savior's arms.

One day as we were going on our way, we were in Marion county then, he called my attention to a splendid out-crop of coal on the banks of a little creek. The discovery, for such it was to me, at once knocked all the religion and piety out of my mental machinery, for the time, and set me wild with visions of millions of clear profits from easy and simple speculation. Ah! surely "the love of money is the root of many evils." How difficult it is for us ever to learn that gain is not godliness! Notwithstanding I had, with prayer and meditation, deliberately resolved to consecrate myself to the sacred work of the ministry, the sight of so much undeveloped, unappreciated and practically unclaimed wealth in this dreary and uninhabited country, at once carried me quite beyond myself. I wanted to buy all the country at once, build a few railroads and manufacturing towns and then sell out the whole thing at a handsome profit. But the good old man took no interest in my scheme. Would God, I had always, in after life, had present with me in similar temptations the restraining influence of his blessed presence. Was not God providing for us, he said? Had we not enjoyed a good lunch and refreshing rest to-day? Did we not have a good place in view to stay to-night? He supposed what I described would all be done some day; but God would so order the doing of it as to have it done by the men best qualified for that sort of thing. We did not have any money to buy that country with, and neither of us knew how to build a railroad, make a manufacturing town or dig coal. We know the Bible says: "He that believeth and is baptized shall be saved; but he that believeth not shall be damned," and many people who understand all those other things better than we, do not know this as well as we. And with many such words did the old man exhort me, till my faith, and piety, and zeal resumed sway over me and I felt in a happier mood for preaching that night than at any other time on our trip. It is speaking in the face of all observation and experience and discounting a long list of well authenticated facts, to say there is no good in the life and influence of such a man.

The last time I met him, was but a short time before his death. I found him living with his daughter in a log cabin under the over-hanging brow of a great mountain. Close by the cabin was one of the excellent springs characteristic of the country. He was no longer able to meet with the brethren at church; but never a Lord's day passed, he told me, without a joyful meeting at his own home. Members of all churches, and of no churches, came each Lord's day to see how he fared, and never did he fail to make them a talk on religious subjects, and warmly exhort them to be faithful to the Lord. We walked to-gether to the spring, I supporting his feeble body. Long and earnestly did he speak to me then, as he had often spoken before, of the goodness of God and the joys and consolations of a living faith. He was feeble of mind and scattering of thought, yet from life-long habit he kept steadily to the one subject always uppermost in his meditations, *viz:*

the love of God and the joys of religion. I had traveled far over a rough road on horse-back to see him; but I felt richly repaid for the worry of the trip by the communion of soul and spirit which I enjoyed with him. No monument, not even a stone, marks the spot where rests the mortal body of John Taylor; but from many a heart the joys and gratitude of living faith ascend in thanksgiving to God daily as a far more enduring monument of the blessed old man's life and labors.

CHAPTER V.

Theophilus Brown Larimore was born in the hill country of East Tennessee, July 10, 1843. In July, 1868, he was preaching, in company with John Taylor, in the mountain region of North Alabama. It would be difficult to give a connected chain of events in his obscure life between these two points even if the reader were interested in the subject. His life in childhood was similar to that of other very poor boys, and a tedious recital of commonplace incidents would certainly prove a dry and uninteresting subject to readers. Besides, it is difficult to learn much about his childhood. He talks but little about himself, and has always been peculiarly reticent in regard to his early life. In an intimate acquaintance and confidential friendship extending over twenty years, I have seldom heard him speak of his childhood. I have learned enough, however, to know his lot was an unusually hard one. The very recollection of it seems to be painful to him, hence he avoids, as far as possible, any allusion to it. Once I told him everybody was anxious to know something about his childhood, and asked him to tell me some of the most striking incidents of his early life. He looked troubled, there were tears in his eyes, and he heaved a great sigh. Then he said, and his voice trembled with emotion as he said it: "Those days were all so dark and gloomy, one incident was scarcely more striking than another." In a letter, in January, 1881, he wrote: "From my very childhood, life with me has been burdened with cares and shrouded in gloom. I do not dread nor fear death. When it is God's will for me to go, I shall tenderly kiss the hand divine that severs the silver cord of life, and joyfully lay my burdens down at the foot of the cross. I have often thought that I would unbosom myself to you some time of all my trials in life, but may never do so." He was in great trouble when he wrote that letter. He was struggling under heavy financial embarrassments connected with Mars Hill College. He was carrying a heavy debt in bank by his personal honor and integrity, and could see no way to meet it. He was also troubled by some irregularity in the discipline of the school.

In January, 1888, he wrote:

"I know the deepest depths of poverty. I have nothing in my record of which to boast. I can not, like some great evangelists, refer to a life of crime and lawlessness before I became a Christian. Desirable as such a record may be, I can not claim it. I have tried all my life to do right and to live an exemplary life. I never knew what it was to have the advice, protection, and support of a father. In my childhood, we never had a horse—never; a cow and calf being all our stock. In February or March before I was ten in July, I was put on a farm to learn to plow, getting three meals a day and all I could learn, for my work—possibly good pay. They told me I might plow old Granny, a little, old, shabby bay pony; and told me to give her ten ears of corn for breakfast. I was afraid to trust Granny too far; so, turning her out of the stable, and shutting the door when I went in, which I did not venture to do till she got out, I proceeded to break up the corn into 'nubbins' on the edge of the trough so Granny could eat 'em. The racket brought some one who astonished me by declaring—unreasonable and incredible as it was to me—that Granny could eat 'em whole! That very year we rented a little field, and Granny and I made a 'crap' of corn—I getting one half of the corn and Granny and the field the other half. The next year, 1854, I got $4 a month from early spring till 'craps were laid by.' I changed from renting to hiring, going to free school ten or twelve weeks each year, till I could get—*did* get—$6 per month."

This last letter was written soon after his second great meeting in Nashville, Tennessee. He was evidently in one of his most cheerful moods, and disposed to indulge his sense of humor, which is very acute and subtile under favorable circumstances. These two extracts from private letters are suggestive of the characteristics of the man, as well as glimpses into the mysterious life of the boy. He is pre-eminently a man of moods and tenses. When hopeful and cheerful as to the success of his work, he meets the world with a smile on his face and a twinkle of humor in his eye. But when he is discouraged in his work and depressed in spirit, he looks approaching disaster squarely in the face with a heart unmoved by fear and fortified by faith perfectly sublime in the providence of God. As a preacher, when in the former mood his eloquence is irresistible, and will cause an audience to resolve at once to storm the fort of iniquity with songs on their lips and joy in their hearts. But in the latter mood, his voice swells and throbs and trembles with plaintive pathos as he pictures the Christian's trials on earth and triumphs in death, until his hearers fall into those feelings of helplessness which drive the soul for refuge to an unwavering faith in God, an unquestioning obedience to His commandments, and a confident reliance on His promises.

Speaking of the year he received $6 a month for work, he says:

"I remember distinctly that we plowed in a field more than a mile from where we slept at night. We were usually in the field before daylight, ready to start our plows the moment it was light enough to see our way. And from daylight till dark we did not stop, save a few moments for lunch at noon. We carried our lunch in a little tin bucket. There was a creek in the field, and at noon we ate our lunch by the creek, drinking creek-water 'as a beverage.' There were three of us—two negroes and myself. We all ate out of the same bucket. That was in the days of slavery."

He was a delicate child, and often suffered severe hemorrhage at the nose. He once said. "I remember to have followed my plow, when a boy, while bleeding at the nose till the part of the plow next to me would be all covered with blood. I would grow weak and dizzy from loss of blood, and, half fainting, would stagger like a drunken man as I walked."

Once he told me he did not remember ever to have failed to give satisfaction as a hireling but once. He had worked hard all the spring on the farm, and, crops being finished, he had started to school. But in the middle of August dire necessity compelled him to stop from school and seek some kind of employment. He was hired at a brick-yard to bear off brick. His failure is thus described by one whose information was accurate, and whose statements are entirely reliable:

"The heavy lifting and stooping posture under the scorching rays of an August sun, caused severe bleeding at the nose; yet the pale-faced, frail-bodied little boy tried hard to keep his place among the workers. Back and forth with measured step he walked with others who were bearing off the bricks. Each time his strength grew more feeble, and his bricks were all covered with blood. Suddenly there was a break in the ranks of the laborers. The men gathered excitedly around a prostrate form. Some one called for water. And then, pale and bleeding, the unconscious little boy was carried off the ground. But the confusion was only for a moment. The boy had fainted.

Consciousness soon returned. The busy laborers moved on at their work, and soon forgot the incident. With a heavy heart, a gloomy soul, and tear-dimmed eyes, the boy received his pay and gave up his place. He had failed, but not from any fault of his. To meet his mother and acknowledge his failure, was a trial infinitely greater than all the hardships he had endured. This little incident made a deep and lasting impression on him. He related it to me in 1888, just after he had closed one of his most successful meetings. His name was in all the daily papers, and the brilliance of his mind and the pathos of his oratory were sweeping the world before him. But when he spoke of this trial and failure of his childhood on the brick-yard, his voice trembled with emotion, and his eyes grew misty with tears."

When he worked out for wages he carried meal for his mother and family from the mill to their home on his shoulder. He would take a sack of corn from the place where he worked to the mill, wait for it to be ground, and then carry it home. He could carry enough at one trip to last them a week. He would start with his corn at dark, after working hard all day. After getting home he was allowed to spend the rest of the night with his mother, provided he would get back to his work by daylight. Speaking of those trips home, he once said to me: "I did not think it any hardship at all to walk home late at night with a sack of meal on my shoulder after a hard day's work. I was so anxious to see mother that I looked forward to such trips with inexpressible joy. I knew she would be up and waiting for me, no matter how late I might be in getting home."

When I think of such hardships of his childhood, and then turn in wonder and admiration to the contemplation of the triumphs of his manhood, I can but feel contempt for those who higgle over nice discriminations between castes in society. Why should any one feel lifted up with pride because of favored opportunities in life? It is in the *man* true greatness is found, and not in the circumstances of his birth or the opportunities of his position in society. We are all created in the image of God, and endowed with the principle of immortality. We all dwell together in the magnificent earthly palace of our God. The heavens are garnished in beauty and bespangled with light alike for us all. No matter what may be our various fortunes in life, each one is but performing his part in the universe of God. There are workmen of honor and of dishonor, it is true; but whether a man be the one or the other, is simply a question of individual manliness. No circumstances of birth or hardships of life can enter into the estimate. If honest and true at heart, the poor little boy that works by day and carries meal to his mother by night is one of God's honorable workmen, while the monarch who wields a scepter in sin is dishonorable and contemptible.

CHAPTER VI.

There is one passage in one of his private letters concerning the poverty and wretchedness of his childhood which I find it difficult to decide whether it is best to give to the public. It may do no good; it can certainly do no harm. Perhaps some readers will appreciate it because it satisfies their curiosity; others because it preserves the facts of history. To all it will teach a valuable lesson on the horrors of intemperance. His language is:

"The very best blood, both maternal and paternal, is blended in my veins. I was born in an humble hovel, right where two royal roads of ruined wealth and shattered fortunes met in the shadow of security debts and midnight of the reign of the intoxicating bowl. In other words, my ancestors on both sides were rich, intellectual, influential, successful, and popular. Just as the converging lines came together, some immense security debts had to be paid. There was no shirking. Every dollar was paid; but it took every thing—negroes, land, stock, money, home; every thing to pay it. Result—nothing, absolutely nothing, left but poverty and honor. Just then I was born—just when the shadows were deepest. Men, hurled from such heights to such depths, turned from these troubles to worse—to strong drink; then the gloom of the darkest night began to gather around my cradle. I can well remember when the yell of the drunken one coming home in the otherwise still hours of night, would start all of us from the hut to the woods, where, for hours, we would hide in fallen treetops and darkness, till the yells and shrieks were cut short by the drowsiness of the maddened brain. Then the beastly drunken one beng no longer dangerous because of the stupor attending the state we call 'dead drunk,' we would slip, like little partridges after a scare, back to the gloomy nest. Brownlow and Prentice together never knew language black enough to blacken the picture, the shadow, of the reality along this line. Born in such shadows, cradled in such darkness, and reared in such poverty, whereas my natural sphere was just the reverse, it is perfectly natural that there should be an indescribable gloom in my soul, often depressing my spirit, making me fearless and reckless, inclining me to delight in the softest and sweetest notes of minor melancholy music and the highest flights of oratory—flights that defy sun, moon, and stars, and fear not to flit to the sublimest heights and fan the flame of glory that envelops the throne of God. Moses in Egypt's kingly court, having been carried on the bosom of a princess from a servant's sphere there, was not higher above his natural sphere than I below mine. I mean not to murmur. I am not complaining; but simply talking to a friend—that's all. My shadow now falls toward the east. I fully realize that I am past the noon of life. Once out of debt, then forever free from debt, doing all the good I can, I intend to see the silvery lining of life's dark cloud if I can. Debt and drunkenness have depressed me and caused me to be dejected all my life."

There is the passage, just as he wrote it. I hope the reader will make the most of it, and learn from it how much misery and wretchedness may come from debt and drunkenness. It is due him to remark that he never thought, at the time he wrote, that what he was saying would be read by any one save the confidential friend to whom he was writing. He has since then given his full consent for any thing he has ever said, to be used in this book if it is deemed of use or interest to the public.

It is worthy of special note that, though he often came in contact with very depraved people when he was a hireling, he never contracted any bad habits. His mother says that if he ever used a profane, obscene, or indecent word, drank a drop of intoxicating liquor, or used tobacco in any way, she does not know it. While he had no opportunity to go into high society during his boyhood, he always had a natural suavity and polish of manners which distinguished him as a boy of refinement. He was diffident, but not cowering; awkward, but not menial. He felt keenly the humility of his condition; but never lost his self-respect. The days of his childhood's hardships were, to him, days of pilgrimage. He was not living in them; but merely passing through them. He never calculated to remain in that condition; he felt intuitively that he was designed for some nobler position in life. He never identified himself in fact or feeling with that sphere in life.

Referring to this period in his life, I find in one of his private letters this language:

"I always felt like I wanted to be an orator. From my very earliest recollection I would go out into the forest alone, stand up with as much dignity as a senator, repeat meaningless sentences, and imagine I was addressing a vast concourse of fellow-citizens. At the very hardest time in my childhood, when I was working as a hireling for a mere pittance, a physician proposed that if I would come and live with him he would take me into his office, teach me something about medicine, bear all my expenses through medical college, give me a good horse and saddle-bags, and start me into the practice when I reached twenty-one. But I did not feel that I could be content in life as a doctor. I wanted to be a lawyer. I would go to the court-house, when a very small boy, and remain in my seat all day, not leaving for dinner for fear I would lose my seat."

No doubt but that it was such feelings and aspirations as these which kept him from contracting any evil habits from his childhood associations.

He once told me that the severest trial of his childhood

days was the death of their only cow. It was in dead of winter, and they had no feed for the cow. He went out in search of work that he might buy some provender; but the weather was severe, and no one had any work to do in such weather. He walked all day through the rain and the cold, but in vain. He was turned away from every house with a sinking heart. Just at noon he called at the house of a well-to-do farmer. They were at dinner; but they bluntly turned him away without offering him any thing to eat. He could not have eaten, however, if they had given him the most pressing invitation. He reached home at dark, cold, hungry, and tired. His mother met him at the gate, and, with tears in her eyes, told him the cow was dead. He told me this after he had become a great preacher, and he said that if he owned the whole world he could see it all swept away in a moment and yet not suffer the feelings of loss which he experienced the night his mother told him their cow was dead.

He has never forgotten those trials and hardships of early life. They taught him how to sympathize with the poor and the unfortunate in life. And it is his deep and tender sympathy for suffering humanity that makes the people love him so. Once his own children were laughing in his presence at the ludicrous appearance of some tramps they had seen passing the road. A look of pain and sadness came over his pale face, and, in a voice pathetic and tender, he said: "Don't laugh about that, little darlings; you do not know what it is to be cold and hungry and homeless." And yet he never talks even to his own children about the hardships of his childhood. The subject is so gloomy and painful to him that he does not wish to darken their joys by alluding to it. They will perhaps learn for the first time from this volume what a hard time poor papa had in childhood.

In an intimate acquaintance of twenty years, I have never heard him use an expression which would indicate that he had any feelings of bitterness or resentment toward any one. He has often spoken to me of unkind treatment received from others, but never has he manifested any feeling of anger toward them. I have never heard him speak of any one in a way to arouse bad feelings on the part of the one spoken of even if overheard. When speaking of what he considered bad treatment, his words were always so carefully chosen, and his voice was so modulated by manifest feelings of tenderest love, that those of whom he spoke could not have felt aggrieved had they overheard all he said. Once I alluded to this in a private letter, and, in reply, never suspecting what he said would ever be published, he wrote:

"While I have friends who would gladly bear my every cross for me, you know I have some enemies. While I can not understand why I should have such friends, I do not see why I should have enemies. I am an enemy to no one. Long ago I solemnly resolved no one should lose an enemy when I die. That exact phraseology came to me in a dream in our Nashville meeting in 1885. I was in the shade of a tree near the old school-house of long ago, 'ciphering' with Daniel Deakins, school-mate of my childhood. He made a mistake. I made a little witty remark about it. His countenance said he was offended. Laying my arm around him, and pressing him gently to my breast, I said: 'No one shall lose an enemy when I die.' The dream was over; but I had, in few words spoken in dream-land, a sincere sentiment of my heart, dear to me years before that dream came to impress it. It stays. My heart has always been too tender to allow me to intentionally injure any one. The first picture on the page of my memory is this: 'Walking along the road with my mother, I found a dead dove. I picked it up and carried it as long as she would allow me, crying all the time, and trying to get her to explain to me why any one should kill a dove.

"I delivered two discourses in the penitentiary at Nashville recently. Ten confessed Christ at one discourse, and seven the next, I believe. After the audience was dismissed the convicts made a rush for me, seeing I shook hands with all near enough. Well, had I been Gov.—I wouldn't be though—I think my inclination would have been to call the unfortunate army in stripes before me, preach Jesus to them, pardon every one of them, resign my position, and evangelize."

CHAPTER VII.

He was in his sixteenth or perhaps seventeenth year when he worked with the two slaves as a hireling at $6.00 per month. At the end of that year he left home to attend college. His educational advantages up to that time had been very meagre. As already quoted from one of his letters, he went to school only ten or twelve weeks in the year; but by studying hard at night while he was away from school and at work he managed to keep his place in his classes. Hence when he entered college, he was as well informed as other boys of his age who had done nothing but attend school all their lives. After speaking of the hardships of his early life, he says, in a private letter: "Such was my life till I had progressed somewhat in my teens, when the hand of Providence touched a hidden spring which hurled me headlong, bewildered and amazed, into one of our very best East Tennessee colleges—Baptist." It is like him to believe all good things are Providential blessings. He is a firm believer in special Providence, and, no matter how long and patiently he labors and waits for a thing, he is sure to consider it wholly God's blessing when it comes, and to receive it with reverent thankfulness as such. He never counts himself entitled to it as of merit because of all he has done, but receives it by faith as of grace from God.

In another private letter I find the following concerning his entrance into college: "I did not accept the first chance I had to go to college. Several chances offered which seemed to promise well for me, but I declined them because I could not see in either of them a chance to carry my mother and sisters along with me in the order of promotion. In the opportunity which opened before me in my seventeenth year, however, there seemed to be a chance for us all to better our condition in the future, though I was compelled to leave them for a time. I left home at early dawn on foot and walked forty miles before I slept. That was how I went to college."

When he was a very small boy he went with his mother to spend the night with some neighbors. There was a flock of geese in the barn-yard with which little Theophilus was greatly pleased. Some young ladies told him that if he would catch one they would cook it for supper. They had no idea the little fellow could catch the goose, so the whole matter soon passed out of the minds of all present. No one missed the little boy till, to their great astonishment, he came up packing a great struggling goose in his arms. He gave it to the young ladies, and, after the amusement subsided, the goose was released and nothing more thought about it till they came to supper. They stood little Theophilus up on a stool at the supper table and said:

"What will you have, Theophilus?"

"If you please, mam, I will have some of the goose."

"But the goose is not cooked yet."

"If you please, then I will wait till you cook it."

"But it is too late now to cook a goose for supper."

"If you please then, if you aint got no goose I don't want no supper."

He had set his heart on having goose for supper, and,

while he was not ill behaved about it, he did not for the moment think of any thing else he could eat.

This little incident made a lasting impression on his mother. So when the son of her love and the support of her life announced his determination to leave home to attend college, she thought of the disappointment of his childhood in not having goose for supper. It requires no stretch of the imagination to see why she thought of it. It was a time to think of his whole life with her. Now that she was about to lose his companionship, she could but think of the happiness she had enjoyed with him during all his life from an infant in the cradle to a man by her side. She resolved to give him a surprise as great as was his childhood's disappointment. So she procured a young goose all unknown to him, and prepared it for his lunch on the road the day he was to leave home to go to college. She also put into the basket with the goose all the delicacies of his choice, and, the morning he left home, she put the little lunch basket in his hand and kissed him a loving good-bye. He walked steadily all the morning, and, about noon, reached the brow of Cumberland mountain overlooking the fertile valley below. A few moments brisk walking down the mountain brought him to a beautiful spring by the road-side, and there he stopped, weary, hungry, foot-sore and home-sick, to rest, eat his lunch and think of his mother. But when he opened the little basket, the fountain of tears broke loose and he wept like a child. What his mother had prepared for him was, he knew, so much better than she had for herself, that he was completely overcome by his emotions and found it impossible to eat a mouthful. He tenderly recovered the basket and gave himself to serious meditation. In a private letter I find this touching passage concerning his reflections:

"The mountain was between me and my mother. The valley was spread before me in beauty that beggars description. The river, like a silver thread of life, wound its course through the valley below me. Towering cliffs and solemn mountains were all around me. Before me was college with all of its advantages so tempting to my youthful ambition; but behind me was mother in her loneliness, dearer to my heart than all else beside. As I pondered and wept, I almost resolved to retrace my steps, give up my aspirations and die in obscurity by my mother's side. Nothing but the knowledge that it was her desire for me to go to college and that she would be displeased if I returned to her, caused me to decide to go on. So taking up my precious basket I continued my journey down the mountain, finishing the walk of forty miles by night without eating a mouthful of any thing." I have never read any thing more touchingly beautiful than this. It was not written for publication, but it is too good to be lost. I have thought of that scene a thousand times and every time with increased admiration. There, by the spring in the woods, the solemn mountains around him and the beautiful valley spread out like a picture before him, the boy of destiny trembled and wept as he thought of his mother. His success in life has been phenomenal, but not accidental. What he has done others may do. The destiny of men in time and eternity is determined by principles as inflexible as the laws that govern the stars. It is not in the nature of things for a boy whose mind and heart are guided by such noble principles to fail in life. The boy who starts in life with such love for his mother and such devotion to what he believes to be right, has the element of success in him. The current may seem to be against him for a time, but if he holds true to those principles he will certainly succeed in the end.

CHAPTER VIII.

Mossey Creek Baptist College was a scientific, literary, and theological institution, N. B. Goforth, President, when T. B. Larimore entered it as a student, about the year 1859. While there, he was universally popular with the students and a favorite with the faculty, and always sustained a good reputation for general morality, studiousness, and courteous deportment. President Goforth said he was a gentleman by nature and a student of unusual promise. The most interesting part of his life there was his religious experience. He was peculiarly susceptible to religious impressions by nature, and the warm friendship and close attachment which the teachers and pupils felt for him brought him fully under their influence. The members of the faculty were all religious, and many of the students were young men preparing for the ministry. Under such influence he became interested in the subject of religion, and when a revival meeting was started he was among the first ones who put themselves forward to seek religion. He tried very hard to get religion, but did not succeed. To put it in his own words:

"I did every thing they told me to do, and abstained from every thing they told me not to do. If I had owned the whole world, I would have given it all, and would have been perfectly willing to die the next moment to experience religion as they described it."

Those who professed religion at that meeting were baptized into the church. Of that baptism he says:

"Nothing short of the despair of doomed souls in the last day can compare with my agony when I saw those young converts baptized at the close of that revival and compared their feelings of security with my own fears of endless ruin. So great was my suffering that President Goforth, in the goodness of his heart, offered to baptize me and receive me into the church, saying my life had always been so exemplary conversion had perhaps taken place gradually and imperceptibly. But such a course then seemed to me to be an empty mockery and a shallow hypocrisy; I thought then the Bible clearly taught a man had to get religion before he was fit to be baptized."

It is interesting to hear him describe his earnestness during that revival:

"I fasted and prayed for days in succession. When others went to their regular meals, I remained in my room to pray. Often did I go alone at the solemn hour of midnight to some secluded spot, and there, under the silent stars, pour out my soul in prayer to God. I went to all the public meetings and earnestly begged all good people to pray especially for me."

Of course he was greatly distressed because he could not get religion; but I have often heard him say he considered his experience during that revival the best part of his preparation for the ministry. Like Dickens' celebrated "How not to do it," that experience has enabled him to lead many groping sinners out of their difficulties, because he can assure them from his own experience that such is not the way out of trouble.

When he failed to get religion, he resolved to pray regularly, read the Bible constantly, and do every thing it required of him. Clearly it was his duty to do that much, and he could not see what more God could reasonably require of him. He has been following out that resolution ever since, and he considers it a solution of all religious difficulties. God has expressed his will concerning man in the Bible. No man has a right to teach any thing in religion not taught in the Bible. Those who do all God requires of them in the Bible will have employment enough to keep them busy. Sinners are confused in revivals about what they think God is going to do for them, and not about what God has required of them.

There is danger of very grave results from failure to get religion in revivals if the seeker does not firmly set aside all theories and implicitly follow the Bible. This danger is aptly illustrated in the case of a warm personal friend of his, a senior student, who sought but did not find religion in that same meeting. One day they went to a secluded spot to pray together. To use his own words again, that young man said:

"They tell me that those who surrender entirely to Jesus, and seek religion with all their hearts, shall find it. I have not found it, and I can not find it. Either the doctrine is wrong, or I have not sought with all my heart. Surely I can not be mistaken as to my own purposes. They may defend the doctrine by impugning my motives and denying my sincerity; but I know I have been honest with myself, and have sought with all my heart."

Certainly that was putting the case logically and clearly. The man never stopped to consider whether the Bible authorized all those revivalistic extravigancies or not. He assumed that the doctrine was from the Bible. He was, therefore, putting the case between his own consciousness and the truthfulness of the Bible. There was a plain contradiction between what he knew on the one hand and what they said the Bible taught on the other. Such a conflict could have but one result. To use his own language:

"When he reached that point in his reasoning a look of sadness and despair, such as I hope never to see again, came over his face. He looked at me as if hope had fled from his heart, then turned away without another word and walked slowly back to his room. He never seemed himself again during the few remaining days we were together there. We parted soon; he became a commissioned officer in the Confederate army, and, while leading his men in a gallant charge in one of the bloody battles of that war, a ball pierced his bosom and forever ended his doubts and troubles on earth. I saw a notice of his death in a paper, which closed with the merited tribute, 'A braver heart never ceased to beat.'"

It remains to be said that he holds a diploma from Mossey Creek Baptist College. He has never shown it to any one save a few confidential friends. It is doubtful whether his wife and children have ever seen it. Discussing it once in a private conversation, he assured me it had never been seen by as many as twenty people since it came into his possession. This is characteristic of the man. He seems to have a dread of being considered scholarly by the public. He stands entirely upon his merits as a man and a preacher, and in no sense relies upon diplomas or titles for success.

CHAPTER IX.

About the beginning of the war he enlisted in the Confederate army for "one year or during the war," and was ordered to report for duty to Col. McClellan, at Knoxville, Tennessee. It is unnecessary to raise any question here as to the right or wrong of secession and the war which followed. We are not so much concerned, in this case, about the merits of the war as the motives of the soldier. It is enough to say he enlisted from a sense of duty, and if he committed an error it is no matter of surprise in one of his age. From Knoxville, he moved to Mill's Springs, in Kentucky, with advance guard of Zollicoffer's brigade. He was at the battle of Fishing Creek; but was on special duty and not in the fight. He went with General Buckner under flag of truce for the body of General Zollicoffer after the battle of Fishing Creek. While he was on this duty the command retreated to Murfreesboro, Tennessee, where he again joined it.

He was at the battle of Shiloh, and was put in command of special picket squad to guard the river above Pittsburg, to prevent a flank movement by Federals landing at a point higher up the river. He wrote the dispatch which gave Johnson notice of the passage of the first Federal gun-boat above Pittsburg. Johnson is said to have remarked that the dispatch was a model military document. On Monday he was ordered off picket to report for duty on the battle field. He found the army in full retreat and with the others, fell back to Corinth.

From Corinth, after the battle of Shiloh, he was detailed for scouting duty up the south bank of the Tennessee river. The Federals moved up the north bank of the river at the same time. At Bain Bridge, the scouts crossed the river, to obtain, if possible, full information concerning the movements of the Federal army. This was considered a very dangerous expedition; but, with a few picked men, he went as far as Rogersville, in Lauderdale county, Ala., from which point they returned and recrossed the river at Bain Bridge. This is a point just above Florence, where the Government of late years has carried on extensive works in opening the channel of the river for navigation. In after years it was his custom to take the pupils of Mars Hill college, a holiday excursion in May, every year to Bain Bridge. Once, some of his school boys, on one of those annual excursions, were discussing whether a man could swim the river at that point. They appealed to President Larimore, who was leaning against a young tree and meditatively contemplating the river and the country beyond, whether he thought a man could swim the river there.

"Well, young men," he said, "I did swim it just about here once; but it was in a case of pressing emergency."

This created much interest among the students, and was the chief topic of conversation with us for many days; but all efforts to get any further information from him failed. It was years afterwards before I learned that the case of pressing emergency was on a scouting expedition during the war, when the Federal cavalry pressed him so close he was compelled to abandon his horse and swim the river where it was fully three-fourths of a mile wide.

While the scouting party of which he was a member was in camp on the South side of the Tennessee river just above Tuscumbia, after he had returned from the dangerous expedition across the river, they received information that the Federal army was crossing the river. It was necessary to investigate the matter, and four volunteers were called for, to go out and see whether the report was true. Larimore, another boy of about the same age and two older men offered their services. They were instructed to cross the open country of nearly a mile in width from the camp to the river, and determine by careful observations along the bank up and down the river whether any Federal troops were crossing. The camp of the Confederate scouts was under cover of timber, and when the valiant four came to the open country and were compelled to expose themselves the rest of the way to the river, the two older men failed in courage and refused to go any further. The two boys, however, went on to the river, and, seeing no Federals, they dismounted and walked out on an old ferry boat which was grounded on the South bank of the river. Now, it so happened that sixteen Federal sharp shooters were ranged behind a large log on the opposite bank of the river, who, resting their guns on the log, fired simultaneously sixteen shots at the two boys in gray. The boys escaped untouched; but their clothing was riddled in many parts by the balls from the boys in blue. Afterwards, two of those same sharp-shooters were captured by the Confederate scouts and they inquired particularly whether either of the men on the old boat escaped without mortal wounds, and when assured that neither of them was touched at all they could scarcely be made to believe it. They said every one of the sixteen sharp-shooters would have bet any amount that each of the sixteen balls fired simultaneously across that river could have been put into the head of a flour barrel by the marksmen who did the shooting.

From Tuscumbia, he went with the scouting party up the Tennessee river valley as far as Chattanooga. When they reached Chattanooga, the two contending armies were seemingly gathering their forces for another great struggle. There was much scouting duty to be done on both sides, and young Larimore, having won flattering recognition by his efficiency and reliability as a scout, came in for his full share of it. He was ordered into Sequachie Valley, where he felt perfectly at home. He knew all the country and its inhabitants, having lived there all his life. One day the scouts were marching through McLemore's Cove, riding double file up a long straight lane. To the right and left were fields, and to the front the road passed over a rugged hill. They had no information that any Federal soldiers were near, and hence were enjoying a leisurely ride, engaged, the while, in pleasant conversation. Suddenly, and without warning, a Federal battery was drawn into position for action on the brow of the hill immediately in front of them. Taken completely by surprise, there seemed, for the moment, no chance of escape. To advance with only a squad of scouts in the face of the battery, not knowing what was behind it and beyond the hill, was not to be thought of. To retreat down that long straight lane with a battery at their backs and sweeping their retreat the full range of the guns, was simply butchery. The clear command of the leader, to break ranks and every man take care of himself, showed them the only chance of escape. The column parted as if by magic, the fences gave way on each side of the lane as the stampeded army surged against them, and the frightened horses gallopped recklessly across the fields bearing their bewildered riders out of the very jaws of death, just as a volley from the battery on the hill swept down the deserted lane. Three days later, he was captured by Federal scouts while dodging from place to place in the hope of eluding them and making his way back to his command at Chattanooga. He was sent to Federal headquarters, and there offered his choice between taking the non-combatant oath and being sent to Federal prison. He saw no chance of further serving the Confederacy to profit in Federal prison, and he could not believe it was his duty to leave his mother and sisters without support or protection when it was impossible for him to be of service to the cause he had espoused. So he took the non-combatant oath, and thus ended his career as a soldier. However, he found it impossible to maintain a neutral position without being suspected by each side of aiding the other. The non-combatant oath, therefore, only deprived him of the right to fight on either side while he was exposed to attacks and violence from both. Once he was arrested by four drunken men who took a formal and solemn oath never to allow him to escape alive. At night they camped in an old house, and slept two on each side of him. In the middle of the night, while they slept heavily in their drunken stupor, he cautiously arose and made good his escape. He made a crop while remaining neutral; but evil minded men destroyed it before it was harvested. Still, he was too honest and conscientious to violate his oath, and so he suffered all such indignities without once thinking of employing any violence even in self defence. While his mother was absent from home, doing what she could to care for some sick people who were very poor, their house was burned with every thing they had. Seeing it was impossible to remain their unmolested without violating the oath he had taken, he resolved to seek less hostile regions. With his mother and sisters, with the few articles of apparel yet left to them, loaded into a two horse wagon, he left Tennessee and crossed over into Kentucky. He stopped near Hopkins ville, Ky., where he remained till he entered Franklin college as a student to prepare himself for the ministry after the war was over. Of his life at Hopkinsville, I shall speak more fully in another chapter.

His war record is eminently creditable for a boy of his age; but he never now alludes to his life as a soldier. Many of his most intimate friends have never learned he was in the war at all, and it is doubtful whether his own children know that he was once a confederate soldier. One day at Mars Hill college he called attention of a class in history to some inaccuracies in the text book concerning the late war, and Miss Minnie Beaty, of Mississippi, asked him if he were in the war. Some of us who had tried before to get his bearings on that subject felt that the Mississippi brunette was manifesting more curiosity than discretion, and were not surprised, therefore, to hear him answer, evasively, "Well, to a limited extent, I was in the war." Not satisfied with this, she again asked, "Which side were you on?" Her flushed cheek and flashing eyes showed too plainly that she had not forgotten "the blue and the gray." With a kindly smile he remarked: "I was, fortunately, one of the few who neither hurt any body nor received any serious hurts themselves." The class smiled audibly, at this, Miss Minnie looked disappointed, and he requested the next student to proceed with the recitation.

I have heard him say he was in the war, in active service, about a year, that he obeyed every order he received to the best of his ability, that he never shirked any duty, that he was with the army during the time several important battles were fought, and yet, with all this, he never fired a gun while he was a soldier. It so happened that he was always detailed for some special duty while the army was engaged in battle so that he never had occasion to fire a gun. He considers this providential, and says if he thought it possible that he might have killed or injured any one, his life would be miserable. But God, he thinks, has so ordered his life that he positively knows he never injured any one in all his life.

CHAPTER X.

We had hard times in Dixie during the war. Only those who had actual experience of such times know any thing about the privations we suffered. Often we were compelled to resort to substitutes for the commonest necessaries of life as unsatisfactory as they were ingenious. As our story leads us through that historic period, it might be of interest to note, in passing, some evidences of the destitution of that war-afflicted country. In a private letter referring to the hard times during the war, he says:

"In 1863 I dug up the ground in smoke-houses, put the dirt into hoppers and drained water through it as we do to get lye from ashes, and then boiled down the water to make salt. Such salt was ready sale at $1 to $5 per pound; indeed, it was almost impossible to get it at any price. I got a small portion of the salt I made for my labor in making it; but never got enough to have any to sell. Such salt was as dark as the darkest brown sugar, and dirty enough for all practical purposes. No smoke-house in all that country escaped the hopper."

Ben N—— was something of a local celebrity down in Alabama during the war. He was a noted bar-room wit, possessed of many good qualities of head and heart, and well calculated to make a useful man in any community, but for his inordinate love of drink. Dr. Talmage would have called him "a man of low wink and filthy chuckle;" but with all that, Ben was not wholly bad, nor yet entirely destitute of inventive genius. He submitted without a murmur to the inconvenience, and even hardships, of making salt out of dirt and coffee out of acorns; but when his favorite beverage began to be scarce in the land, he earnestly protested against any further efforts to continue the war in the midst of the wide-spread ruin and hopeless desolation that deluged the country. However, the war continued against his protest, and times went from bad to worse, till absolute and inevitable prohibition was an established fact. Ben and his associates gathered around the old saloon in Frankfort, where they had so often regaled themselves with enlivening drinks in the good times of old, and, like unhappy ghosts in an abandoned grave-yard, they wandered gloomily about the desolate ruins of the forsaken old house. It was a crisis which seemed to call for an inventive genius to provide some special means of deliverance. Ben was equal to the emergency, and, with all the enthusiasm of originality, he said:

"I tell you what, fellers; wek'n dig the dirt out'n' this old house 'n' bile it down 'n' make licker!"

But the suggestion was not favorably received, and no effort was ever made to put it into execution. Poor old Ben! With more than an average intellect, and a heart as tender as a woman's, he wasted his life in genial worthlessness around cross-road saloons. When he was old, he was touched by the story of the cross, and became a disciple of Christ. A sad sight it was to see him weeping over the ruins of a misspent life; but a blessed thing to see him so earnestly devoting the influence of his last days to correct the mistakes of his youth.

There were no stores in the country, and nobody had any store-clothes, unless it was an article now and then that had been bought before the war. There was but one store-hat in all that part of the hill country of North Alabama.

It was hopelessly disfigured in shape, and seriously damaged in color; but it distinguished its owner, and helped to make him the envied nabob of the country around Rock Creek. And yet pride of dress and rage for fashion were just as prominent then as now. The hats worn by men and women were platted by hand out of oats straw or wheat straw, and yet we talked as flippantly then as now about hats in style and hats out of style. It never occurred to us as any thing ridiculous to plat two hats out of the straw of the same sheaf of oats, and call one a fine hat for Sunday wear, and consider the other one a coarse hat for rough wear.

A man we will call D——— lived near Russellville, Franklin County, Alabama. Eccentric, ridiculous, and good-humored, he was known throughout the county as an original character. As times went from bad to worse, he tried various experiments to discover satisfactory substitutes for such articles as could not be obtained. He had a large family, and at times could get neither meat, salt, breadstuff, lard, nor coffee. His ingenuity was put to the test to get up a mess of pottage for a gang of hungry children in such straightened circumstances. He had a never-failing spring of pure water, near which grew some large beech-trees, and he boiled a pot of young beech leaves in clear spring water, by way of experiment, as salad for the children. It was amusing to hear him say, in after years, with many antic gestures and ridiculous grimaces:

"It beat nothin' bad; but it needed salt and seasonin' to give it stren'th!"

I smile when I think how we used tea made of parched rye, corn, meal, sweet potatoes, acorns, okra, and such things, as substitutes for coffee. There was no coffee in the country during the last days of the war.

The few old men left in the country because unfit for service, spent most of their time explaining to each other how the war ought to be managed. When times came to the hardest, those old decrepits were all in favor of an aggressive campaign. They did not always use words in exactly the same sense Webster gives them; but they felt that a crisis had arisen which could be successfully met by desperate means only, and they expressed themselves in the *harshest-sounding* words they could command without regard to the *exact meaning* of such words. Old Mr. W——, who was an authority among them on military tactics, said:

"Lee's got ter cross the *She*nander river, make a raid through the North, and order his men to commit *suicide* as they go, or the Southern Confederacy's busted!"

Of course he thought suicide meant destruction and dire calamity to the enemy.

The country along the Tennessee river was hotly contested ground during the war. The Tennessee river, through the Mississippi, opened direct steam-boat transportation to the base of supplies for whichever army held possession of it. By holding the Tennessee river, the Confederate army could reach the rich agricultural regions of West Tennesse, Arkansas, Mississippi, and Louisiana, and communicate with such important supply-centers as Paducah, Memphis, and New Orleans. With the same facility the Federal army, if in possession of the river, could reach Paducah, St. Louis, and the Ohio river to Evansville, Louisville, and Cincinnati. For these reasons the country along this river was one of the great battle-grounds of the late war, and second in importance only to the famous valley in Virginia, where Lee and Jackson fought their great battles. The two armies never ceased to strive for the mastery of the Tennessee river till the soldiers on both sides were mustered out of service. At one time the Confederate troops would drive the Federal army back and destroy all railroads and bridges leading up to the river from the north; and then again, unable to hold the territory they had gained, the two armies would come surging back over the country, fighting over every inch of ground, till the Confederate forces would be driven back several miles south of the river, and all railroads and bridges leading to it from that direction completely destroyed. Each army managed to hold possession of the river at points enough, for the greater part of the war, to prevent the other from transporting supplies and munitions of war over it; but neither could get such control of it as to make it of any use for purposes of navigation. In the struggle for possession of the river, each army had managed, by destroying railroads and bridges, to cut the other off from its base of supplies by over-land transportation. With the river blockaded by each against the other, and railroad transportation seriously impeded when not destroyed altogether, the two armies were compelled to fight out the issues of the war along that river, and gather their supplies almost wholly from the country in which they were fighting.

Early in the war the planters in all that country sent their negroes and mules, in charge of reliable overseers, further south, to save them from confiscation by the armies. It required but a few months of such fighting as we have described to lay in waste hundreds of miles of fencing, thus throwing out hundreds of thousands of acres of farm lands.

The Confederate army called for all males over seventeen and under fifty years of age, and patriotism prompted many younger boys and older men to volunteer their services in the army without a call. Madison County, Tennessee, was only one of many counties that furnished more volunteers in the army than there were voters in the county. There were more boys under twenty-one in the army than men over twenty-one out of it. Negroes and mules all gone, much of the fencing destroyed, and all of the men in the army, women and children, with a few helpless old men, were left to manage as best they could the difficult problems that confronted them at home.

In the hill country adjacent to the valley of the Tennessee river there were poor people before the war. They solved the problems of hard times in Dixie during the war easy enough. The hardships of lives of poverty for generations back had afforded them valuable experience. But the valley of the Tennessee river was one of the garden spots of the South, and noted for its palatial country-residences and the luxurious lives of its inhabitants. It has been supposed that Southern women, brought up in such luxury, their every whim gratified in delicacies of food and ornaments of dress, are lacking in fortitude, industry, and practical business management; four years of hard times in Dixie exploded that theory. Women are women, and whether you find them in the frozen regions of the North, or fanned by the balmy breeze of the South; facing wild beasts in the jungles of Africa, or gracing parlors in the most refined society in American cities; wherever they are found, they are ready to make any sacrifice or submit to any hardships which fidelity to the object of their love may require. To help child, brother, father, husband or lover, she will do what she can while she lives, and in death look up through her tears and sigh because she can not do more.

Women who had never even arranged their own toilet before the war without the help of waiting-maids, had to take charge of a country laid waste by war, and, with the help of a few children large enough to work, and the care of a great many too small to do any thing, support themselves, supply two armies, provide for the helpless, aged, cripples and invalids, and suffer the ravages of war and pillage of robbers. Yet they never faltered for a moment. Dressed in the coarsest of material, made by their own hands, they went through heat and cold, dust and rain, from daylight till dark, laboring at all the rough and heavy drudgery of farming. They guided the plow, built fence, harvested hay, gathered corn, fed stock, drove teams, and chopped wood.

To appreciate the disadvantages under which they labored, it should be remembered that there were no manufactories of any kind in the South. Every thing had to be made by hand. The South made no buttons; no nails; no sewing-needles; no pins; no sewing-thread; no knives and forks; no cups and saucers; no tumblers or goblets; no dishes of any kind; no matches; no hair-pins; no knitting-needles; no writing-pens; no lead pencils; no writing-paper; no plows; no axes, saws, hatchets, augers, chisels, hammers; no pocket-knives; no hoes; no tin buckets; no indigo, coperas, blue-stone; no quinine, nor medicine of any kind; no drawing-chains. These, and hundreds of other things of common use, were not to be obtained at all in Dixie during the war—particularly that part of it now under consideration.

When our fire went out, we had to borrow of those who had it. As substitutes for pins, the women used thorns; and for hair-pins, the large thorns from locust-trees. Buttons for the heavier clothing were made of leather, and the smaller buttons of thread. Sewing-thread was spun by hand, and the few needles in the country were those only that were bought before the war. There were but few of them in each neighborhood, and each one was kept going night and day. The time of a needle in any family was limited, and the breaking of one was lamented as a public calamity. Tumblers were made from round bottles. The process was to pass a stout cord around the bottle and see-saw it till the friction produced a hot ring, and then dash cold water on it. This caused the bottle to break smoothly where the cord was sawed, making a fair substitute for a tumbler. Such table-furniture had the advantage of variety, as hardly any two tumblers were of the same size and color. Common combs were not to be obtained at all, and the only substitutes for them were bungling imitations made by hand from cows' horns. Such were some of the disadvantages under which the women and children in Dixie labored and suffered in the dark days of a war which cost our lovely South-land her fairest homes and noblest sons.

It is difficult to tell where so many robbers came from; but it is easy to establish the fact that they were there. Whenever neither army was present, robbers seemed to literally infest the land every night. They took away every thing of value they could find, and made night hideous with ghastly crimes of murder and arson. If any one was even suspected of having any thing of value concealed, the robbers would murder him by slow torture or have it. One night they came to the home of old Mr. Wilson and demanded a few hundred dollars in gold which they suspected him of having concealed. He declared he had none, but they would not believe him. They stripped him of all his clothing, bound his hands and feet, tore leaves from his family Bible, saturated them with turpentine, spread them over his naked body and burned them off. This they repeated many times, till he was quite dead. He was one of the best old white-headed fathers in all the country. This is only one of the incidents of common nightly occurrence in the absence of both armies.

Surrounded by such difficulties and terrorized by such dangers, the women of Dixie struggled through four years of war without a murmur or complaint. It was not patriotism, but womanly nature. They were not struggling for any great principles of statesmanship; but sacrificing their lives in behalf of those they loved. The soldiers on both sides were brave men and true; but the women of the Sonth met and overcame obstacles that would have wrecked both armies and ended the war, if *men* had been required to suffer such hardships instead of *women*. Such was the state of affairs T. B. Larimore left when he moved from Tennessee to Hopkinsville, Ky. Coming near to Hopkinsville, he fortunately met B. S. Campbell, an elder in the Christian church. Elder Campbell was favorably impressed with the young man from the first, and arranged for him to have a temporary home near his farm, four miles from Hopkinsville. His mother was a member of the Christian church in Tennessee, and had with her a church letter. Elder Campbell describes her, at that time, as a woman of prepossessing appearance and splendid intellect. He tells the story of his life in Hopkinsville briefly in one of his letters in after years in the following words:

"I cut and hauled wood at a dollar and a quarter a load during the winter and spring of 1864. I tried to give honest measure and good wood, and if any one ever mistreated me, or took advantage of my straightened circumstances, I either did not know it or have forgiven and forgotten it, as no such impression is now upon my mind. I never asked anybody to trust me for any thing, nor did I contract a single debt I never paid. The people in general treated me justly, and Elders Campbell and Hopper were especially kind and generous to me."

Everybody who knew him at Hopkinsville speaks in the highest terms of him. He established and maintained a general reputation as being honest, industrious, studious, courteous, and especially devoted to his mother. He studied under the private instruction of a retired Presbyterian preacher, whose name I do not now remember, during the winter and spring of 1864, of nights; and through the influence of that gentleman and other friends he secured a country school to teach in the summer. He attended church regularly with his mother, and July 10, 1864—the day he was twenty-one—was baptized by Elder Hopper in Little river at Hopkinsville. Elder Hopper was not a preacher, nor was there any preacher present when he made the confession. About sunset, Saturday evening he decided to be baptized next day, and accordingly presented himself for that purpose at the ordinary church-meeting, without any preaching. The vow he made at the close of the Mossey Creek College revival caused him to make the decision to be baptized. That vow was to pray regularly, read the Bible constantly, and do every thing he understood it to require of him. Careful reading and constant prayerfulness had impressed him that it was his duty to confess his faith in Christ and be baptized, and he decided to do it.

MARS HILL, ALABAMA, FEB. 19, 1889.

DEAR BRO. SRYGLEY:

You can not make your chapter "Hard Times In Dixie" too strong. Women and children worked as slaves and lived in constant dread of robbers, murderers—the knife and the torch—anxious for news, but always afraid to hear it. Women who had spent all their ante-bellum days in ease, affluence and luxury, followed the plow, fed hogs, hid their bread and meat in cellar, loft and field, spun and wove their clothing, used thorns for hair pins, made hats of shucks and straw, made coffee of corn bran, carried corn to mill, hid their horses in the bushes—in short, sun-burnt and hard-handed, lived, labored and looked like *squaws* of the forest—dragged down by cruel war, but bravely battling against hard times, loving God, serving their generation and giving their *lives* for those they loved. Mrs. Larimore says she and her sisters, though blessed with competency before the war, took in the whole list of hard work, except cutting grain with a cradle—they "drew the line" at the reap hook—sickle. They plowed, grubbed, made, gathered and hid the crops, made rails (handled ax, maul and wedge), built fence, etc., etc. They dug a deep hole, in dead of night, in their smoke house, carried off the surplus dirt and hid it, buried their meat in that hole in a box, covered up the place nicely, sprinkled ashes over the place, to conceal all traces of the grave, and when absolutely necessary, to prevent starvation, they would, at midnight's solemn hour, while some of them "stood picket" resurrect some of the meat and again close the grave with previous care. All this and much more, when *any moment* the torch might be applied to their hard-earned, humble home. We laud the Carthaginian women, who, ages ago, gave the hair of their heads to make bow-strings for their soldiers; but neither Greece, nor Rome, nor Carthage, nor Jerusalem, nor this wide world, has ever developed sublimer specimens of true, genuine heroism, than "Hard Times In Dixie." Though the fountain of times onrushing stream be not dried up in ten thousand ages, neither tongue, nor pencil, nor pen, nor all combined with human and angelic wisdom and skill can ever do justice to "Hard Times In Dixie," especially the trials of the fairer, feebler, purer, truer and braver, sex.

Fraternally and truly,

T. B LARIMORE.

CHAPTER XI.

He was baptized July 10, 1864, and made his first public talk in prayer meeting Jan. 10, 1866, from second chapter of James. His second public talk was in prayer meeting Feb. 7, 1866, from Luke vi: 17–49. April 1, 1866, he made an address to the Sunday-school which is still remembered and highly commended by those who heard it. That address distinguished him as a ready and fluent speaker, and caused the elders of the church to encourage him to exercise his gift as a speaker, in the ministry. Accordingly he made his first public talk to the church on Lord's day meeting, May 6, 1866, from Rom. xii: 1. Encouraged by the favor with which this first effort was received, he consented that a regular appointment be made for him to preach. His first sermon was delivered May 13, 1866, from Luke xii: 13–29, at the close of which Miss Editha Ritter made the confession. I find the following note, in his own memoranda, concerning that sermon:

"Miss Editha Ritter made the confession—my first. This was the beginning of a meeting in which forty came to Christ—J. M. Long and others doing the preaching. I brought on the fight; they swept the field and gained the victory."

He did not count himself one of the preachers in this meeting.

These efforts were all made at Hopkinsville, Ky. In

the fall of 1866 he entered Franklin College, near Nashville, Tennessee, to pursue a course of study under the talented and lamented Fanning with a view to specially prepare himself for the ministry. The next memoranda of public work is to the effect that C. G. Payton, of Hart county, Ky., made the confession at the close of a sermon he preached at Burnett's Chapel, Davidson county, Tenn., June 2, 1867. They were schoolmates at Franklin College, and by request of Payton went to-gether to Green's Chapel, Hart county, Ky., where the baptizing was done June 16, 1867. This was the first person he baptized. The first funeral service he ever conducted was at the burial of "sister Sinclair's little baby boy, age six weeks, near Thompson's station, Tenn., July 12, 1867."

During the protracted meeting period in the summer of 1867, he traveled with R. B. Trimble through Maury, Hickman and adjoining counties in Middle Tennessee. Sometimes they traveled on horse-back, sometimes in a buggy, but never by railroad. Their meetings were all with country churches and at places in the country where we had no churches. That was before the time of town churches and city pastors among our people in that country. They preached in private houses, under the trees, in school houses, at country churches—any where they could get a congregation to hear them. With a Bible and hymn book in one end of saddle-bags and a clean shirt and collar in the other, they traveled through the country on horseback, counting themselves fortunate if they found a place to preach and a congregation to hear them. There were many good church members scattered over that country, and at several points there had been strong churches; but the war had disorganized most of the churches, discouraged many of the members, and greatly impoverished the country.

R. B. Trimble was a merchant tailor by trade in early life; but in later years a preacher of decided ability. His sermons were noted for clearness of conception, force of expression and close adherance to the teaching of the Scriptures. He never drifted into unprofitable speculations in doctrine, nor attempted extra adornment in speech. He tried to preach the gospel plainly in the spirit of its divine author, and in many places in protracted meetings his labors brought large numbers into the churches.

At one point in their travels, they found certain brethren who had come to doubt the existence of the old fashioned hell, as they termed it. Bro. Trimble declined to argue the question with them, and said, as he was not traveling in that direction it mattered but little with him whether the place should be kept up or abolished altogether. Before preaching, however, he took for his Scripture lesson Luke xvi, and when he came to verses 22 and 23 he read slowly and with emphasis:

"And it came to pass, that the beggar died, and was carried by the angels into Abraham's bosom"—then pausing a moment he looked over the audience and said: "Brethren, he was or he wasn't." With even more deliberation and emphasis he continued reading—"The rich man also died, and was buried, and in hell he lifted up his eyes"—again he paused and looked over the audience in deep solemnity, and said: "Brethren, he did or he didn't." This time the shot went home. And while it was having its effect, he remarked, by way of fastening the impression—"Brethren, while this is a matter of no moment to us, as we are not traveling in that direction, it is a subject of living interest to the man who is taking any chances along that line." This little incident he related to me as characteristic of R. B. Trimble's pointed manner of preaching.

He preached but little while with Bro. Trimble. It was not a time to trust an inexperienced boy to represent a doctrine so bitterly denounced and so obstinately opposed on every hand when the work could be performed by one as well qualified as was R. B. Trimble. Occasionally, however, he preached when the congregation consisted mainly of brethren and friends. Of one of those efforts, I find this memoranda of his own.

"Preached at Cathey's Creek, Maury county, Tennessee, night of Aug. 4, 1867, and told 'em all I knew. The brethren gave me $25, and kindly asked me to preach again; but, knowing nothing more to preach, I fled from the field of my glory, having divided between the sheep and the goats all the food I had, and fleeced the flock." In his memoranda of this period of travels with Bro. Trimble, I find one other note, which I decipher as follows:

"August 23, 1867, rode a mule to Bond's Mills, Hickman county, Tenn., to try to fill appointment for Bro. Trimble. Bro. Bond introduced me to one of the elders who was a tanner and at work on some hides when we found him; surveying me sadly, he said to Bro. Bond, in my presence, with a sigh: 'Well, we'll not be *entirely* disappointed.' But Bro. Trimble, fearing it was not expedient to risk me, decided to come himself a few hours after I left him. He came to my rescue before the conflict commenced, and there was *no* disappointment."

Bro. Trimble says he was the most devoted and self-forgetful young preacher he ever knew. He seemed to have but one desire, and that was to do good. In one of his early efforts to preach he advanced an idea not in perfect harmony with the Scriptures. It was of little consequence, but Bro. Trimble felt it his duty to call his attention to it privately. He received the correction thankfully; but was greatly distressed about it for several days, and even wept bitterly, fearing he had committed a mistake he could never fully correct, as an erroneous idea once communicated is so hard to recall.

It was through Bro. Trimble's influence that he came down into Alabama. According to his own memoranda, he left Franklin College early in 1868 for Alabama. So it would seem that he returned to Franklin College in the fall of 1867, after spending the summer of that year with Bro. Trimble. He always had a high regard for the talent of his teacher, Tolbert Fanning, at Franklin College. As a forcible speaker and finished orator, he thinks he had few equals and no superiors. After hearing Senator Daniel W. Vorhees in a celebrated murder case at Fort Smith, Ark., in 1888, he said of him: "He looks and talks more like Tolbert Fanning in a speech than any other man whom I have ever heard."

He came to Alabama to teach at Mountain Home, in Lawrence county, where the brethren under the leadership of Bro. J. M. Pickens were trying to establish a college. He remained there till the summer of 1868, when he came down to preach with old Bro. Taylor in Franklin and Lauderdale counties, during vacation of the school.

CHAPTER XII.

An account of his preaching during the summer of 1868 with John Taylor in North Alabama will be found in a preceding chapter. August 30, 1868, he was married to Miss Esther Gresham, near Florence, Alabama. In the fall of that year he resumed teaching at Mountain Home, where Brother J. M. Pickens was trying to build up a church college. The enterprise failed, however, and in the beginning of 1869 he went to Mansell Kendrick's, West Tennessee, to teach. He taught there six months, and at Stantonville, Tennessee, ten months, when he removed to his present home near Florence, Alabama, and opened Mars Hill Academy, January 1, 1871. While at Stantonville, he preached acceptably at various points in the surrounding country, and during vacation of school in midsummer, he held several very successful protracted meetings in John Taylor's field of labor, in North Alabama; but no data can be found as to the exact dates of meetings or number of additions. At his second visit to Rock Creek, in 1869, W. B. Blackburn, a local preacher in the Methodist Episcopal Church, South, and a man of much general information, and more than local reputation and influence in his church, submitted a list of forty questions to try to entangle him in his theology. These questions were read publicly, and a day set to answer them. There was general interest in the occasion, and an immense audience assembled to hear the questions discussed. Mr. Blackburn was present, and, by mutual agreement, each was to have a chance to speak on the questions submitted. The day passed pleasantly, without a discourteous or unkind word being spoken by either against the other. The audience was perhaps about equally divided in opinion concerning the merits of the doctrines advocated, but unanimous in the feeling that it was by far the most lovely and brotherly religious argumentation ever heard in that community.

I must be pardoned for a word of digression concerning W. B. Blackurn. In general religious intelligence, he lived a generation in advance of his day in that country; in encouragement and warm-hearted helpfulness for young men in every good work, he stood without a peer in that age and vicinity; in religious convictions, he was a Methodist. He was my friend, faithful and true, till the day of his death, and many a time has my heart beat the lighter and my soul quivered with a new joy for the fatherly resting of his hand on my head while his patriarchal "God bless you, my son," sounded with strange gladness in my ear. No doubt he would have loved me all the more if I had become a Methodist preacher; but for this I only reverence him the more, because it shows he was true to his convictions. But who will say he would have *tried* harder to deal with me *justly* and fairly? I do not believe it. He had faith in the boys of that mountain country. He knew them to be honest and persevering, and he believed they would some day be distinguished. He also had faith in the Methodist church, and perhaps never fully understood that it was not of divine origin nor identical with the scheme of redemption in Christ. When two objects of the heart's love and faith drift thus apart, who has an unkind word or thought for the heart's distressing agony? Nothing but sympathy and love for a heart thus rent asunder by conflicting emotions will comport with the spirit and teaching of Christ. To be firm in convictions, yet not severe in bearing, is a gift all too rare, especially with young men. I always understood that W. B. Blackburn was my uncompromising enemy in religious doctrine. He believed I was wrong, and it would have been the joy of his life to have brought me to his way of thinking; or failing in that, his next best joy to have prevented what he considered my heresy from leading astray any others whom he loved. But I loved him for his abundant labors in behalf of us all; I loved him for his steadfastness in what he believed to be right; but for the error I firmly believed possessed him in doctrine, and from which I never hoped to see him released—for these things I gave him the unmeasured sympathy of a heart that never ceased to reverence him in life.

W. B. Blackburn was not a man without faults; but in his country and time, he possessed a depth of piety and wealth of general information which went far to mitigate the faults he possessed in common with others of his generation less gifted in graces than himself. To get the true measure of a man, he should be studied in connection with his local surroundings. If his faults are all common to his associations, they are not so much to his personal demerit; but stand rather as defects of his generation. If his virtues are likewise held in common with all his associates, they are to the merit of his surroundings rather than to the commendation of his personal character. Thus judged, W. B. Blackburn had the demerits only of his surroundings, but the merit of personal virtues.

We turn now to the work of T. B. Larimore. His effort to establish Mars Hill College may be regarded as the greatest enterprise of his life. The extent to which he succeeded in the undertaking may be considered little less than miraculous. It will forever stand as a monument of his indomitable perseverance, unswerving faith, untiring industry, and matchless gifts of leadership. Considered from a purely business stand-point, it is questionable whether such meagre resources were ever before made to accomplish such immense results. In 1870 he was little more than an inexperienced boy. But recently out of college, he was not known in the church at large as a preacher or scholar. The site he selected for the college that was to be, was a cluster of little hills covered with stately oaks and watered by living springs, four miles from Florence, and scarcely more than a stone's-throw from Hopewell, where they so unceremoniously declined to hear him preach but two years before. He had not money enough to buy a postage-stamp—in fact, he lacked a few dollars yet being out of debt. The college was to be a *church-school*, and there was not a church nearer than Memphis, one hundred and fifty miles, that was able to sustain a preacher. If there was a meeting-house worth $300 owned by that church within a hundred miles of that place at that time, diligent inquiry has failed to discover it. The impoverished condition of the country has been alluded to in a previous chapter, and it had improved but little when he began his enterprise. The low standard of education in general may be inferred from remarks in a former chapter, and the intense religious prejudice all over the land was still further strengthened and enraged by this bold effort to establish a school to teach the doctrine of the sect everywhere spoken against. Confronted by all these obstacles, he undertook to establish a church-school, and to what extent he succeeded remains to be seen.

On the summit of one of the cluster of little hills, a site

was selected for the school-building. Mrs. Larimore received this spot of ground, worth perhaps $250, from her mother's little estate, and this was all their earthly possession. They had never kept house, and hence did not have enough furniture to start a home on the most economical plan. The first building, a three-story house of twelve large rooms, three halls, each ten by forty feet, and four open porches, each ten by fifty feet, was finished at a cost of $5,000 in round numbers. To suitably furnish this building, inclose the campus, and put up the necessary out-buildings, cost, perhaps, $5,000 more. If the reader will now take the pains to study the resources of the field on which he had to depend for support, the intense religious prejudice he had to combat, and the general indifference to education he had to overcome, it will certainly seem clear enough that, to successfully manage a $10,000 debt and meet the running expenses of a well-appointed school, would require unusual ability in an inexperienced boy but a few years out of his 'teens. But this was not all. Other buildings were added, additional ground was purchased, and a monthly paper started for gratuitous distribution, published on a very expensive plan, and as many as 20,000 copies issued and distributed in one month. The college property at the beginning of 1875—only five years after the beginning of the enterprise—consisted of over 600 acres of land, more than twenty houses, and a splendid collection of school furniture—all of which cost not less than $30,000. The college was successfully managed seventeen years, and never a dollar of debt contracted that was not paid to a cent. It was a church enterprise depending for patronage upon a people who had threatened to stone John Taylor for preaching, shaved the tail of his horse, and refused to "grunt" when he prayed. It was an educational enterprise depending for support upon a country where a citizen had brought up thirteen children on thirteen days' schooling, without so much as learning there was such thing as free schools, and where the local preachers in consultation expressed doubt as to whether any man ever lived long enough to read every thing in as big a book as the Bible. It was an immense financial enterprise involving the expenditure of thousands of dollars, and depending for support on a country in which a citizen was forced, by the general impoverishment produced by the war, to offer his hungry children beech leaves and spring water for diet. It was all these combined under the management of an awkward boy considered too ignorant, two years before its commencement, to preach in a country church within little more than a stones'-throw of the site on which it was located. If his success, under all these circumstances, does not demonstrate that he is a man of superior ability—yea, a consummate genius—then success in any thing can never be an evidence of merit in the leader. It will not do to say he deserves no credit for all this because the people did it for him. As well might it be said that Napoleon had no merit in military tactics because it was his *army* that shook every throne in Europe. Does it require no ability to get the people to do great things under adverse circumstances? Let those who have tried to lead men in great and noble enterprises answer. No man is readier than he to consider his success due to the co-operation of his friends. He not only claims no merit in himself for the stupendous work he has accomplished, but he does not seem to consider it any evidence at all that he possesses superior ability. He censures himself for every mistake or mismanagement in his life work, and renders sincere thanks to God and unstinted praise to his friends for every measure of success he attains. By what methods he succeeds where no other man would think it necessary to ever try in an enterprise, must appear from the simple story of his life and labors. It is the purpose of this volume to make a simple statement of facts, and leave each reader to amuse himself in analyzing his doings, to discover, if possible, his methods. Fortunately, from the starting of Mars Hill College, the story can be told from the stand-point of a personal observer, and even confidential adviser, for the most part. The writer was for years a member of his family, was fully informed as to the financial condition of the college, knew what debts were paid, what running expenses had to be met, how much money was received, and from exactly what sources it all came. It is impossible to point out the peculiarities of the man and his methods without giving a detailed statement of every thing he ever did. Every thing about him is peculiar, yet nothing is eccentric. He is unlike everybody else in every respect, yet not the least offensively individual in any thing. He is one of the most agreeable men I have ever known, and yet he has a way of his own about every thing, and always does things his own way. He seems always open to suggestions from everybody, and yet everybody seems to prefer his way to any other. He seems to follow his own way, not particularly because it is his way, but because everybody likes it best. He does not lead men in the sense of compelling them, or even asking them to follow him; but he leads them because they love to follow him. Indeed, there is no alternative for him but to lead, for the people *will* follow him. For this reason he is a great man and a successful preacher.

CHAPTER XIII.

He succeeds in what he undertakes because he *will not fail.* He has great faith in God and man, and believes any thing can be done that ought to be done. He makes no allowance for failures. If a thing ought to succeed, he believes God will do every thing man can not do for its success. His perseverance is absolutely indomitable. He never gives up. In an announcement concerning the college in 1875, he said:

"Trusting in Jehovah's strength, we know no such word as fail. With us, Webster's Unabridged is next to the Bible, and the word fail has been erased from our copy of that."

His valedictory address on leaving college is so characteristic of him in this respect, it can not fail to be of interest in this connection. It should be remembered that it is a schoolboy's production and therefore not entirely free from the defects in style peculiar to such documents. While no literary merit is claimed for it, considered in the light of his subsequent life some of its utterances seem almost propthetic. It abundantly shows that he is capable of long continued adherence to a principle, and not a mere superficial fine talker swayed by short-lived emotions.

[Following is the Valedictory Address by T. B. Larimore, of Hopkinsville, Ky., student of Franklin college, Tennessee. Delivered June 6, 1867, at Hope Institute, Tennessee, during the commencment exercises of that school and Franklin college. —Ed.]

My Dear Friends and Fellow-travelers to Eternity:

It has fallen to our lot, this fair and lovely summer's morn, to deliver you a farewell or *valedictory* address; the performance of which very solemn duty would fain have been neglected, but for the promptings of a desire to render implicit obedience to the requirements, and gratify the desires of a worthy and (justly) dearly beloved teacher, whose every command is just, and ought to be obeyed.

It is not in consequence of an *unwillingness* to address you, that the subject is approached with so great a degree of reluctance and diffidence, but because of a consciousness of incompetency to do justice to the occasion.

Had we the ability, we would be proud to say any thing in our power which might be, in the *least* degree, advantageous or encouraging to our fellow-beings, while marching through this dismal land of sorrow and despair.

But, since duty has made it obligatory upon us, we shall endeavor to draw your attention for a few moments to the subject of *Perseverance*—a quality which as surely tends to raise the mind of man above the trivial affairs of earth; a quality which as surely tends to raise the *soul* of man above the vices and low, degrading practices of his day, and ultimately exalt him to "a home above the skies," as the gas with which a balloon is inflated, tends to force it to quit the clouded scenes of earth, mount high upon its airy throne, and wend its way, in grandeur, through the ethereal realms above, entirely regardless of every wind that blows—a quality, the *absence* of which is just as *sure* to confine a man to a level with the dust from which he sprang, as is the absence of *wings* to confine the *stately eagle*, the "*king of birds*," which surpasses every other species of the feathered tribe, in the dexterity of its movements, and the velocity and height of its flights—called the "Bird of

Jove," because it majestically soars aloft, FAR beyond the reach of the limited vision of man, and there calmly and gracefully traverses the "blue fields of space," 'mid destructive thunderbolts and lightning's angry flashes; thus seeming to bid defiance to "Heaven's fiery messengers," and sport with Jupiter's implements of destruction—to a level with the *reptile that crawls in the dust!*

The *warrior*, who, perchance, has washed his unhallowed hands and dyed his martial robes in innocent blood, may, while seated upon the summit of the towering heights of fame," and looking down, like a grim monster, upon a subjugated world prostrate beneath his feet, boast of his *bravery!* The *historian*, who, with pen and scroll in hand, has almost spent his life in sketching down the great events of ages past and gone, may boast of his *ancient records.* The *poet*, who, in colors *bright*, has painted many a *scene*, and oft described, with great *delight*, things that have never *been*, may boast of the grandeur and sublimity of his *compositions.* The *orator*, who oft has stood before the great and powerful of earth, and held them, by his magic power, *completely* 'neath his *sway*, may boast of his *eloquence.* The *devotee of wealth*, who's filled his coffers up with gold, and dressed in costly robes, may boast of his fortunate *skill.* The *haughty potentate*, who's held for years his royal *seat* upon a royal *throne*—his temples bound with chaplets rich, beneath a golden crown, may boast of his *matchless power*—but *all* are bound to surrender the "palm of victory" to *Perseverance*; for, had not this indomitable and never despairing spirit presided over their career, they would never have been celebrated upon the pages of history as men of *chivalry*, *talent*, *wealth* and *renown.*

The *alluring*, *deceptive*, *defrauding*, *peace-blasting*, *war-making*, *blood-shedding*, *soul-destroying*, and *Heaven-defying* spirit of *wealth*, may sit enthroned for a while, surrounded by blind, deluded admirers, who worship at her shrine, having crowned her as queen, in their endeavors to exalt her. *Idleness*, that pauper-making spirit, by God long since condemned, may for a while, upon her faded brow, wear a wreath of withering flowers, *culled*, as well as *woven*, by the slaves of indolence. *Pride*, that egotistic, that self-esteeming fiend—that tyrant, who is holding so many 'neath his sway, destroying youthful vigor, health and beauty, too—may *flourish* for a while, and bask with seeming pleasure in Flattery's sunny rays. But the conquering genius, *Perseverance*, is destined to proudly triumph over *all*—sit enthroned HIGH above them—wear a glittering diadem, by integrity adorned with gems of fitting splendor for one who justly reigns, and gain the *merited* applause of all who prefer *true* worth to that which is only *visionary* and *deceptive.*

Wealth may, if rightly *used*, be an *auxiliary* in forming and developing the character of men. Pride may inspire him with a *desire* to succeed; but *they*, (though wealth be mountain high, and pride its equal be,) in the absence of *perseverance*, will prove as useless as hidden treasures which have never been discovered. They, with *all their attendant* train, are as far inferior to *perseverance* as the transient bubble which plays upon the limpid bosom of the rippling lake, and which the least slight rustle of the wind may cause to burst and disappear for ever, is to the pearl that lies unheeded beneath its liquid throne; and the man who is the possessor of *these alone* without the unerring guidance and faithfully supporting power of *perseverance*, like a ship without sails, compass, or ballasts, is uncertain in *all* his *movements; far out* upon a stormy sea, yet steering for no port; liable to be drifted upon the perilous rock of misfortune, and there disastrously wrecked by every *wind* that *blows*, and every *wave* that *rolls!* But *perseverance*, in the absence of *both* these *auxiliaries*, will triumph over, and trample under foot, every thing that might impede his progress, and bring him off a victorious conqueror, in *every laudable enterprise.*

It matters very little what may be the *pecuniary* circumstances of a youth when he enters upon the "theater of life;" if he is endowed with ordinary *intellect* and *perseverance*, to cause him to *press forward*, he *will* succeed. Though his birth-place be an humble *cottage*, a miserable *hovel*, or the *stall* of a *stranger*, as was our blessed Savior's; though he be considered by his superiors in *rank* and *fortune* as being *almost* upon a level with the "*beast of the field*," or the *dust* which he treads beneath his *feet;* though the youth of fortune may *disdain* to *associate* with him—*still*, if he will press forward with *unwavering energy* in some *laudable pursuit*, he is as *sure* to triumphantly arise from his humble position, to occupy a station in life which the favored sons of earth might envy, as the tender sprout which shoots up from the tiny acorn is to become a sturdy oak, and overshadow the grass which once towered above it, but, like the indolent, was forced to yield, in meek submission, to the beauty-blasting frosts of each successive autumn; and the day *will* come when those who, in *base, ignominious* idleness, contemptuously spurned him from their presence, in his youthful days, will be proud to gather round him to receive instruction from the "crystal fountain" of his superior knowledge.

But, on the other hand, though a youth be greatly *blest*, in every respect; though his share of earthly wealth be large as he could wish, it will vanish soon, and all be gone, unless he *persevere;* and though he be endowed with almost a *supernatural intellect*, his position will *always* be an *humble* and *degraded* one, unless he *cultivate* it. *Yes*, with *all* these advantages, if he yield himself a slave to *slothfulness*, he is *inevitably* destined to drag out a *miserable, brutish* existence which a wandering Arab would *blush to claim*, or a *Peon* scarce would envy! Let no one, then, lull himself to rest by the delusive hope that his strong and powerful mental faculties will guide him safely through this world, while he enjoys rest. *No;* although the *richest boon of Heaven*, they are *useful* but when *used.* It is not the *real, specific value* of a substance or quality which causes it to be *admired*, but the manner in which it is *polished.* The *pearl* that is buried *far* down beneath the "briny wave," over which untold millions glide, unconscious of the wealth that lies beneath their *path*; the *diamond*, sleeping in its rocky bed, a thousand feet below the surface of the *earth;* or the gold that is mingled with *old California's dust*, although of the same *intrinsic* value—although *just as bright*, in their present dark and gloomy positions, as if they adorned a *conqueror's brow*, or decked a *monarch's diadem*—they will *never* present their glittering beauties to the *eye of man*—*never* draw forth the applause of the thousands who admire gay apparel and gaudy show, unless *brought to light and polished by labor.*

Just so with the *mind of man.* Though he possess the *loftiest* intellect, the highest capacity for *every* honorable achievement; though he be endowed with the *natural* abilities of a *Webster or a Clay*, with the *bravery of a Leonidas*, and the *physical* powers of a *Hercules*, they will *all* prove comparatively *worthless* to him; and instead of becoming an intellectual giant, his brilliant intellect will perish unadmired, like the lovely flower that withers in its bud, in some dark, secluded spot, where the cheering rays of the sun have never penetrated, to develop its beauty, or "the gentle dews of heaven" descended, to bathe its lovely face in nature's sparkling gems, unless *developed by perseverance.* Yea, these heavenly gifts, neglected, will prove to be a curse! I verily believe that the man who, in the possession of such talents, spends his days in idleness, and fails to cultivate them, is *tenfold* more miserable than the one who scarcely possesses sufficient reason to guide him in the most *common* affairs of life; for no one can be entirely *unconscious* of his ability. And should he spend his days in idleness, and fail to cultivate those talents, the possession of which he is *conscious*, his conscience will continue to reprove him for his unfaithfulness *as long as life remains.*

How *strange*, then, that *man*, created in the image of his Maker, and granted dominion over *every* thing that dwells upon the earth, should be content to fall as far short of that station which God designs him to fill, as he must *inevitably* do, if he allows idleness to fill the seat designed for perseverance! *especially* when he knows that *sorrow* and *remorse of conscience* will thereby be incurred, and while, at the same time, *all nature* testifies, with one united voice, that *every thing desirable* may be obtained by *labor;* while nought but *degradation* to *indolence* is given! The *bee*, that sucks the fragrant flower; the *bird*, that cleaves the air; the *beasts*, that roam the forest; the *stars*, that shine on high; the *moon*, that *wanes* and *waxes*; the *sun*, that gives us *light*; the *earth*, that on her *axis* revolves both day and *night—all*, by their example, inculcate *perseverance!* There is not a *single star* that *dwells* among heaven's shining host, that's spent a day in idleness, *since God created it!* There is scarce an *insect, known to man*, that has no work to do. By use, the *magnet's* power is *increased;* in *idleness* it *wanes.* By use are *metals* made to *shine*, while in *idleness* they *rust.* By constant *flowing*, water keeps its clear and pure state; but when in *idleness* it stands, it forms a *loathsome pool.* By work, the *cheek* is made to *blush*, which in *idleness* grows pale.

To prove that perseverance *will* develop the latent spark concealed in the bosoms of the most humble and unfavored ones of earth, we only have to move the veil from the brow of ages past, and take a retrospective glance at the truths thereby concealed. By a careful perusal of the history of the most celebrated and successful of our predecessors, we will find that *none* of them were *naturally* great; but that they—*every one*, without a *solitary exception*—scaled the "towering heights of fame" by *faithful perseverance.*

For proof of this, let us go in our imaginations back to the bright and sunny plains of the chivalrous and far-famed land of Greece, in the days of her ancient glory, and there associate, for a few moments, with her noblest son and brightest jewel, *Demosthenes*—the greatest orator the world has ever known—one who stood before an iron-hearted consul, who knew not how to pity, and pled for a *poor, friendless, penniless* convict, in such an overpowering strain of eloquence, that the consul—his frowning face becoming pale, his body weak and faint—unconsciously relaxed his grasp upon the death-warrant which he held in his trembling hand, and, letting it fall to the floor, ordered the heavy shackles, which held his victim bound, to be burst from off his fettered limbs, and him to be released, while the saving words of the orator still echoed through the hall!—one who completely eclipsed all his cotemporaries; one who shone in the constellation of oratory with such brilliancy, that others seemed but glimmering stars, compared with an unclouded sun, in his presence; one to whom the youths of all succeeding ages have been referred, as a model of greatness and oratorical perfection! Do we find him, from infancy to age, dwelling in a lordly mansion, living in pomp and splendor, surrounded by inestimable wealth, and followed by a train of servants, to do his *every* will? No! We find him a *poor, humble orphan,* not only destitute of *wealth,* but laboring under the oppression of *natural* defects, which render it *highly* probable that he can never be successful! We find him of a *delicate constitution,* which causes his fond mother—influenced by the promptings of that pure, holy, and undying love, which finite skill can never fathom, and none but a mother ever know—to neglect his education, thinking that he is unable to endure hard study! Besides, he has an *impediment* in his speech, which renders it *highly* improbable that he can ever be proficient in that profession which he is most desirous of following! In addition to all this, he meets with great discouragements in the very *dawn* of his career. Upon his first appearance upon the stage, so *ludicrous* is his effort, that, after the utterance of a few stammering sentences, we behold him driven from the rostrum, and even from the *presence of the assembly,* by the sneers of the audience. But do we find the energy of our young hero crushed by these misfortunes? No; they only cause him to *double* his labors, summon *new courage,* approach the scene of his former disaster, to renew the conflict with increased energy, and with a firm determination to *never despair,* but patiently to persevere, under the cheering light of *fortune,* or the gloomy cloud of *woe.* And, true to the promptings of his persevering spirit, we next behold him out yonder upon the seashore, *far away* from the contemptuous gaze of the busy throng, surrounded by naught but surging waves, towering cliffs, and forest trees, with *earth* for his *stage,* the *heavens* for his *covering,* and *God* for his *audience,* delivering orations to the foaming billows as they burst with loud roar upon the rocky *beach,* with pebbles in his mouth to assist him in overcoming the stoppage in his *speech!* Again we see him, for months in succession, confined to his little dark and gloomy subterraneous studio; with no *companions* save his *books*; no *food*, save *bread and water*; with naught to cheer his lonely hours, except a glimmering lamp; an exile (banished by himself) from all the world without, applying himself *diligently* and *perseveringly* to his studies, till at last he comes forth from his dismal abode, the champion of his age, *well* calculated to bear away the "palm of victory" from *every oratorical contest!*

But, for an example of more modern date, go, if you will, to the birth-place of the renowned *Franklin*, and follow *him* in his eventful career through life. See him, an *humble illiterate* youth, at home with his father, a *poor* man, in the most *humble* occupations of life. No *books* to read, no *time* to study! Behold him in the capacity of an *apprentice* and a *journeyman*. View him in these humble circumstances for a moment, and then turn your attention from these discouraging scenes to the lofty positions which he *afterward* filled. See him in the French Court, the Minister of the Colonial Government—intrusted with the transaction of the most important business that arose before his country in her darkest and most perilous hour—admired by the American at home and the foreigner abroad, for his integrity, wisdom, and learning. See him penetrating the hidden recesses of knowledge, and bringing up to light, from their lowest depths, principles of vast importance to man—of which *none*, not even the wisest sage that ever surveyed the canopy of heaven, had ever *dreamed* before! See him stretching forth his Herculean arm of knowledge —snatching the fierce, forked lightnings from the brow of the dark and lowering clouds, along whose rugged battlements they play, with fearful speed—bringing them down from their boundless domains to the circumscribed limits of earth, and forcing them, thus caged and tamed, to cease their frantic sports, and yield, in meek submission, to the stubborn will of man! See him controlling the electric spark, thus taken from its home in the stormy bosom of the heavens, in such a manner as to be enabled to transmit intelligence from *State* to *State*, from *continent* to *continent*, from *clime* to *clime*, with lightning speed—swifter than the march of *victorious Time!—yea*, *almost* with the velocity of *thought itself!* and *then* ask yourselves the question, Should we *despair*, or should we be encouraged, by these examples, to *persevere?* If we refer to the history of the *mighty conquerors* of *all ages*—whether to that of a *Pompey* or a *Cæsar*, an *Alexander* or a *Napoleon*, or *any others*, who have caused the earth to tremble with their power, we will find that perseverance has been the key to *their* success.

But, my dear young friends, I do not refer you to the history of these *bloody* men because I would have you imitate their example in *all* things. *No, never!* I would not have *you*, like an Alexander, look out over a conquered world which you had devastated; over a sword-smitten world; over a world which you had "clothed in sackcloth and ashes;" over a world which you had stripped of her noble sons and valiant warriors; thus leaving mothers' hearts to bleed; thus reducing *loving wives* to *mourning widows*, and *affectionate children* to *helpless orphans*; over a world which you had filled with the lamentations of the bereaved, of every age and rank, and *weep yourself*, not through sympathy for the bereaved and broken-hearted, but because there are no more *opposers* to *slaughter*; no more *nations to subjugate*; no more *lands* to *drench in blood;* no more *cities* to *reduce to ashes;* no more *wives* to be *bereaved;* no more *children* to reduce to *orphanage*; no more *mothers' hearts* to *break;* or, at least, no farther *pretext* for this *heart-rending work!* And then suddenly usher your *wicked, discontented* spirit into eternity, by the inordinate use of *wine*, which oft, perhaps, had cheered you on in your dreadful work of carnage!

I would not have *you*, like a *Cæsar*, weep because you had never imbrued your hands in human blood; then rush forward, *like a furious beast of prey*, or an *evil spirit determined on destruction*, to the slaughter of a million of the human race; lead a million into miserable captivity; carry desolation and destruction into the midst of three hundred nations; plunder eight hundred quiet cities; push your conquests to the homes of poor, humble, innocent people, of whom you had never *heard* before; there take the father from the presence of his unhappy, helpless, weeping little ones; tear the husband from the fond embrace of his doting wife; hurry him off from the home of his childhood and friends of his youth, whose familiar faces he is never again to behold; barely giving him time to take one farewell, longing look, while the tear rolls down his manly cheek, to behold his little cottage—dear to *him* as a *palace* to a *king*—wrapped in *destroying flames*; drive him on, like a *beast of burden*, "through cold and heat," to dwell among strangers in a far-distant land, and there rivet the "galling chains of slavery" upon him and his posterity for ever! And, having thus spread consternation throughout the inhabited world, be *one day* looking for a *crown*, and the *next*, *weltering in your own life's blood*, drawn by the swords of bloody assassins, whom you considered your *best and dearest friends!*

Nor would I have you, like a Napoleon, to strew your mangled and lifeless thousands over rugged, frozen mountains and sanguinary fields; and then, in the midst of your career and prime of your life, be banished by a conquering foe far away from home, country, and friends, to spend the remnant of your days in lonely exile, upon a desolate island, in the bosom of the "stormy deep!"

I would not have you endeavor to inscribe your names upon the "scroll of fame" with a sword dipped in the blood of the innocent! I would not have you immortalize your names by desolating countries; by reducing *hamlets to smouldering ruins*, and *fruitful fields* to forests; by bathing continents in the blood of their sons and tears of their daughters, and whitening their hills and valleys with the bones of the slain, who have fallen before you, on their own native soil, while defending whatever they held dear! No! Never! Never! There is a more *noble*, a more *glorrious* work for you to perform; a work which will yield you, on earth. unspeakable bliss, and a treasure unfading in heaven.

The most of you—my fellow-students, especially—are "*Christians;*" you are "*disciples of Christ;*" you have dissolved your allegiance to Satan; are no longer under his dominion; hence you are to conquer by *love*, and *not* by the *sword.* The only sword that you can use, consistent with your Christian profession, is the "sword of the Spirit." You have taken up the cross, and set out upon your pilgrimage from the "city of Destruction" to that blest abode reserved for the righteous, God-loving and God-serving of all ages. You have enlisted under Christ as your Captain; that meek and lowly one who never took revenge; that pure and holy heir of heaven, who suffered himself to be nailed to the cross and cruelly slain, when he could have instantaneously summoned "more than twelve legions of angels" from their starry abode in the presence of the "Omnipotent Father on high," to his rescue! He has a work for you to do which you must perform if you would receive the reward of faithful laborers. Think not that you can spend your days in idleness while on earth, and yet receive the reward of laborers in heaven. If thus you think, you are *deceived.* We must nourish the "tree of life" in time, if we would pluck its fadeless flowers, taste its delicious fruits, and recline beneath the sacred shade of its ambrosial boughs in heaven. We all have a work to perform. Our Omnipotent Father in heaven has given to each of us an intellect, which it is not only our duty to cultivate, but to devote to his service. Though we be not as intellectual as others, still it is our duty to make a proper use of the talent with which we are each intrusted, and our reward will be just as great as that of those who are more favored. The servant who gained two talents by the use of two received the same reward as the one who gained five by the use of five; but the one who received *one* and *buried* it was condemned for *slothfulness;* though the inference is plain, that if he had gained *one* talent by the use of the *one* with which he was *intrusted,* he *too* would have been rewarded by being made partaker of the joys of his Lord. Where little is given, little is required; but something is required of all. If you have power only to minister to the necessities of one of "the least of the disciples of Christ," though it be but the giving of a cup of cold water, it is your duty to do that, and no more, and God will reward you for it. But if your Heavenly Father has blessed you with an intellect which will enable you to "stand on Zion's sacred walls," and speak words calculated to shatter the supporting pillars of infidelity, and cause that mighty fabric to crumble into dust, burst assunder the strongholds of sin, remove her galling chains, and liberate a captive world, it is your *imperative duty to do it.*

As season follows season, so generation follows generation. As the leaves of each succeeding summer supply the place of those which by autumn's frosts are killed, and by winter's blasts dislodged, so the individuals of each rising generation must supply the place of those blighted by the frosts of time, by the hand of death removed. But did the buds not grow in the winter, nor swell in early spring, sunny summer ne'er would have bright foliage for her trees. And unless the youthful mind is trained to think, and persevere, it will never be prepared to fill another's place. One by one, the hand of death is removing the useful men of our age from among us, and soon, very soon, my young friends, the duty will devolve upon you and your contemporaries, of filling all the high and useful stations in society, and of rallying beneath the "banner of salvation," to carry on that glorious work, by Christ on earth begun. But you cannot be prepared to assume these great responsibilities, without first training and educating your minds. Hence it is your duty, in the *first* place, to hoard up an ampel stock of knowledge, thus preparing yourselves for the fulfillment of the mission of man on earth, and for the discharge of the duties which God has made incumbent upon you. True, the "hill of science" is long, steep, and rugged; but this should not *discourage* you. You should remember that the greatest men who have ever adorned the world, were once little boys, with no better prospects than you have at the present. Yes, many of the brightest intellectual gems of earth were born and reared under circumstances as dark, compared with *yours*, as *midnight* when compared with *noon*. You should remember that all the wise and powerful men of earth were once *little boys*, playing round their mothers' knees, learning to lisp the first sweet accents of a mother's love, or learning their letters, one by one, as they reclined their little heads upon a mother's breast. The paths they trod are open still, and you can walk therein. By *perseverance* they arose, and you can do the same. Be not discouraged because there seems to be fearful difficulties arising before you in your journey. They are not insurmountable. They may appear formidable, when beheld through the misty veil of the dim distance; but be patient; you will overcome them all, and come off victorious in the end. "Make your mark high." Keep your eyes upward. *Persevere.* Remember, too, that no great, worthy, or desirable object is to be gained, without time and exertion. Rely upon God; meet difficulties with a determined spirit, and be not discouraged, because you can not reach the desired object immediately. An education is made up of letters, syllables, and words, and must be acquired letter by letter, and word by word. Be patient, then, and *persevering;* content with gaining a *little* every day. Cents compose the fortune; atoms make the mass. Every thing is formed of particles. That gigantic mountain, which rears its lofty, cloud-capped summit high in the blue ether above, till it seems to be lost in the skies, is formed of little grains of sand! That vast ocean, which stretches out far beyond the limits of the telescopic eye, washing the shores of every continent, from the frozen regions of the North to the sunny plains of the South, is formed of tiny drops! The whole universe, this earth, and all the glittering planets that adorn the "blue vault of heaven," are formed of mere insignificant particles! Then we should certainly be willing to treasure up a reasonable portion of useful knowledge, little by little; especially when we remember that God has given us the minds to contain it, and men (some of them guided "by wisdom from on high') the books from which it may be gathered!

We may learn an important and encouraging lesson, upon this subject, from the insect world.

What man is there, who—never having heard or thought of such a thing—would not be surprised, yea, startled, when told that the beautiful, fruitful, flowery, fertile isle upon which he dwells; upon the production of the alluvial soil of which he depends for his "daily bread;" and within whose shady groves he has roamed from childhood up—was formed, yea, its very foundations laid, and its mass erected, by mere insects? Yet this might often be the case.

Let us, by the eye of imagination, behold a group of little coral insects, *away down* in the depth of the fathomless ocean; mere *insignificant* insects! Let us observe the labors of these little creatures. Patiently and perseveringly they prosecute their work. Day by day, and year by year, they toil diligently and incessantly. Though great the work they've thus begun, they never will despair. Daily and hourly the little cells are erected, one upon another, rising slowly and imperceptibly, but steadily upward. After a long succession of years, we see the surface of the water disturbed by its progress; and lo! in a short time, that mighty column rears its massive head in triumph above, and looks down with an air of pride upon the proud billows which have for ages rolled triumphantly above its humble builders!

In *vain* the ocean's crested waves may rage and surge around! That structure, thus by patience built, can *never be overthrown!* The rain may fall in torrents; the thunders shake the sea; the waves may rise like mountains, to meet the angry clouds, and with wind and vivid lightnings, on that mighty fabric rush; but harmless is each allied blow, for still it stands secure!

Soil and seeds are wafted thither, from distant climes, and neighboring islands. The acorn and other seeds are imbedded there; and, in course of time, the sturdy oak and lofty cypress rear their towering branches majestically upward, and bow their graceful forms to the breeze, to give, as it were, a welcome salute to the weary sailor as he sails around that flowery spot, which, to seamen of past generations, was but a common part of the "briny deep," having nought to give the weary traveler but a cold and watery grave, but which now invites him to anchor there, assuring him of protection from the furious blasts of the reckless storm, and offering him *pure water* to quench his painful thirst, delicious fruits to regale his appetite, and pretty birds and roses to charm his *weary eyes*!

Thus we see that these little creatures, by their patient and energetic labors, have erected a monument which will not only be vastly beneficial to "generations yet unborn," but will proclaim to the world, and perpetuate, from generation to generation, and from age to age, the story of their untiring *energy, perseverance, and industry,* as long as Time, from year to year, keeps up his solemn rounds!

Then, my dear young friends, if you would write your names high upon the scroll of fame, in indelible characters; if you would be able to guide the weary sailor on life's boisterous sea, and direct him on to the shining mansions of eternal rest; if you would be able to assist in shielding Christianity from the furious blasts of the reckless storm of infidelity; if you would be able to stand upon a foundation as firm as the "*Rock of ages*, and battle with and vanquish the allied hosts of Satan, in all their wicked onsets, take courage from such examples as these; press forward diligently, patiently, and resolutely, in the acquirement of useful knowledge; devote it to the advancement of the cause of

God, and the good of your fellow-man, and success will inevitably crown your commendable efforts.

He who his duty seeks to know, and always does the same,
Will not be kept confined below the portals of immortal fame.

Young ladies, you, too, have a work to perform, a *mission* to fill, a *duty* to discharge.

If, when God from chaos the universe had formed, to all the shining worlds on high their daily work assigned, and in his own great image had made the creature man, he saw his work was incomplete, his glory's height not reached, and, as his *last*, his *crowning* act, he made your mother Eve, and placed her by his new-made image, as a jewel to adorn it, then "bowed to view his mighty work," and saw 't was "*very good,*" *surely woman*—the *climax*, the *culminating* point of the drama of creation, at the end of which, in the language of Job, "The morning stars together sang, and all the sons of God shouted for joy"—was not created merely as an ornament for Eden's lovely bowers, and beatifying companion for man, without some worthy part to enact in all God's righteous plans! No! While man has been pronounced "the lord of the earth," the "glory of man," which the great apostle declares the woman to be, has resting upon her the greatest responsibility of which we can conceive. It is not your duty to occupy the foremost station in the "army of the Lord," and there contend with uplifted voice, against the fiery darts of infidelity, in the warfare waged between Christianity and sin. *No!* Such work is not suited to your delicate nature. But it is your duty—like angels of mercy from heaven dispatched, like the two Marys, your sisters of old, who lingered long behind the crowd who had crucified the Lord, the last to quit the rugged cross on which he bled and died, the first to visit, ere the sun had driven night away, the closely guarded sepulcher in which the Savior lay, and first to tell the glorious news that Christ had conquered death, or like her who bathed his feet with a shower of tears and wiped them with her flowing tresses—to visit and sympathize with the sick, afflicted, poor, needy, and distressed; soothe their afflictions by your tender care; comfort and console them in their distresses by suitable acts of kindness and gentle expressions of love; encourage young "soldiers of the cross" to strive to gain the prize; in short, to perform all those sacred duties which are best performed by creatures of finer feelings than man is apt to possess. And, above all, to shape and train the youthful mind for future usefulness. For that circle, within the bounds of which the young are all beneath your care and influence, is the ante-chamber of the Church, which is the vestibule of heaven; and those whose minds are filled with false impressions and wicked thoughts in the antechamber, seldom enter the vestibule through which to pass to heaven. Then who can overrate the importance of your mission?

If you would be prepared for the discharge of these sacred duties; if you would be beloved by your associates in life, and have your names held in fond remembrance by succeeding generations; if you would speak words which would extend their hallowed influence over the forlorn and distressed of following years as a soothing balm in the afflictions and fiery trials of life, to raise their minds from gloomy and desponding reflections of despair to glittering beauties of the paradise of God; if you would perform acts which, like the anointing of the Savior's head by Mary, would be proclaimed to the remotest bounds of earth, as a perpetual memorial of, and token of regard for you, press forward *perseveringly* in the acquirement of useful knowledge, to be devoted to the honor of God, and the good of your race, and you will not only be successful and happy in this life, but you will thereby gain admittance into the portals of heaven, there, with the beatified and redeemed of every age, country, and clime, to enjoy the glories of that happy clime, and each to wear a glittering star-spangled crown of immortal glory!—a crown which as far outshines that worn by the haughty monarch on his throne, as yon brilliant sun, whose glorious, unborrowed light sends its radiant rays to the remotest planets known, outshines the *fading jewels of earth!*—a crown which shall shine with radiant, undimmed splendor when all the thrones, crowns, principalities, and powers of earth shall have been tried, condemned, and cast aside as worthless rubbish, rolled beneath the last tread of the ponderous wheels of Time in his final farewell circuit, and buried in the wrecks of everlasting oblivion!

O may you each for that heaven prepare;
And there, 'mid shouts of "the victory's won,"
Each such a glorious diadem wear,
When Time's fleeting ages are done!

While it is a pleasing task to linger in the presence of near and dear friends; while it causes my humble bosom to swell with joy, and with emotions of gratitude to God for permitting me to be placed in so favorable a situation in life; while it is a source of gratification to me to know that a part of the morning of my life has been spent with those whose purity renders them well worthy of the highest stations in life, there is a part of my task which causes my heart to throb with emotions of sorrow. That part, that *painful* part of my task, is yet to be performed.

It is my sad and solemn duty to-day to bid a last, yes, a last farewell, to those with whom I have associated, and whom I have learned to love as a band of brothers.

Though short has been our acquaintance; though we have associated together but for a few months, still it thrills my heart with sorrow to know that, in a very few hours we must separate, to meet no more on earth. What a change can be wrought in a few fleeting days! When, but a short time since, we, by the goodness of God, were permitted to assemble here to dwell beneath the same roof; to partake of our daily refreshments at the same board; to take our evening's recreation in the same grove; and, above all, to receive instruction, both scientific, practical and divine, from the same worthy and inexhaustible source, we were strangers. No love then burned within my breast for any one of you more than that I owe to all of Adam's race. But, since that time, by your kindness and attention to me, you have enstamped foot-prints of the gentle spirit of love upon this humble heart of mine, which all the storms and commotions, wars and destructions, trials and troubles, conflicts and afflictions, which Time, in his conquering march, scatters broadcast among the "sons of men," *never can erase!* No! Time can not destroy the love which I cherish for you, or erase the remembrance of the happy hours which we have spent together here, till this mortal frame shall have been swept from the stage of existence! Though we be separated far from each other, and from the endearing scenes which cluster around us here; though lofty mountains, unfathomable seas, rushing rivers, and desert wastes, separate us; though I seek my home upon the billowy ocean; though I make my abode among the lovely flowers, fruitful fields, and sunny plains of the far-distant South,

Where the forest's ever fragrant,
Where the orange ever blooms,
Where the birds sing sweetly evermore;

or among the icy fetters, barren wastes, and eternal snows of the dreary North,

Where the ocean's ever frozen,
And the mountains clad with snow,
Where the sun never thaws the dreary shore;

though I roam to the remotest bounds of earth, still memory, fond memory, will unconsciously flit back and convey me, upon the silvery wings of imagination, to this (to me) ever sacred spot, and to the side of those with whom I am bound by that "golden chain" which eternity itself can never sever!

But, beloved associates, this is the common lot of all. All the ties of nature must in time be severed. All must, sooner or later, "take the parting hand." No tie of nature can prevent this. The fond mother must wipe the cold death-drops from the tender brow of her dying infant, and press for the last time its cold and silent lips, as she surrenders it up to the care of that blessed One who said, "Suffer little children to come unto me, and forbid them not, for of such is the kingdom of heaven." The loving sister, whose love is second only to that of a mother, must clasp for the last time the hand of her departing brother. The devoted wife—though it inflict a wound upon her delicate heart which must soon bring her sorrowing to the grave—must receive the parting hand of her companion, as he submits to the stern summons of the common conqueror of all. But, notwithstanding all this, notwithstanding we must be separated, my dear friends, there is a place where we can all meet, even while on earth. Though we be scattered to the "ends of the earth," we all have the blessed privilege of meeting around the same "blood-bought mercy-seat." Though we no longer dwell beneath the same roof; though we no longer partake of our refreshments at the same board; though we no longer take our evening strolls over the same grassy lawn, and beneath the shade of the same waving branches; though we no longer assemble in the same hall to receive instruction; yet we can all offer our morning and evening sacrifices upon the same sacred altar, to the same benevolent Heavenly Father, with the same assurance of his divine acceptance; and, if we continue to do this, and to discharge all of our other duties to God faithfully, we will meet erelong beyond the stormy waves of time, where perfect peace eternal reigns, and "parting is no more."

Not only does it grieve me to know that the hour has almost made its arrival when I must for the last time see the faces of my fellow-students, but I behold many fair and lovely faces here which have become familiar to me, from having frequently met them in the chapel, where we have assembled from time to time to discharge some of our special duties to God, and to unite our voices in singing the praises of the Redeemer. Although deprived of the pleasure of conversing with you, and thus forming your immediate acquaintance, being enlisted in the same holy cause has caused me to cherish love and respect for you which I never can forget. May the spirit of hope ever spread its balmy wings o'er you! May the spirit of happiness ever shed its cheering rays upon you! May your pathways, through this stormy land of sorrow, disappointment and deception, ever be strewn with fragrant flowers of the sweetest odor! May the spirit of sorrow never cast one gloomy cloud upon your pure hearts! Ever through life's journey,

> May your friends be many, faithful, and true;
> Your foes, if any, weak, and but few!

May the guardian angels of heaven ever hover around

you; guide you among the "thorns and thistles" in roads with roses strewn; guard and protect you from the wicked intrigues, devices, and deceptions, which always beset the innocent, lovely, and fair, during their pilgrimage here; and enable you (bright gems and angels of earth) to live a spotless life in this world, and enjoy the association of the angels of heaven in eternity!

But while these are the earnest and sincere desires of our heart, we can not cherish the hope that they will all be realized. Trouble, in some form, and at some time, visits every heart. Even now 't will not be long till tears will wet your cheeks. You are seated close together now, with quiet, happy minds; but a few more fleeting moments will be your last together! The sun, now looking down from the zenith upon us, will not have sunk to rest behind the western hills, till a never-ending farewell shall have fallen from the quivering lips of some of you, followed by a tear from all! When you separate here, some of you separate *forever*. You will never all meet again, never see your kind teachers and loving matron again till you meet beyond "death's chilling flood." You will never hear your kind, fraternal preceptor speak of "the realms of the blest" again. No more will you sit beneath the sound of his eloquent voice, and listen to his earnest admonitions as he entreats you to be faithful, and warns you against the snares which the emissaries of the evil one are ever ready to prepare for the innocent and unsuspecting posterity of Eve. No more will you see him till you meet on eternity's wave! Oft, in after years, will you look back to these happy days with tearful eyes, and sigh for the pleasures enjoyed here. While dwelling here together, your misfortunes and pleasures were shared in common. If one were afflicted or distressed, all others sympathized with her; shared her grief by mingling your tears with hers, and calmed the emotions of her troubled breast by the healing balm of "the perennial spring of everlasting love." But soon, alas! how changed it will be! You 'll soon be fanned by the breezes of different parts of earth, far away from these endearing scenes. You can neither know nor share each other's troubles then. If in prosperity, you 'll rejoice then alone. If in adversity, no beloved school-mate will be there to sympathize with you, and mingle her tears with yours. If sickness oppress you, they will not be there to soothe your afflictions, or cool your fevered brow. When bowed down by time, age, and trouble, they will not be there to cheer your gloomy path. When languishing on the bed of death, they will not be there to smooth your pillow, speak sweet words of comfort, breathe a prayer for your future welfare, or sigh for your relief. But, notwithstanding your afflictions will be known to each other no more, they surely will come. As withering autumn divests the bright foliage which grows, and the odorous flowers that blow, in summer, of all their charms, so the blighting hand of after years destroys youthful strength and beauty. Your blooming cheeks will soon begin to fade! They will soon exchange the blushing rose for the withered lily! Your sparkling eyes—bright orbs of light—erelong must lose their beaming luster! Your glossy curls, so exquisitely beautiful now, will soon be mantled by the venerable frosts of time! Your erect and graceful forms, so stout and nimble now, will soon be bowed down by the pressing hand of cares and time! It will seem as but yesterday to you, when you look back from old age, from the verge of the grave, and shore of death, through the dim, intervening mists, to the happy associations of to-day!

Then, my dear young sisters, regard the pleasures of this

world not as permanent realities, but as fleeting bubbles which burst as soon as caught; and look to a higher, a nobler source for happiness. Treasure up, in your pure hearts, the divine, the heavenly lessons which you so oft have heard while here, and prepare to meet each other, with smiles of joy, shouts of victory, and "songs of praise," in that "better land," in that land of beatified spirits above, where "sickness and sorrow, pain and death, are felt and feared no more," to dwell in that blest abode which the Savior has gone to prepare, and from which he has promised to return to take his ransomed people home—"that house not made with hands, eternal in the heavens."

> There your beauty 'll never fade!
> Your pleasures never cease!
> There, in shining robes arrayed,
> You'll dwell in endless peace!
>
> My sisters, strive to gain that land,
> And meet each other there;
> Where you can all for ever stand,
> Nor know one anxious care!

Farewell!

There is another theme—"the last, but not the least"—which I would not forget. My teacher! How can I express the gratitude that I owe to him for all the loving kindness and attention that he has lavished upon me, with a "prodigal hand," from the day in which I was so fortunate as to become his pupil, to this, the day of our separation? Was I sick? He visited me and offered every assistance, gave all the good advice, and uttered every comforting and consoling sentence in his power. Was I bewildered in my studies? He was ever ready to assist me, ever ready to remove every difficulty, explain every point, expound every theoretical principle, and—by his quick perception, and superior ability in the elucidation of difficult problems—shed a halo of light around the most obscure proposition, which would render it "clear as the noonday sun in the heavens." May he ever receive that honor and respect which he so justly merits!

My teacher, farewell! May it ever be your good fortune to be surrounded by friends as kind and attentive to you as you have ever been to me! May richest blessings from above ever be showered down upon you, to cheer and comfort you as the dews of heaven revive the wilted flowers of spring! May success ever attend you! May the spirit of fortune ever be with you! And may you ever be the happy recipient of those golden blessings which are so justly thine! Farewell!

Strangers, friends, and fellow-students, farewell! To-morrow we part to meet no more in time! A few hours more, and we shall have taken the "parting hand," and gone to our respective homes. A few years more, and we will be scattered, like the fragments of a wrecked vessel, to the "four winds of heaven;" no one, perhaps, knowing the location, fortune, or destiny of another! A few years from that time, and we, though in the bloom and vigor of life to-day, will all have passed from the "stage of action" into the boundless ocean of eternity, to meet no more till the archangel's trump shall "shake the globe from pole to pole," and summons the hosts of all ages to appear before the "judgment bar of God!" But O, let us all be faithful! Let us all prove true to the trust which God has given us! Let us all endeavor to live free from, and never become entangled with, the wicked devices and intrigues of this sinful world! O let us all endeavor to so live that, when that memorable day shall arrive; when conquering Time shall end the race that he so long has run, and like a weary traveler when the evening's sun is low, fold up his weary, outstretched wings, and take himself to rest; when all things earthly shall, in a moment fade away, and the universe "like a scroll" be folded up, our ransomed spirits and glorified bodies united, may be admitted into that celestial abode on high where, free from all the storms, trials, troubles, persecutions, afflictions, and disappointments of this world, we can exultingly sing the praises of the Redeemer, as we in harmony surround the throne of God, amidst the triumphant shouts of angels, and of the redeemed of all ages for ever!

Farewell!

CHAPTER XIV.

He always taught us in school there was a difference between perseverance and industry. Perseverance is industry steadily directed toward the accomplishment of a well-defined result. Many industrious people fail to accomplish any thing in life for want of perseverance. They lack continuity of purpose, and are unstable in all their ways. He had both industry and perseverance. His plans were carefully formed and unwaveringly pursued. People followed him because they knew he was going somewhere. He was a worker as well as planner at Mars Hill College.

While carpenters were building the college, he worked with the men every moment he could spare from other business. He handled lumber, shoveled dirt, made mortar, sawed timbers, carried brick, hauled shingles, chopped logs, and cheered the men. He seemed to be the very life and motive power of the body of workmen.

During the session of college, he worked every moment of time he was not engaged in the class-room giving instruction. He chopped wood, carried water, swept the class-rooms and study-hall, carried stove-wood, rang the school-bell, built fires for young lady boarders, helped arrange the dining-room, helped in the kitchen, worked in the garden, fed the stock, and helped to dress the children. He seemed to do every thing with the consummate skill of genius inspired by professional ambition. He was always in a hurry, never in a fret, and always on time.

No one had any idle time at Mars Hill, if he kept his

place in the programme of daily work. He rang us up at 4 o'clock every morning, and kept us busy as ants till 9 o'clock at night when he rang out the lights. How much he slept himself we never knew, for he was always up before we awoke in the morning, and we left him up when we retired at night. Four o'clock in January was long before day, and 9 o'clock was rather late into the night. At 4 in the morning we assembled for worship, and always found the chapel warmed and lighted. He built fires in the stoves, trimmed and lighted the lamps, and made every thing comfortable for us before ringing us up. He met us with a bright face and a cheerful "Good morning, children," which at once warmed our hearts and drove all drowsiness from our eyes. After singing and prayer, he always gave a morning lecture which kept us engaged till breakfast. After breakfast we had barely time to arrange our rooms, carry water, and prepare wood for the day, till the recitations began. At noon we had one hour for dinner, and then regular recitations hurried us on till late in the afternoon. We came together every afternoon, after recitations were finished for the day, to sing. We met in the chapel for singing, and spent an hour every afternoon in this lung exercise under the leadership of a competent teacher. And that was singing, too, and no foolishness about it. If anybody thinks over a hundred students, each with a book, and all with a good leader, can not make a joyful noise unto the Lord after a hard day's study and close confinement, he has never been to Mars Hill at the singing hour, that's all. An operatic singer would not have considered our voices highly cultivated; but he would have admitted that we had voices, plenty of them, and strong ones too. We did not stand much on the *quality* of our singing, from an artistic stand-point; the *quantity* of it was our main hold. We met critics like the merchant met the lady customer who declined to purchase his cloth because it was too narrow: "Not very wide ma'am, I admit; but great Cæsar! just look at the *length of it!*" Yet we did not sing in disregard of all rules; on the contrary, we were carefully taught the principles of vocal music, and thoroughly drilled in pitch, time, and accent. Indeed, those who had voices and talent for music attained a high degree of proficiency in the science and art of good singing. But the great bulk of the school, being deficient in natural gifts, profited little by good teaching and constant practice. Still, as the singing hour was a recreation we all delighted in, he never would consent for the pleasure of a single child to be sacrificed for the sake of a few artistic songs faultlessly rendered by select singers. He wanted everybody to sing, and everybody did try to sing, though some of us occasionally missed the pitch, lost the time, and wandered from the tune. But there were always good singers enough to keep steadily and vigorously on in the proper pitch, time, and tune, and as for the rest, we all rounded up at the end with a glorious mingling of glad voices that moved the listeners wildly, making them feel like swinging their hats and yelling hurrah! If we may judge by the compliments we received, and the effect our singing had on competent judges of music, it was good singing. People often drove out from Florence to hear us sing, when the weather was good; and often have I seen those who had listened for years to faultless singing artistically rendered by trained choirs in city churches, perfectly elated at our singing. They would go away declaring they had never heard any thing equal to it. He is a believer in, and advocate of, congregational singing. A favorite expression of his, printed in the order of worship on cards and distributed through the congregation in many of his meetings, is, "LET ALL THE PEOPLE SING."

He took his place in the singing class every evening "with the boys," and received instruction as a pupil. He perhaps tried harder and learned less than any other one in the class. He had by far the strongest bass voice in the school, and when he could get off on the right pitch he was "a whole team," as Charley Carter expressed it, "till the line crooked." The songs we sang were, for the most part, simple compositions, the bass usually being perfectly straight for several measures in succession. If he could only get the right pitch on such stretches of straight notes, his bass would give strength to the performance; but when the pitch changed he would often shatter the concord and produce an explosion of laughter by striking off alone on a wrong pitch. He took it all in perfect good humor, and seemed to enjoy the fun we had at his own expense quite as much as any of us. Such blunders were mostly confined to the practice of new pieces; for after repeated efforts he would master the few crooks in the bass, and then his matchless voice was the very strength and beauty of his part of the song. We always had fun in practicing a new piece, and he was too wise a teacher to suffer us rebuked for laughing at the ludicrous mistakes so often made by awkward members of the class.

One evening a young man who had made many ridiculous blunders, and seemed to have no talent for any thing else, became mortified and discouraged over his failures, and in a tone which showed his feelings were wounded, asked to be excused from any further efforts to sing. We all felt rebuked, and were ready to cry in pity for him. Professor Larimore showed his consummate skill as a heart-comforter by saying, in his kindly manner:

"Do not be discouraged; you can soon learn to sing. These boys and girls used to laugh at my blunders when I first began to sing, and see what a great singer I have made."

The absurdity of the thing was too much for us, and we all exploded with laughter, in which the wounded-hearted young man joined heartily. Everybody knew Professor Larimore could not sing a tune that had a crook in it. The wound was healed at once, and the young man resumed his seat in the class, saying:

"Well, Professor, if you succeeded in spite of the fun they had at your expense, I certainly ought to be willing to try."

The singing exercise closed the day's work. Immediately after singing we had supper, and after supper an hour for recreation. Then the bell for study called us to our rooms, where we applied ourselves to our books till the lights were rung out at 9 o'clock. This was the order of school-work every day except Saturday and Sunday.

Saturday we were called together the same hour in the morning as any other day in the week, but not for the same routine of work. We spent half the day in the usual school exercise of speeches, compositions, recitations, etc. At noon we were dismissed for a half-day of recreation. We were permitted to spend Saturday evenings in whatever way seemed best to us. Usually the young men who were preparing for the ministry had appointments to preach Saturday nights and Sundays at country churches, in different neighborhoods around the college, and young men who were not preparing to preach would go along "to make the thing interesting," as it was commonly expressed. This was a sly way they had of hinting that such preaching as "the boys" could do needed something "to make it interesting." The usual means of conveyance to these country appointments conformed strictly to the apostolic plan, viz: walking. It was customary for about four to go to each appointment—two preachers to do the preaching, and two who were not preachers "to make the thing interesting." The preachers may not always have given entire satisfaction in their part of the work; but no case has been reported where the other two failed to do their part satisfactorily, even if it had to be at the expense of the two preachers. The four usually made a lively quartette in song, and the "non-professionals" took the business management of the programme in hand in a way that guaranteed good fare on the trip—they made a judicious selection of places to stay Saturday night and to take dinner Sunday.

One Sunday evening the usual quartette returned from Stony Point, four miles distant, much earlier than usual. G. P. Young was the main preacher on that trip, and we all considered him the "big preacher" of the school. Supposing he would preach one of his very biggest sermons that Sunday, we were not expecting them back till late, and Prosessor Larimore said, in some astonishment, "Why, young gentlemen, you are back unusually early." With an air of general disgust, one of the "non-professionals," his coat on his arm and his handkerchief in his hand, strode wearily by, mopping the perspiration from his forehead, and remarking in answer to the Professor's expression of surprise: "Yes; Mr. Young preached for us today, and he just put the thing right through." Further inquiry revealed the fact that Mr. Young's big sermon would not materialize that day, and, after a few unsuccessful efforts to make it visible to the naked eye, he gave up in despair and dismissed the congregation. That "nonprofessional" had been induced to walk to Stony Point to hear the big preacher's big sermon, hence his disgust. G. P. Young is now president of Orange College, Stark, Florida, and notwithstanding the failure of his big sermon at Stony Point, he is one of the big preachers of the South.

The students who remained at the college Saturday evening gave a public debate Saturday night in one of the literary societies of the college. Sunday morning, at 9 o'clock, we had Sunday-school, and at 11 o'clock a sermon from Professor Larimore. Sunday night the young men who were preparing for the ministry held prayer-meeting. This closed the week's work. Every thing in the working of the school was regulated by the clock and a deep-toned big bell. The college bell weighed 1,800 pounds, and could be distinctly heard from five to eight miles. Each hour of the day, from the time recitations began till the hour for singing, was struck on that bell, and every thing connected with the workings of the school moved exactly to time with the regularity of the clock.

CHAPTER XV.

The order of exercises in Mars Hill College given in the last chapter, refers to the first years of the school. The lecture before breakfast was abandoned in 1877, and some other changes were made at the request of some of the best friends and patrons of the institution. The school was not established as a business to make money; but as a means of building up the church. The one idea and ambition of his life centered in the progress of Christianity. The school was established and conducted to help his preaching; but never allowed to supplant it. The sessions began in January and ended in June—only six months each year—so that he might have the rest of the year for preaching in protracted meetings. This arrangement suited those who were preparing for the ministry well enough, as they could attend school six months and preach the rest of the year; but it never was entirely satisfactory to other departments of the school. For reasons already given, his chief interest was in the Bible Department, and to that he gave his principal attention. The other departments in the school lagged in interest and fell off in attendance year by year, till the sessions came to be little else than a school for the small children of neighbors and a course of instruction and practice for young preachers.

With him, the design of the school was to build up the church, and the object of education was to make Christians. Many a time have I heard him say in the presence of the school that he would rather see his own children grow up in ignorance of even the English alphabet and be Christians, than to graduate with highest honors from Yale or Harvard and live out of Christ. He never lost an opportunity to impress pupils with the brevity and uncertainty of this life. He never talked to us about school days being the time to prepare for the great battle of life; but rather reminded us of life being the time to prepare for the great issues of eternity. Under his teaching and example, we soon came to consider life as our school time, and Christianity our curriculum.

His pupils were all Christians. Those who were not members of the church when they entered school, with few exceptions, were baptized before they were many weeks under his instruction. I do not now remember but two young men, and not a single young lady, who ever remained at Mars Hill a whole session without being members of the church. It is probable that in the seventeen years he conducted Mars Hill College he never parted with as many as a dozen pupils at the close of sessions who were not members of the church. Nor did it end with becoming members of the church. He made every one feel that Christianity was the most important of all professions, and to preach the gospel, the solemn duty and exalted privilege of every Christian. Every pupil wanted to be under his special personal instruction, and as his entire attention was given to the Bible Department, every body soon began to want to learn to preach. It was very difficult to hold pupils in other departments. All other professions seemed insignificant in importance as compared with preaching the gospel. Why should a boy prepare himself for a profession that pertained only to this life, when even better opportunities were offered him to prepare for a profession the results of which were to be as lasting as the eternal throne of God?

"What shall we eat and what shall we drink and wherewithal shall we be clothed," were questions we never canvassed. Every session was a genuine religious revival under the enthusiasm of which we went out to preach the gospel during vacation without one thought about all those little conveniences of food and raiment after which the Gentiles used to seek. Yet we fared sumptuously every day, receiving liberal remuneration in money from the people where we labored, besides having the very best of every thing where we went. It is hardly proper to say we trusted in God for a support, nor yet in the brethren nor least of all in a missionary society. The truth of the whole business is, as well as I remember, we never thought any thing about it. We were wrought up to a point of religious zeal and enthusiasm, under his personal influence and the power of his preaching, so intense and constant, that we felt impelled to preach the gospel, nor thought of any thing else.

Through such preaching, churches were established in almost every neighborhood in the country for many miles around the college. The work, however, was confined almost exclusively to the country. Very little preaching was done in towns, and but few churches were established save in country neighborhoods. No conventions were ever called, nor any system of co-operation ever attempted. Each church, when established, was independent of all others, and attended to its own business and order of worship, not forsaking the assembling of its members together on the first day of the week for prayers, exhortation, reading the Scriptures, singing, breaking of bread and fellowship. To this day, there are efficient and working churches, each independent of all the others, all over that country established years ago by the labors of Professor Larimore and "his boys" during vacations of Mars Hill College.

His own preaching grew in favor with the people each year, and his reputation spread rapidly throughout the South. He received letters by every mail begging him to come to different places to hold meetings at the earliest possible day. All such letters were laid aside unanswered till a few weeks before the close of school, when a list of appointments would be made covering every day of his time during vacation. It was a very rare thing to allow more than one Sunday to each appointment. Usually his meetings would begin on Sunday and close about Friday night following, leaving Saturday to reach the next appointment. The appointments would all be arranged and decided before any one was sent out. The great pile of letters calling him to places he could not go would then be answered by a line on postal card saying it was impossible to accept the call. It is impossible to estimate the amount of real labor he performed in vacation in such unbroken series of protracted meetings.

Each year the calls for his meetings increased in number and importance, till it began to be a grave question whether Mars Hill College was as great a help as hindrance to his work. While he could do more for the church in the school than in the pulpit during half the year, when he was unknown as a preacher and his labor not in special demand, many of his warmest friends and confidential counselors began to think a wider field of usefulness was now open before him. The anxiety to hear him in all parts of the country was simply distressing. The writer decided in 1880 that the interests of the church could be better served by constant work in the pulpit than by longer continuing Mars Hill College. Each year strengthened that conviction, and results since 1887, when the school was suspended, have abundantly demonstrated its correctness. Mars Hill College never failed; but was abandoned because a wider field of usefulness opened before him. The school declined in interest and patronage, it is true; but only because the immense pressure upon him in pleading letters by every mail to preach the gospel, diverted his attention from the details of college work. More than once have I seen him shed tears over piles of letters begging for preaching when he was confined by college duties at Mars Hill. He would say he had no heart to be there teaching children English Grammar when a perishing world was pleading with him to tell them of Jesus and his love. Those of us who knew his feelings and understood the situation, advised the suspension of the college. After more than seven years steady persuasion on our part and serious, prayerful consideration on his part, the school was abandoned. Like an uncaged bird, he went forth, the Bible in his hand and the joy of glad tidings for a lost world in his heart, "to turn sinners from darkness to light, and from the power of Satan unto God."

He is strangely reticent by nature concerning every thing pertaining to himself. It was generally understood that he began at Mars Hill without money and he was known to be considerably embarrassed with debts during all the years he taught there. It has been supposed, therefore, that the school was suspended from insolvency. This is an error he has never taken any pains to correct. He was in debt and greatly needed money when the school closed; but his financial condition was no worse than it had been from the first. He had managed to carry heavy debts and sustain the college through all the years of its life, and he could have continued to do so. Indeed it is a most remarkable fact that he had almost unlimited credit in bank at Florence throughout his most depressing financial embarrassments, and could at any time get loans of money for the asking. This credit he never abused, and would have seen every thing swept away by the pressure of debts rather than accept a loan he could see no way to repay. It may be stated, once for all, that when the school was suspended, his debts, in the aggregate, were less, and in a condition to be easier managed, than for years before if not indeed during the whole life of the college. He was entirely solvent, and none of his creditors had any fears of losing a dollar he owed.

The attendance was smaller when the school suspended than earlier in its history. This was largely due to causes already given. The details of college work were tolerated as a hindrance rather than entered into as a help to his work. He felt that God was calling him every day to preach Jesus to the world, and every effort to build up the college seemed out of the line of his plain duty. Perhaps there are not a half-dozen people who knew then his feelings on the subject. But those who were in his confidence as counselors, understood perfectly that he had no tears to shed over the falling off in attendance at Mars Hill College. His friends and admirers outside of three or four confidants, could not understand why he would not abandon Mars Hill and accept the presidency of some one of several colleges tendered him in better locations. Well established colleges in Tennessee and Kentucky urged him to accept the presidency on good salaries, and it was a puzzle to many why he steadily declined. They did not understand that he wanted to be freed from college work so that he might devote all of his time to preaching. When he decided to suspend the school, he wrote that after an absence of only a month in meetings, he returned home at the time to begin another session and found ninety-nine letters and postal cards calling him to as many different places to preach, while only a few students had arrived to enter school. Clearly the demand for his labors in the pulpit was immeasurably greater than in the school room. He called the school together, arranged to satisfy every one present as to the terms and conditions of closing the school, and then announced that as soon as the agreement could be faithfully carried out on his part, Mars' Hill College would be suspended indefinitely.

CHAPTER XVI.

Let no one conclude that the preachers who went out from Mars Hill were mere religious enthusiasts of superficial ideas and smattering information, fit only to preach in rural districts to backwoods congregations. Such was by no means the case. Many of them were men of brilliant intellects and fair education, and could preach acceptably in any city in the South. They had an unusual amount of religious zeal while under Professor Larimore's influence and matchless preaching, it is true; but when they went about their work in the pulpit, they were never too religious to be both sensible and decorous. They preached in the country to the neglect of towns and cities, it is true; but from necessity rather than choice. The necessity was not for lack of ability to preach acceptably in cities; but for lack of suitable places to preach and interested audiences to preach to. Their doctrine was a new thing in that country, and towns and cities having heard of it through their preachers, had unanimously decided not to hear it. Being more fully under the influence and dictation of the reigning clergy than the rural districts, it was far more difficult to get a hearing there than in the country.

A few men like John Taylor had preached the doctrine here and there for years in the country around Mars' Hill, and had started small churches at several places; but the strongholds of religious thought had never been touched. The work of Professor Larimore and "his boys" was the first movement toward the establishment of the doctrine in that country of sufficient general magnitude and importance to attract the attention of the leaders of religious thought. In ability and general intelligence they compared favorably with the preachers of any other church in the land, and in religious zeal and readiness to preach wherever a suitable place and an interested audience could be found, they lead all other churches in that country. For a few years the reigning clergy kept them out of the towns and cities; but this neither silenced their preaching nor modified the sharp conflict between their doctrine and the accepted theology. It only shifted the battle-ground from the cities to the country. This left the parties to the issue unequally matched to our advantage. Professor Larimore and "his boys" were altogether too many for the ordinary country preachers who had to defend popular theology against apostolic doctrine. We had every advantage in representatives as well as doctrine. It was the strength and flower of our pulpit against the odds and ends of the reigning ministry. Professor Larimore and "his boys" were at home among those people. Their preaching was in the land of their birth and to the friends of their childhood. In argument and exhortation they sought to reach the hearts of friends and relatives dear to them from their earliest recollection. Their opponents, in the main, were strangers to the people and ignorant of the local customs of the country. They were part of an organized ministry, and for lack of any better answer to the preaching of "the boys," they exercised the authority of "preachers in charge" and locked congregations out of churches in many places. But such methods always reacted against them. The people stood up for "the boys," and demanded fair play. They built other houses, and made sure that the keys were not given over to "preachers in charge." It was one of the commendable methods of Mars' Hill College that everybody who received instruction there was encouraged to go home and preach to his own people. With such advantages in our favor, but one result could be expected. Our cause succeeded throughout that country, and its success in the country created a demand and opened up opportunities for preaching in towns and cities. The work began in the country and radiated into towns and cities. Some close observers argue that this is the way religious movements always begin; but other great leaders say a better plan is to begin in important cities and radiate into the country. It may be stated as a fact that in this case the order was to begin in the country and radiate into towns and cities; but we are not warranted in concluding from this one case that such is a uniform law of religious movements.

While the advantages we had are plain enough to be seen now in looking back over the contest, neither party in the struggle saw them at the time. The logic of the situation was clearly in our favor; but it was not of man's planning. Some would call it an *accident;* but *he*, in reverence and awe, would say it was *Providence.* The advantages we gained by being turned away from towns and locked out of churches, with *him*, are but so many practical illustrations of the text: "All things work together for good to those who love the Lord."

Those advantages were quite as much to the growth of "the boys," as the success of the cause. Their success made them reputation, and opened to them wider fields of usefulness. A successful meeting at any point always creates a demand for the preacher in further regions. To a young preacher, success and reputation are encouragement, inspiration, and growth. If they do not "turn his head," they are more valuable "than gold, yea, than much fine gold;" "sweeter also than honey and the honey-comb." Without some measure of success, young men naturally become discouraged and lose interest in their work. They lose the inspiration and enthusiasm produced by success and reputation, and gradually drift into indifference, formality, and monotony. The world loses all interest in them, and the church has no patience with them. As soon as the world concludes a man is not a success it has no further interest in him; and whom the world declines to hear, him the church refuses to encourage. Young men can neither succeed nor make reputations preaching in cities. Strong and influential city churches do not call young men to preach for them. They are able to secure men of acknowledged ability and established reputation, and they have neither time nor money to waste on pulpit experiments. City churches that call young preachers are without reputation or influence, and usually destitute of the elements of strength or success. Preaching for such churches is an effectual method of laying young preachers "on the shelf." One successful protracted meeting in a country church is worth more to a young preacher, and to the cause at large, than a whole life-time of unsuccessful pastoral work in such churches. Preaching for such churches is about as helpful to the development of young men as sand-paper and varnish to the growth of a geranium. Aside from all these considerations, there are other prudential reasons why country-bred young preachers should not undertake pastoral work in cities. They are ignorant of the temptations of city life, and in danger of falling into hurtful sins. They scarcely know how to take care of themselves, and how can they take care of the church? Is there nothing to be learned from the clerical scandals that have blighted so many brilliant young preachers and humiliated so many churches? When a young country-bred preacher accepts a call to serve a defunct city church, the eternal fitness of things suggests the familiar lines beginning:

"Now I lay me down to sleep;
I pray the Lord my soul to keep."

Professor Larimore and his boys stuck to the horseback-and-saddlebags way of doing the thing. Not till his first great meeting in Nashville, Tennessee, in 1885, did he himself ever preach any of consequence in important cities. And as for the boys, their preaching was entirely in the country, and for the most part each one preached around his own home. While this all seems to have been for the best, for reasons already given, it was not of any man's planning. It was never taught at Mars' Hill as unscriptural for a young man to accept a call to preach for a city church. The inexpediences of such a thing, as discussed in this chapter, were never even so much as mentioned among us. There were no city churches to preach to in that part of the world, and for that reason alone, trivial as it may appear, Larimore and his boys never preached to any city churches.

"Like priests, like people," is a familiar truism of universal application. A low standard of general intelligence is to be expected under the reign of an uneducated ministry. Whatever tends to elevate the standard of pulpit intelligence advances the grade of general education. All churches believe in their preachers, and consider them guides for the people. To know as much as the preacher is a high accomplishment in any church; to know more than the preacher is an unwarrantable presumption in all churches.

Through the successful labors of Professor Larimore and his boys the standard of general education in rural districts was elevated in all the regions around Mars' Hill. Country places built better churches, supported better schools, employed better teachers, and cultivated better singing in church services.

Earnestness was one of their chief elements of success in preaching. They believed all they preached, and preached all they believed. They preached it because they believed it, and preached it exactly as they believed it. No playing at preaching or mere pulpit performances were encouraged at Mars' Hill. Sensational themes and studied formality in preaching were never mentioned but to be condemned. In a letter to one of the boys on "how to preach," he said:

"Fortunately, I have never been drilled in elocution, oratory, gesture, etc. I escaped all that in my boyhood days, and providentially was spared that ruinous torture after I grew up. To my mind, it would be a wonderful advance in the right direction to spend all the time wasted in colleges and other schools in teaching how to gesture, etc., in teaching how to kill snakes, how to get out of a neighbor's water melon patch when you hear something '*drap*,' how to 'pull a hen off the roost,' and other useful and practical things of that kind. The way to preach is to *preach*. Just get full of spirit and truth and turn yourself loose. As a good old brother once expressed it, 'Just fill the barrel *full*, knock the bung out, and let 'er come.' That's the way to preach."

They stuck to the Book. They preached neither less nor more than the Bible, and in the very words of the Bible. They looked upon all divisions among professed Christians as not only grave errors, but grievous sins. They believed all such divisions, as well as all the confusion in the world concerning what churches to join, originated in departures from the teaching of the Bible. The plainest and only way to remedy such evils was to remove the cause of them. No man has a right to make a test of fellowship of any thing which God has not made a condition of salvation. No man should be denied fellowship in the church on account of any thing which will not deprive him of admission into heaven. No man has a right to require a sinner seeking salvation to do any thing he cannot read in the Bible. Man's opinions are his own private property, and no man has a right to deprive him of them. But no man has a right to trespass upon another's liberty in Christ by making his opinions tests of fellowship. No man has a right to preach his opinions; there is no salvation in them. Christ commissioned the apostles to preach the gospel, and not opinions. The gospel, and not opinions, is the power of God unto salvation. Concerning a question that was extensively discussed in church papers, one of the boys once asked him: "How shall we stand on this question?" He answered:

"Better not stand on that question at all; stand upon Christ and him crucified. If you *must* do *any thing* with that question, sit down on it. It is not a good thing to stand on."

They preached the gospel in gentleness and love. No word of bitterness or semblance of anger ever marred one of his sermons. Earnest and uncompromising in what he preached, and loving, gentle, and pathetic in the manner he preached, minds were enlightened and convinced and hearts touched and subdued by his sermons. Those who accepted his preaching had deep and intelligent convictions as to their faith, and fervent and consuming piety as to their motives, in rendering obedience to God's commandments. They *believed* something, and they knew what it was and why they believed it; they *felt* something, and they knew what it was and why they felt it. Churches built of such material do not spring up in a day and perish in a night. They are founded upon a rock and built to stand.

CHAPTER XVII.

The foregoing general observations touching the preaching of Professor Larimore and "his boys" may be illustrated by brief sketches of the labors of some of the Mars' Hill preachers.

J. H. Halbrook, of Lewis county, Tenn., was at Mars' Hill two years, and on leaving school he settled at New River, Ala., where he still resides. He was somewhat advanced in years, and was married, when he entered school. He has preached extensively through Fayette, Lamar, Tuscaloosa, Walker, Marion, Lawrence, Franklin and Colbert counties, Alabama, and has also made preaching tours to Tennessee, Mississippi, Missouri, Arkansas and Texas. Except the tours to Missouri, Arkansas and Texas, he has traveled almost exclusively on horseback and in buggy. He has held two debates, and many very successful protracted meetings. He has baptized hundreds of people, and has been instrumental in establishing many good churches. As a preacher he is earnest, Scriptural, original, argumentative, and ready in wit and repartee. It has been no unusual thing for him to baptize over forty people during a meeting. His leg was broken in 1877 by his horse falling on it while on his way to an appointment. He is a good financier, and when preaching does not support him he turns his attention to something else that will, and preaches what he can. He is neither profound scholar nor a finished orator; but a man of fair education and general information and a clear and forcible speaker.

When the Alabama Christian Missionary Society was organized, some one connected with it wrote him to know how much could be raised in his field for missionary purposes. He wrote:

"I do not know how much can be raised in my field for missonary purposes this year. I have planted my field in cotton, and it is too early in the season yet to tell how it will pan out; but all it makes is for missionary purposes."

The answer was thoroughly characteristic of the man, and suggests all that needs be said concerning his manner of life. He makes a living, and as for the rest, he cheerfully spends all he makes and himself too in the missionary field. He delights to carry the gospel into new fields.

A man once interrupted him at a new preaching point with the remark:

"Water baptism may do for such folks as you, parson; but if I am ever baptized I want it to be with the Holy Ghost."

Seeing the man was not to be reasoned with, he said, in perfect good humor:

"Well, now, my brother, you better take such as you can get. Any preacher can baptize you with water; but God only can baptize you with the Holy Ghost, and He may not consider you of sufficient importance to require such special attention. Besides, you, and all other men, are commanded to be baptized with water; but to be baptized with the Holy Ghost never was a *command* to any body, but simply a *promise.* If any body is to receive a promise, those who obey commands certainly stand as good a chance as those who refuse to obey."

Having no answer for this clear and unexpected statement of the case, the man simply fell back upon the stubborn and not very courteous retort:

"Well, if you have not been baptized with the Holy Ghost, I would not give much for your religion any how."

This called out another good humored and eminently sensible remark which silenced the critic and left the audience in the best of feelings:

"It is no concern to me whether you would give much for my religion or not. I did not come here to sell my religion any how; but to try to tell you how to live so that you might have religion of your own. My religion is not on the market."

C. F. Russell, of Apple Grove, Ala., was one of Mars' Hill's brilliant young preachers; but unfortunately his labors were cut short by failing health soon after he left school. While yet a student, he held several very successful protracted meetings, and but for the failure in health would unquestionably have taken high rank in our Southern pulpit. He was modest, quiet and unassuming; original, earnest and untiring. Professor Larimore once had an appointment he could not meet, and asked brother Russell if he could fill it for him. With characteristic modesty and willingness to do his best, he said:

"I don't think I could fill it for you, professor; but if it will accommodate you and do any good, I am willing to go and wriggle about in it."

His labors were principally confined to Alabama and Mississippi with an occasional tour into Tennessee.

R. P. Meeks, of Stantonville, McNairy county, West

Tennessee, finished his course at Mars' Hill in 1875. He is a man of splendid talent and thorough education. Unfortunately, his voice failed and he was afflicted with chronic throat trouble for several years, immediately after he left school. He has never fully recovered in voice and throat; but has been able to preach regularly for several years. But for the impairment in his voice, he would have ranked with professor Larimore himself as a pulpit orator and successful evangelist. His preaching now must of necessity be simply a statement of the gospel in a carefully modulated conversational tone. Still he has been eminently successful, having baptized hundreds of people and established scores of good churches. For several years he was the District Evangelist of the West Tennessee co-operation meeting during which he preached extensively throughout West Tennessee, and occasionally in North Mississippi and Alabama. In 1887 he moved from Stantonville, Tenn., to Jackson, Tennessee to preach for the church in that city. His work there was greatly hindered by sickness of himself and family, and in 1888 he moved to Henderson, Tennessee, to take a professorship in West Tennessee Christian College. He is now at the head of the Bible Department of that college, and is endeavoring to perpetuate Mars' Hill methods of instruction for the benefit of young men who desire to prepare for the ministry. Professor Meeks is a man of living faith, studious habits, deep piety, modest demeanor, spotless reputation and universal popularity. It is no unusual thing for him to baptize from thirty to fifty persons during a meeting. In addition to preaching extensively in rural districts and building up many strong country churches, he has preached successfully in almost all of the towns of that part of Tennessee as well as in many in Mississippi and Alabama.

He has been instrumental in establishing the cause in almost all the towns he has visited.

H. F. Williams from Maury County, Tennessee, took a pretty thorough course at Mars' Hill. He had the misfortune to be sadly mangled in a sorghum mill when a boy, by which he lost both hands and one arm. As a student he was patient, painstaking, conservative, persevering, and conscientiously submissive to all the requirements of discipline. As a friend he was true and unwavering; but frank and manly in reproof when necessary. In religion he was emotional, but not without deep and intelligent convictions. He discriminated between gush and repentance, and never mistook tears of mere sentiment for deeds of genuine love. He believed correct and intelligent convictions as to the truth would crystalize into a Christian character and bring forth a rich fruitage of a godly reputation. He considered all life a process of growth, and renounced all stagnation as a form of death and destined to early decay. On leaving Mars' Hill he married and began to teach and preach in Giles and Lincoln Counties, Tenn. His wife has been a true helpmeet for him, furnishing hands to complement his physical defects, and love and sympathy to encourage and strengthen his mind and heart in their great works. He has preached extensively through Tennessee, Alabama, and Mississippi when not engaged in teaching. His preaching has resulted in the conversion of many souls; but its greatest value has been in its effects upon Christians. In 1889 he gave up teaching and accepted an editorial position on the *Gospel Advocate*, of Nashville, Tennessee. He is a clear and forcible preacher, and eminently sensible and practical in every thing.

J. C. McQuiddy, from Marshall county, Tenn., took the full course prescribed for preachers at Mars' Hill, and afterward a thorough course in language, mathematics, and English literature, at Winchester, Tenn. On leaving school he accepted a call to preach for the church at Columbia, Tenn. He conducted several successful protracted meetings in Tennessee and Alabama before he went to Columbia. In 1883 he became editorially connected with the *Old-Path Guide*, of Louisville, Ky. He traveled extensively in Middle Tennessee and South Kentucky in the interest of that paper. In 1885 he became Office Editor and Business Manager of the *Gospel Advocate*, and moved to Nashville, Tenn., in which position he still continues. He has developed remarkable talent for wise and energetic business management, and proved himself an editor of no mean ability. He is a ready and fluent speaker, a zealous Christian, and an accurate scholar. In Columbia he was successful in developing the church, and popular as a preacher. In Nashville his time is principally occupied with editorial and business duties; but when he finds time to preach, his labors are always in demand with the many churches in the bounds of his acquaintance. At Mars' Hill we called him "Little Mack," and we all liked him for his nice manners and obliging disposition.

George P. Young, of Lauderdale county, Ala., finished a thorough course in English, Latin mathematics, and the Bible at Mars' Hill in 1876. He entered school at Mountain Home, by Professor Larimore's advice, in 1868, and was a close and constant student up to 1876. He spent vacations teaching and preaching, and missed a few terms on account of having to earn money to pay his expenses; but he kept steadily on till his education was finished. He preached extensively, and with good results, through Alabama, Mississippi, and West Tennessee during the time he was teaching and going to school, and on leaving school in 1876, he located at Stark, Fla., to preach and teach. In 1879 he moved to Texas, but in a year he returned to Stark and resumed his work. He has preached extensively through Florida, established and successfully managed Orange College up to the present, and accumulated a very neat little fortune in orange groves, nurseries, and other valuable property. He is a man of untiring energy, indomitable perseverance, sound business judgment, ceaseless industry, practical common sense, and thorough education.

J. R. Bradley, of Lauderdale county, Ala., was at Mars' Hill in 1878–9. He was well along in years, and married when he entered school. His education in younger days had been entirely neglected, and he was wholly without financial resources, and his only means of support was hard manual labor on the farm, as a renter or hireling. In school he applied himself closely, and attained a fair degree of proficiency in English grammar, logic, rhetoric, and general outline of history. He developed an easy and impressive delivery, acquired a correct knowledge of the doctrine of Christ, and came to understand the leading doctrine of the different religious sects of modern times with tolerable accuracy. On leaving school, he settled in Giles county, Tenn., where he still resides. He has preached constantly and very successfully in Giles, Lawrence, Maury and Wayne counties, Tenn., and Lauderdale, Colbert, and Limestone counties, Ala. He has baptized hundreds of people, and has been instrumental in establishing many strong country churches in his field of labor.

D. A. Mills, of Lauderdale county, Ala., was over fifty years old when he entered Mars Hill College as a pupil. He had a wife, but no children. He was one of the tallest, straightest, and biggest frame men in the country. He had served as a soldier through the late war, and had been babtized only a few years before he came to Mars' Hill. As I remember him, he seems to have had a fair English education when he entered school. He gave his time almost exclusively to the study of the Bible. He was a fair speaker, and very prepossessing in appearance in the pulpit. He had preached some before he came to Mars' Hill, and he improved wonderfully as a preacher while there. He preached a few years after he left school in Lauderdale and Colbert counties, Ala., and then he moved to Texas. He was a true man and a fair country preacher; but I have lost sight of him of late years. Wherever he is, if alive, I feel confident he is faithfully preaching the old-time gospel of Christ—he was not the sort of man to surrender in a good cause.

T. L. Weatherford, of Limestone county, Ala., was at Mars' Hill in 1878. He was a man of advanced years and burdened with the care of a large family. He was very poor, and dependent entirely upon hard labor on the farm for support. He had preached some before he came to Mars' Hill. He was greatly benefitted by a session at this college, and has accomplished much good by his godly life and unremitting labors in Lauderdale and Limestone counties, Ala,, and Giles and Lawrence counties, Tenn. He is a ready speaker, clear reasoner, and pathetic exhorter. He is a good man, tender in sympathy, warm in friendship, unselfish in zeal, spotless in reputation, constant in faith, and self-sacrificing in good works.

M. A. Beal was the gentle-spirited and sweet-voiced songster of the memorable class of 1878. Disguised in the ragged garments of an outcast, he sang the famous temperance solo, "Shivering in the Cold," commencement night, with a pathos and heartfelt earnestness I have never heard equaled even by professionals. He unquestionably had remarkable gifts for music; but he was burdened with the care of a large family, his education had been sadly neglected, and he lacked means to cultivate his splendid talents. But what matters it? He was not long for this world any way. One summer evening, soon after he left school, he sat under the trees in the front yard of his humble home and sang "Sweet by-and-by" as the sun went down; on he sang while the twilight deepened—and still he sang "In the sweet by-and by" when the stars came out, and the moon smiled sweetly over the hills in the east. When the morning light came again he was cold in death; but who shall say he was not singing in sweeter voice and happier soul than ever before, with those who are always in "The Sweet by-and-by"? His sudden death was from hemorrhage of the lungs. He was not specially gifted as a preacher; but he was measurably successful in the few protracted meetings he conducted.

H. North, was a man well advanced in years, of limited means, with a large family, and without a common school education when he came to Mars' Hill in 1878. He was a man of great faith, deep piety and consuming zeal. He made a fair preacher, and moved to Texas. He believed in prayer. While he was in school one of his children was sick, nigh unto death. He called the elders of the church together at his house, had them to pray for the recovery of the child and it recovered. He never for one moment doubted but that, the prayer of faith saved the sick.

Brother Walker was another member of the class of 1878 who was advanced in years and married. On leaving school he remained in the vicinity of Florence, and was a helpful worker in the church at different points in the country around, and is still living at Mars' Hill

---

H. H. Turner, of Collierville, Tenn., came to Mars' Hill in 1878, and remained till about 1882 or perhaps 1883. During the time he was in school he preached at several different points in the country around the college. He moved to Texas in about 1885, and from Texas he went to New Mexico.

W. B. McQuiddy, of Marshall county, Tenn., was a skillful and practical telegraphist and in the employment of a large railroad corporation before he came to Mars' Hill in 1878. He remained in school two sessions, and developed into an acceptable and successful preacher. On leaving school he preached a while in Middle Tennessee, and then accepted a field of work in Texas. On account of the failure of his wife's health, he gave up preaching in Texas and returned to Tennessee in about a year. He resumed his position as telegraphist for the railroad; but has continued to preach with splendid results as he has had opportunity. He is one of the unadvertised and not very widely known, but very useful, men in his part of the country. He is a true man, a good scholar, a fair speaker and a good preacher in the truest and best sense of the word. He is of the steady, reliable, patient and faithful kind of men whose chief value to the cause of Christianity is in giving permanence to the work of less stable, but more brilliant preachers.

J. A. Taylor, of Franklin county, Ala., was at Mars' Hill in 1877–8. On leaving school he preached for a time in Franklin and Colbert counties Alabama, and then moved to Arkansas. He made teaching his means of support and preached as he had opportunity. He was a valuable man to the cause wherever he was located up to the time he moved to Arkansas, and for ought I have ever heard to the contrary he is still maintaining his usefulness in the church where he lives

---

J. T. Underwood was another member ot the class of 1878. He continued in school till 1879–80. On leaving school he located near Bellgreen, county-seat of Franklin county, Alabama. He was helpful in building up several country churches in Franklin and Colbert counties, Alabama. He is now located at Barton, in Colbert county, Alabama, and preaches regularly in the country for miles around his home.

W. J. Hudspeth, of Prescott, Arkansas, was at Mars' Hill in 1878–9–80. He preached extensively through Lauderdale, Limestone and Colbert counties, Alabama, and Giles, Maury, Lawrence and Wayne counties, Tennessee, while in school and during vacation. In 1881 he located at Bairdstown, Texas, and preached for the church at that place. He also held several successful meetings in Texas in the summer of 1881. In 1882 he returned to Arkansas and preached for the church at Hope. In 1883 he became editorially connected with the *Old Path Guide*, and for two years represented that paper in Arkansas. He traveled extensively, and became widely known in Arkansas, as a successful evangelist, untiring worker in the Sunday-school cause and an able, self-sacrificing preacher of the gospel. In 1885 he began to suffer from throat trouble and for two years was unable to preach regularly. In 1888 he was employed by the Arkansas Christian Sunday-school Convention to labor as State Sunday-school evangelist. In 1889 he moved to Texas again to preach for the church at Sulphur Springs. As a preacher he is especially noted for his social qualities, deep and abiding piety, earnest exhortations, strong faith and untiring perseverance. He is a good singer, and a most successful leader of song service in congregational singing. He is warm-hearted and emotional by nature, and exhorts sinners, with tears in eyes and pathos in voice, to come to Jesus.

James B. Street, of Mississippi, was at Mars' Hill two terms, and during the summer of 1878, after school, he conducted a few successful protracted meetings. He had flattering prospects of a useful life; but in the time we all least expected death, he was visited by that ever unwelcome messenger. He was the pride of his home church, the idol of his mother and the hope and joy of his father, sisters and brothers. Young in years, but abounding in faith and rejoicing in hope, he died like the Christian that he was. Rest to his soul, peace to his memory, good cheer to the loved ones bereaved, and blessings, patient continuance in well doing and faithfulness unto death, to those he taught the way of salvation. In college he was my room mate beloved, and to the day of his death my friend and brother, faithful and true.

D. R. Hardison, of Maury county, Tenn., was the youngest of all the preachers in the class of 1878, if indeed it be proper to call him a preacher. He preached some, and with excellent effect in protracted meetings after he left school; but finally settled down as one of the substantial and successful farmers and stock-raisers of his native county. He was a boy of excellent heart, brilliant mind and cheerful disposition. Quick to see the ludicrous in every thing, he was rather more inclined to levity than piety, and readier to laugh than to pray. If any thing is to be said against this trait of his nature, it should be lamented as a misfortune rather than censured as a fault. Generous hearted, original, witty and a great mimic, I am half inclined to think his laugh often did more good for the desolate-hearted and unfortunate sufferers of earth, than more pious men's prayers. However, undue levity is not to be commended or encouraged, and a deeper piety would have added greatly to his usefulness in the church. Fortunately, the defect is one which increasing age tends constantly to remedy, and his usefulness should continue to increase as the weight of years adds steadiness to his many other excellent qualities. He is a true man, and ought to be a valuable worker in the church.

Walter Norwood, of Landersville, Ala., was at Mars' Hill two terms, and on leaving school began teaching and preaching at and around his home church. In 1886 he moved to Hickman county, Tennessee, where he has since resided. He is popular as a teacher and successful as a preacher. His work has been hindered to some extent by sickness in his family; yet he has done much to establish the cause in his field of labor.

F. C. Sowell, of Maury county, Tenn., left Mars' Hill about 1883, and settled on a farm near Columbia, Tennessee. He has preached regularly since he left Mars' Hill, and his preaching has resulted in much good to the cause through Maury, Giles and Lawrence counties, Tennessee. Strong country churches have steadily built up in almost every neighborhood in those counties, and such men as he have done far more than traveling evangelists of greater reputations, to give permanence to the work. He is competent and self-sacrificing as a preacher, and thoroughly identified with the people and the country as a citizen. These considerations make him peculiarly valuable to the cause as a leader in whom the people all have confidence. Without such leaders for churches, the splendid revivals preached up by traveling evangelists would be little else than a display of pulpit oratory, or a glow of spiritual fox fire, without permanent results for good.

R. E. McKnight, of Maury county, Tenn., is a man of general and accurate information, unflagging industry, rather excitable temperament and fine personal appearance. In deportment he is a gentleman of polished manners and easy bearing. Tall, slender, athletic and trim in physique; quick, supple and graceful in movement; a rich crown of dark curls disheveled about his brow, and a voice well modulated but flexible and clear; he seems by nature specially designed for pastoral work in aesthetic city churches. After he finished his course at Mars' Hill, he taught one session in that institution, and then made a tour among the churches in several counties in Alabama and Tennessee, soliciting patronage for the college. On leaving Mars' Hill he located at Lebanon, Tennessee, to preach as the evangelist sent out and sustained by a co-operation of churches in that county. After a years' work in that field he moved to Lebanon, Missouri, to preach for the church at that place. From Missouri he was called to preach for the church at Fort Worth, Texas. He remained at Fort Worth two years, during which he accomplished much good. From Fort Worth he was re-called to his former work at Lebanon, Missouri, his present place of abode.

E. A. Elam, of Fosterville, Tenn., graduated at Burritt College, and went to Mars' Hill to teach with the determined purpose to preach whenever the opportuity offered. The attendance being too small to require all of his time teaching, arrangements were made for him to spend part of his time studying the Bible to further prepare himself for his chosen work of preaching. Possessed of a strong intellect, a thorough education, a converted and consecrated heart and a soul abounding in desires for the salvation of all men, he made rapid progress in the study of the Bible and soon began to preach with great ability and remarkable success. He gave up teaching entirely, and devoted himself unreservedly to preaching. On leaving Mars' Hill he located at Lebanon, Tennessee, and for several years preached for the church there a part of his time reserving a good part of each year to hold protracted meetings at such points as the interests of the cause seemed to require. From Lebanon he went to Chattanooga and labored about a year, and from Chattanooga to Gallatin, which is his present address. He has perhaps preached more generally through Middle Tennessee than any other man of his age. His labors have been greatly blessed in the number of persons added to the churches, and he has been especially valuable to the churches in arousing indifferent members to new life and activity in Christian duty. He is in every sense a strong man. He has a strong body, a strong mind, a strong voice, a strong faith and a strong courage. Few men of his age have done as much as he to plant churches, train Christians and combat sin and error. He is a fluent speaker, a ready writer, a clear and vigorous thinker and unremitting worker. He has convictions, and he knows how to maintain them. He is decidedly an uncomfortable fellow to sit down on.

T. H. Humphrey, of Gadsden, Tenn., was a promising student at Mars' Hill; but since he left school his work has been greatly hindered by continued bad health. H has been a useful member of his home church, and has preached acceptably in the country around Gadsden at occasional intervals when his health would permit.

H. N. Harris was a member of the class of 1878, and preached with encouraging success during the summer around the college. He moved to West Tennessee to preach and teach; but probably settled down on a farm in a few years. Last report from him seemed to indicate that he was much interested in the welfare of the church; but on account of other duties not preaching regularly.

T. H. Mills, of Maury county, Tenn., was at Mars' Hill in 1878–9. He was a man of general information and thorough education; but modest and retiring disposition. On leaving school he became principal of Lasea Academy, in Maury county, Tennessee, and, while filling that position, he preached through that part of Tennessee as he had opportnnity. He made a preaching tour to West Tennessee, and conducted several very successful protracted meetings. He gave up teaching at Lasea Academy and moved to West Tennessee to teach and preach. He has done much good work for the cause in Tennessee, and may always be relied upon to do all in his power to extend the reign of Christ over the minds and hearts of the people.

Robert M. Clark, of Moulton, Ala., was at Mars' Hill in the later years of that institution. His father, J. M. Clark, has long stood high in the medical profession in North Alabama, and has also been a recognized factor of considerable magnitude in religion and politics in that country in late years. His uncle, Hon. J. S. Clark, was a leading lawyer and brilliant orator in that country to the time of his death. For several years judge of the circuit court in that district and always influential in politics, he was in a position to offer young Robert strong inducements to turn his splendid talents into worldly channels. But Robert chose that better part, nor for a moment has he ever regretted his choice

At Mars' Hill he was always dignified, and deservedly popular and influential among the boys. As a speaker, he possesses much of the grace and facination of style which distinguished his celebrated uncle as an orator at the bar and on the political rostrum. The great distinguishing characteristics of all the Mars' Hill boys—fidelity to the Scriptures and close adherence to the teaching of the Bible in the pulpit—are peculiarly prominent in him. He is always earnest, zealous and industrious as a preacher. Unfortunately he is a man of feeble health, and physically not able to endure continuous evangelistic work. He now lives in Mississippi. He teaches, preaches and farms, varying his labors, to preserve, and, if possible, improve his health. He has been very successful as an evangelist wherever he has labored in bringing people into the church as well as building up the churches in zeal and spirituality.

Dr. J. W. Hollan, of Troy, Ala., is another one of the Mars' Hill boys of whom the writer has obtained a good report. At school he had the reputation of being tender-hearted, sympathetic, almost inexpressibly averse to falsehood or deception of any shade, wholly free from hypocrisy, unwavering as a friend; loving, trusting, confiding; rather too easily influenced; easily lead by those he loved and trusted, hence sometimes considered rather fickle or wanting in the sterner elements of resistance; but never yielding to do what his conscience condemned as morally wrong. He was prayerful, pious, believed in Providence and was always confident of success in every good work. Since he left Mars' Hill, he has been successful in life, and has enjoyed the confidence of all who have known him.

George Lewellen, of Baldwin, Miss., was one of the best of Mars' Hill boys. After leaving there he attended Kentucky University, from which institution he recently graduated. He is now President of West Tennessee Christian College. He is a man of pure life, modest bearing, strong intellect, tender heart, clear convictions, deep piety and thorough education. He is a preacher of no ordinary ability, and in the high and responsible position to which he has been called as president of West Tennesse Christian College, he seems peculiarly qualified to succeed,

F. B. Srygley, of Rock Creek, Ala., was at Mars' Hill three years, and on leaving school he located at Lebanon, Tenn., to preach in destitute places in that county as the evangelist sent out and sustained by a co-operation of the churches in the county. His preaching resulted in many conversions, and several churches were built up in the bounds of his labors. As he became more generally known, wider fields of usefulness opened before him, and he began to extend his labors into adjoining counties. He has preached with good success in almost every county in Middle Tennessee, has done much valuable work for the churches in Alabama, made two very successful preaching tours through Arkansas, and has done much protracted-meeting work in Kentucky. He is a clear and original thinker, a deliberate and forcible speaker, and a free, social commingler with the people. For two years he has been the regular preacher for the church at Lebanon, Tenn.; but still reserves the spring, summer, and fall to preach in protracted meetings wherever he can best subserve the general cause.

W. W. Vick, of Lawrence county, Tenn., was at Mars' Hill the first years of the school. He was a Christian of strong faith and spotless life, and a student of good ability and great promise. On leaving Mars' Hill he taught several years in Lawrence county, Tenn., and preached acceptably around home. He was a valuable worker in the church, but he chose to teach as a vocation and preach as he had opportunity. In later years he taught for a time at Mars' Hill, and then moved to Texas, where he is still teaching and preaching.

John E. Campbell, of Giles county, Tenn., was at Mars' Hill early in the seventies. He obtained a fair education, and then taught several years in a country school in his native county. In later years he was associated with his brother, G. W. Campbell, in the management of Lynnville Academy, in Giles county, Tenn. This was a flourishing school, and the two Campbells established enviable reputations as educators in its management. John E. Campbell also taught at Mars' Hill in 1877. On account of failing health he moved to California, where he is still teaching. He is a good scholar, a successful educator, and zealous Christian. He is a good worker and a wise leader in the church, though he hardly considers himself a preacher.

A. B. Herring, of Georgia, was at Mars Hill several sessions. He preached around the college with good success while in school; but since his return home I know nothing of him save an occasional report through the papers. He is still preaching, and the papers report good results from his labors. He is a young man of much general information, strong faith, and constant piety, and he can not fail to greatly strengthen the churches wherever he labors.

Brown Godwin, of Tennessee was at Mars' Hill from January, 1882, to June, 1885. While in school he preached occasionally around Mars' Hill, but says, like the other boys, he "did but little preaching of that kind," except where better preachers had not been, as it was a difficult matter to get the brethren who had heard better preaching to board him while he was preaching. In the later years of his college course he preached during vacations in Middle Tennessee—Williamson, Maury, Lewis, Marshall, Hickman, and Perry counties. Here he gave promise of his subsequent great success as an evangelist. In 1885, soon after leaving Mars' Hill, he engaged to preach as an evangelist under the direction of the churches at Landersville and Russellville, Ala. He spent six months in this work, and in that time held several successful meetings. The first half of 1886 he spent at Linden, Tenn., and in July, 1886, he began preaching in Decatur, Texas. After thirteen months' work in Texas, he returned to Tennessee on account of his wife's health. In 1888 he preached at Paris, Tenn., except a few months in protracted-meetings in Middle Tennessee. In 1889 he moved to Princeton, Ky., where he now resides. Besides the preaching he has done for churches, he has held sixty-five protracted-meetings and received into the church more than 800 people. There were 70 additions at one meeting, and in five weeks' preaching there were 125 additions to the church. For a man of his age, his work has been signally successful in building up churches. He has the religious faith and zeal characteristic of his *alma mater* and his distinguished teacher. Few men of his age have done more for the church, or enjoy brighter prospects for the future, than he.

Lee Jackson, of Mississippi, was at Mar's Hill toward the last days of that institution. He had in him the elements of a successful preacher, and nature had endowed him with the energy to develop them. His faith and zeal supplied him with ample stimulus, and a steadfast purpose held him unswervingly to the great object and ambition of his heart. He has preached extensively and with good results through

Mississippi and Alabama, and at present is evangelizing in Lawrence, Colbert, and Franklin counties, Ala. He is proving himself an efficient preacher and safe counselor for the churches in a field where he is much needed.

C. N. Sparkman was one of the promising boys at Mars' Hill in the later sessions of that school. He was from Middle Tennessee, and a descendant of Seth Sparkman of blessed memory and abundant labors in the pulpit in the early days of the reformation. He stood well in his classes, and commanded the respect of all and enjoyed the love of his teacher. He preached some while at school, and his preaching was well received, and gave promise of a successful career. He has been attending school at Kentucky University since he left Mars' Hill, and it is safe to assume he will prove a valuable worker in the church and an able preacher of the gospel

---

B. F. Hart, of Petersburg, Tenn., was at Mars' Hill in the earlier sessions. He is a man of sterling principles and fine ability; he has a good education, and for years has been farming and preaching successfully in his native county. He is well informed in the Bible, and is an excellent preacher. He has done much to strengthen and build up churches throughout his community, and may always be relied upon as a faithful Christian, a wise counselor, a zealous worker, a safe teacher, and a good preacher.

O. P. Speagle, Falkville, Ala., "staid with Mars' Hill to the last, and is now completing a thorough course in Kentucky University" at Lexington, Kentucky. He preached his first sermon near Mars' Hill the day he was eighteen years old. His teacher, brother Larimore, refers to him as "One of the very best and most promising of the Mars' Hill boys—young, fine looking and destined to make his mark in the world." As he is not yet out of school, he has preached but little; still the brethren who know him well think they see in him evidences of great capability and promises of abundant usefulness.

T. E. Tatum, of Wilson county, Tenn., was at Mars' Hill in the latter days of the school. He took the usual course for preachers, and on leaving school preached acceptably in his native county some years, with occasional tours into adjoining counties. He is a man of gentle spirit, easy manners and pleasing address, and his preaching has greatly profited the cause of general Christianity wherever he has labored. In 1888 he was called to Chattanooga, Tennessee, to assist in building up a church at a mission point in that city. He has traveled through Tennessee, Kentucky and Ohio in the interests of this mission work, and his labors promise well for the enterprise. He is a man of faithfulness and persistent endeavor, and may always be counted on for commendable deportment and courteous proclamation of the gospel.

A. C. Williams, of Maury county, Tenn., was at Mars' Hill two years, and afterwards at Winchester, Tennessee, in school two years. He is a man of good character, splendid natural abilities and thorough education. Since he left school he has been teaching and preaching in Lincoln and Marshall counties, Tennessee. He is a man of strong convictions and good executive ability. He has been a constant and valuable worker in the church wherever he has lived, and his labors have greatly promoted the interests of the cause of Christianity.

There are others, many others, who were educated at Mars' Hill and whose lives since they left school have been quite as profitable to the world and as helpful to the church as those of whom favorable mention is made in this chapter. I can not speak even of all I know, as I wish to speak, for lack of space; and of all who were educated there I know but a small per cent. As to the preachers educated at Mars' Hill, it is worthy of mention that probably a majority of them were converted to Christianity by his preaching during vacation, and nearly all of them were induced to preach by him. He was not a mere school teacher who waited for preachers to come to him to be educated; but a preacher, in a country where we had few members and fewer churches, who would go out and convert sinners to Christ and cause men to determine to be preachers, and then bring them into Mars' Hill College and educate them. He spent six months of each year holding protracted meetings and persuading men to preach the gospel, and the other six months in teaching men how to preach. In another chapter I will make mention of a few out of many others who were at Mars' Hill College.

CHAPTER XVIII.

Those who came to Mars' Hill to study for the ministry were but a small part of all whom he induced to preach the gospel. He believes in an educated ministry, and encourages all who wish to preach the gospel to spare no efforts to qualify themselves for the important work by as liberal an education as they can possibly attain. But when it is quite out of a man's power to attend school, he never advises him to neglect the gift that is in him for want of much needed helps he can never obtain. In every neighborhood where he has preached, he has made not only devout Christians, but has established strong churches and called out acceptable preachers. Nor is his work of that superficial and emotional kind that soon passes away. Of all those who attended Mars' Hill, very few do I now remember who in after years lost interest in Christianity and fell back into habitual wrong-doing. Many of them have at times done wrong—no one of them has been without sin, as to that matter. But, most of them, known to me, so far as I now call to mind, have been not only consistent in Christian professions as to their general course of life, but active workers in the church. These sketches and observations would not be complete without some mention of at least a few of his pupils who, though not preachers, have been successful in life and an honor to his institution.

Mrs. Mattie Y. Murdock (*nee* Miss Mattie Young), of Lauderdale county Ala. finished a thorough course at

Mars' Hill in 1875. In 1876–7 she taught at Mars' Hill; in 1878–9 she taught near Saltillo, Miss.; in 1880 she was married to Prof. Murdock, of Saltillo, Miss.; in 1881 she moved to Ellis county, near Waxahachie, Texas, where she and her husband both taught in the county free schools; in 1883 she moved to Ennis, where she has since taught continuously in the city graded free school. Her husband has been very successful as a teacher; but on account of his health he prefers an out-door life, and hence he gives his attention mainly to farming and stock-raising. Mrs. Murdock is a self-possessed and prepossessing woman in demeanor and appearance. She is progressive but not fanatical as to methods of teaching and discipline; practical and thorough in what she undertakes to teach; sincere and unwavering in what she claims to believe; honest and free from deception in what she professes to be. She is esteemed wherever known as a woman of eminent natural abilities, and an educator of consummate tact and varied accomplishments.

M. H. Meeks was a pupil of Professor Larimore at Stantonville, Tenn., before Mars' Hill was established, and went with him to Mars' Hill at the opening of that institution. He attended the Military Institute at Knoxville, Tenn., one term after leaving Mars' Hill, and in 1877 graduated in the Law School at Lebanon, Tenn. In 1878 he was elected Attorney-General for the State in the Eleventh Judicial Circuit, composed of the counties of Hickman, Perry, Wayne, Hardin, McNairy, Decatur, Henderson, Lewis, and Chester. He served eight years in that office, and then removed to Jackson, Tenn. In Jackson he was a member of the law-firm of Pitts, Hays & Meeks, and one of the founders and directors of the Second National Bank. In 1888 he moved to Nashville, Tenn., and became a partner in the law-firm of Pitts & Meeks. He is a successful financier, a brilliant orator, and an able lawyer. As a "stump-speaker" in politics, he has few equals, and no superiors of his age. He is a zealous Christian, and ardent admirer of his old teacher.

Frank Boyd finished his course at Mars' Hill in 1878. In 1880 he began the study of law under Judge Howell E. Jackson, now of the United States Court, at Jackson, Tenn. In 1883 he graduated in the Law School of Lebanon, Tenn., and, on leaving school, located at Waynesboro, Tenn., where he has since resided and engaged in the practice of law. He is an able lawyer and successful practitioner.

J. H. Moore, of South Florence, Ala., finished his course at Mars' Hill in 1876, and subsequently graduated from the Medical College in Vanderbilt University, at Nashville, Tenn., and has since practiced medicine in Alabama, Texas, and Indian Territory.

J. H. Anderson, of Russellville, Ala., was a member of the class of 1878. On leaving Mars' Hill he attended the Medical College in Vanderbilt University, at Nashville, Tenn. He graduated in medicine, and has succeeded admirably in the practice of his profession.

J. J. Coats, of Rock Creek, Ala., was at Mars' Hill in 1877. On leaving college he settled in Marion county, Ala., as teacher of a country school. After teaching a few years he turned his attention to farming, then operated a mill for a time, then figured some as a contractor in a small way in building the Sheffield and Birmingham Railroad, and lastly gave attention to dealing some in real estate. He has been measurably successful in his business enterprises, but has never for a moment forgotten to be loyal to his convictions and punctual in the discharge of his duties as a Christian. He is one of the substantial men in his community.

F. W. Srygley was at Mars' Hill in 1876–7. He completed the course in the Business College, and acquired a fair education in languages, mathematics, and general history. On leaving school, he taught two years at Rock Creek, his native home, and then began business as a merchant at Frankfort, Ala. He has been successful as a merchant, and has wielded an excellent influence for Christianity and general morality in his community.

R. E. McKenney, of Purdy, Tenn., was at Mars' Hill in 1876. In later years he was Clerk and Master of the Chancery Court in McNairy county, Tenn., and afterwards a successful merchant at Jackson, Tenn. He took the commercial course at Mars' Hill, and also a course in languages and higher mathematics. He is pre-eminently a man of business, diligent, practical, energetic, discreet, moral, and exact. He has made life a success by close attention to the details of business. He is now cashier of a bank at Henderson, Tenn.

J. W. Fry, of Lynnville, Tenn., finished his course at Mars' Hill in 1876. On leaving school he settled down as a farmer and stock-raiser, near Lynnville, Tenn,. He is one of the leaders and supporters of an unusually large church at Lynnville. At school, John was lively, cheerful, full of good-humor, and always in favor of having a good time. He is a useful man in his community, and a strong-hold for the church.

Major McDonald, of Mayfield, Ky., was at Mars' Hill in 1878. On leaving school he engaged in business in his native town, and has by constant application to business, attained a fair measure of success. He stands high in the confidence of the people who know him, and has an excellent influence for morality over those who associate with him.

R. H. Thompson completed the course in the Business College at Mars' Hill, and on leaving school accepted a position as book-keeper in Cincinnati, Ohio. In later years he returned to Alabama and engaged in merchandising at Hartselle, in Morgan county. He has maintained a good moral character, continued faithful in his duties as a Christian, and made life a fair business success. He is a worthy member of the purest and best society.

Frank Tankersley, of Marshall county, Tenn., was in the Bible College in 1878, and teacher of vocal music in 1879. He was a good leader of song service and an acceptable preacher. He settled down as a farmer and stock-raiser on leaving school, and has made a useful member of the church and of society where he lives by a consistent Christian life and a free exercise of his gifts in song and in leading public meetings in the church. He is well informed in the Scriptures, and possesses a fair education.

In closing these sketches it is proper to say I have not been conscious of any feeling of partiality toward those of whom I have made honorable mention against the many who are equally worthy but of whom no mention is made. Having been at Mars' Hill only four years of the seventeen years of its existence as a school, only a small per cent. of those who attended school there were ever known to me; and of those I knew, only a very few have been known to me since we left school. These sketches indicate only a part of the work done at Mars' Hill during a part of the existence of the school. As a preacher, Professor Larimore is known to excel in revival work. Modern revivalists have been charged, and not without good cause, with adopting sensational methods for temporary effects. Indeed, it is well-nigh a foregone conclusion that a revivalist who can move a whole community, and baptize scores of people during a single meeting, as Professor Larimore almost always does, should be liberally discounted for emotional and superficial work that is lacking in the essential elements of stability and endurance. No such objections can be urged against him. His pupils will compare favorbly with those of other schools in wearing qualities, and those added to the churches under his preaching compare favorably with any other Christians in depth of convictions, steadfastness in faith, and zeal in good works. These sketches are not written in partiality to those whose works are described, but simply to illustrate the general character of his work as a teacher and preacher. I have written entirely from such information as I have gained and retained by irregular correspondence, occasional newspaper reports and general notoriety, of the Mars' Hill boys. With one or two exceptions, no one of them knows what I have written about him, and but few know that I have written of them at all. While all that is said may be relied upon for general accuracy, there may be some slight errors as to dates and minor details in some of the sketches.

CHAPTER XIX.

It is impossible to follow him closely in all his evangelistic labors during the continuance of Mars' Hill College. He spent six months of each year preaching in protracted meetings, and rarely spent over a week at any place in one meeting. It must suffice to note a few of his many important meetings by way of illustrating the general character of his labors and successes.

In July 1870 he went to Collierville, Tennessee, a flourishing little town twenty-five miles east of Memphis. We had a few members there, but no house in which to have a meeting. He began preaching in a little school house near town. His meeting resulted in eighty-one additions to the church, and immediately afterwards a suitable lot was secured in town and a good house erected on it. A large church was established, and has continued in good working order to this day. During that meeting a Methodist Quarterly conference was held in Collierville, and the eminent John B. McFerrin, of Nashville, Tennessee, was in attendance to deliver a series of his masterly sermons and lectures. But the beardless youth in the old school house near town was drawing immense audiences day and night while the scholarly doctors of divinity with well-trained choirs and comfortable pews could scarcely hold their best members in attendance upon the business meetings of the conference.

From Collierville, Tennessee, he went to Antioch, Lauderdale county, Alabama, a country church fourteen miles from Mars' Hill, in July 1870. He began his series of sermons on Saturday-night and closed the following Friday-night with fifty-two additions to the church. This had been a preaching point for John Taylor and others of his day for many years; but our membership was small, and the principles of our reformatory movement had never been generally understood nor seriously considered. Antioch at once took on new life and began to develop some valuable talent. J. R. Bradley and a brother Smallwood, members of Antioch church, soon began to preach, and not many years afterwards the former became a pupil at Mars' Hill, and is now a successful preacher in Tennessee.

About this time the effects of his first work at Rock Creek began to be manifest in important improvements of various kinds. The old house described at length in a former chapter, was torn down and a good country meeting house built in its stead with glass windows, doors with locks and keys, comfortable seats, stove and ceiling all complete. The grade of the country school there was very much improved, and a flourishing Sunday-school was established. It will save time and space to say, once for all, that similar improvements were made in these respects throughout that country as a result of his preaching wherever he went.

July 11, 1872 he went to Pocahontas, Tennessee, where we had only two sisters. He held a meeting of seven days there, delivered fifteen sermons, and baptized thirty-two people. M. H. Northcross, now of Bunker Hill, Tennessee, and an able preacher, was baptized at that meeting. A good church was established and a commodious, comfortable meeting house was built. A Mr. Adams, who was a prominent citizen there and an out-spoken infidel, donated land for a church site, contributed liberally to build the church, and offered to pay $50 a year to get professor Larimore to preach for them. He said he did not believe his doctrine, but considered his preaching worth that for its refining power in the communnity.

August 25, 1872 he went to Cloverport, now called Greenwood, Tennessee. We had but one member there—a brother Pyrtle. The meeting was held under an immense shelter for want of a house. The "straw" in the "altar" was badly worn by a long "mourners bench" revival that had just closed. The meeting continued ten days and resulted in sixty-one additions. Before he preached the first sermon brother Pyrtle said to him: "you can do nothing here now—you have come too late." The fourth day of the meeting he preached by request of a prominent Presbyterian gentleman from Rev. vi: 17. When he closed the sermon and stepped from the platform the Presbyterian brother, perfectly elated by the power of his preaching, caught him in his arms as if he had been a long lost son just found. A lady who was a sort of sectarian spit-fire and altogether more religious than courteous said to him: "If you are safe, I am too. I have been as deep under the water as you." To whom he replied in his mildest manner—"My dear sister, I hope you are not depending upon water for your salvation. No one can be saved by water alone." Mrs. Dr. T. J. Robinson, now of Mariana, Ark., was out-spoken and emphatic in her opposition at the beginning of the meeting. She and her husband had worked very zealously for the revival that had just closed when he began; but she declared she would not do any thing to help him in his meeting. She said her husband might do as he pleased, but as for her, she would furnish neither chicken, shelter, nor pie "for that other preacher." About the fourth day of the meeting she hunted up her husband when the invitation song was started and went with him to make the good confession. They have both made good members. He was called away from that meeting when the interest was at its very best, and when he had every prospect of sweeping the whole country, to marry a couple at Jackson, Tennessee. He felt in duty bound to attend to the marriage, as he had before promised to do; but he has never ceased to regret the untimely break in that meeting. Writing about it years afterwards he said: "Little things should not be allowed to interrupt a good meeting. It would have been far better for a common squire to have married that couple rather than break off that meeting just at that time." A good church was established at Cloverport, as the result of that meeting.

It is proper to state that he engaged to preach for the church at Jackson, Tennessee all of his time during vacation of 1872, so that the two meetings at Cloverport and Pocahontas were mainly projected and directed by the Jackson church.

Dates are somewhat confused along here, and it is difficult to determine the exact time of many of his best meetings from 1870 to 1880. It seems that his first successful meeting in Lawrence county, Alabama was in the summer of 1871, though it might possibly have been in 1873. It was held in a country church called Prospect, near Landersville. The meeting house, in a general way, was much the same as the old Rock Creek church described in a former chapter, and the membership of the church consisted mainly of J. W. Srygley and family and a few others. This was another one of John Taylor's preaching points. The meeting resulted in over thirty additions to the church, and in after years old Prospect was given up to the owls and bats, a comfortable and commodious house was built in Landersville, to which old Prospect congregation moved, and a strong church still keeps the appointments of the Lord's house there.

About this time he preached with great success at Baldwin, Eureka and Saltillo, Mississippi. His preaching in these towns was a necessary result of a very successful meeting ten miles from Saltillo in the country. He was urged by a few brethren to preach in Saltillo, which he reluctantly consented to do. We had no church there, and but few members. Arrangements were made for him to preach in a school-house, and the meeting resulted in a great number of additions to the church. A good house was built at once and a strong church established there. The church is still prosperous.

Solomon Childers was a prominent citizen at Saltillo, and an infidel. Years before, he tried to get religion, but failed. For eighteen months he almost lived upon his knees, and prayed without ceasing for such manifestations of the Spirits power in his conversion as popular theology taught him to expect. Discouraged by his failure he drifted into indifference, doubts and confirmed skepticism. He had not been to hear a sermon in many years; but the violent opposition to professor Larimore's preaching on the part of preachers and members of other churches excited his curiosity, and he decided to go and hear him. He was at once charmed by the preacher's matchless oratory, soon he was deeply impressed by his earnest reasoning, and not many sermons did he hear till his heart was strangely moved by his pathetic appeals to sinners to submit themselves in obedience to the commands of Jesus. Before the meeting closed, he confessed his faith in Christ and was baptized, and to the day of his death he rejoiced, believing in God.

Solomon Childers was a peculiar man. He could be convinced of an error and he was ready enough to yield to fair argument; he could be deeply moved by sympathy and easily led by love; but he could not be intimidated by numbers nor coerced by fear. Once he was a leader in a neighborhood feud in the vicinity of Saltillo, Mississippi. Each side numbered several men, and the strong-hold of Solomon's enemies was in that Mississippi town. Threats were freely iterated on both sides, and a serious difficulty seemed imminent. Solomon was not inclined to assume an aggressive attitude towards his enemies; but he maintained the daring kind of defensive bearing which is often a more provoking incentive to an open conflict than a mild form of direct attack. In this case Solomon heard that his enemies said "Solomon Childers will not venture to come to Saltillo." One day he bought some tent-cloth, had a tent made, loaded a few simple cooking utensils into his wagon, drove over to Saltillo and quietly pitched his tent. He molested no body, nor offered any explanation except to a few friends whom he requested to inform "the opposition" that Solomon could be seen at his tent any day. He remained there several days and then folded his tent and quietly returned to his home. Such a man was Solomon Childers. For years he was a sincere but unsuccessful seeker of religion, then he became discouraged, then indifferent, then sceptical and finally a confirmed infidel. His conversion was a great success of the gospel over mystic theology, and he made a good Christian to his death which occurred recently in Arkansas.

By request, professor Larimore delivered an address before the Memphis and Shelby county Bible Society in the

First Presbyterian church of Memphis, Tennessee, Sunday evening March 1, 1874 on "God and The Bible." On receiving a copy of this address, Mrs. Alexander Campbell wrote: "I am so glad to see, my dear brother, that you were entirely absorbed in the grandeur of your theme. I notice that the large I did not stand out once before you; but the great I AM occupied your wonder, admiration, gratitude and love. 'God and The Bible' is the most exalted and the loftiest theme that could engage the tongue of man or seraph. Your collation of truths in defence of the Bible and the God of the Bible can never be set aside or refuted by the strongest opposers, either Deistical or Atheistical, upon earth."

It is known to but few that the talented and venerable J. T. Barclay, author of "The City of The Great King" warmly favored the appointment of professor Larimore as consul to Jerusalem. To this end he wrote a strong letter of commendation in November 1871 in which he spoke of him as "a young man of great promise, of first rate education and talent * * * a gentleman and Christian every way worthy of your esteem, consideration and attention." His great desire to visit Jerusalem and to spend a few years among the scenes of sacred memory in the life of Christ, was a strong temptation to apply for the consulate; but he was disinclined to take part in a mere political scuffle for office and so dismissed the idea from his mind. The fact that such an idea for a moment was encouragd by such a man as J. T. Barclay, shows no ordinary general reputation for a boy yet in his twenties and but four years out of school.

In 1874 he delivered a series of sermons in Linden street Christian church, Memphis, Tennessee, then under the pastoral care of David Walk. This was his first preaching in the city, and though the meeting resulted in about twenty additions to the church he never considered it a success.

About this time he held his first meeting of importance in Florence. The meeting resulted in several additions and the beginning of what has since developed into a well regulated church. The increase at Florence has been gradual and not without many discouraging hindrances; but it may be said that we now have a good church there as the result of his untiring perseverance and faithful preaching.

These sketches all pertain to work done between the years 1870 and 1875. Nor do they give a tithe of his work during that short period. No notice at all is taken of the many meetings he held with good results but of less importance to the general cause. In 1875 he began the publication of a monthly paper on a novel plan, and also conceived the idea of enlarging Mars' Hill Academy, as it had been up to that time, into a great University. He went so far with the University idea as to decide definitely the general plan and approximate cost of the building, and even had the site of the building cleared off, the campus inclosed and the young forest trees carefully pruned. If he could have seen his way clearly to carry out this scheme he would perhaps have given his life to the work of continuing Mars' Hill. But when he became satisfied that it was not prudent to attempt so great an enterprise, he began to lose interest in Mars Hill. But as all this pertains to another well-marked period of his life, further comments are reserved for another chapter pertaining to his work from 1875 to 1887.

CHAPTER XX.

The first number of the paper published from Mars' Hill, a monthly, edited by T. B. Larimore, appeared in January, 1875. It was a twenty-four page pamphlet, five inches wide by eight inches long, neatly covered and trimmed. The front outside page of the cover bore the motto, "For what is a man profited if he shall gain the whole world and lose his own soul? or what shall a man give in exchange for his soul?" On this page were also ingeniously arranged the words, "Faith, Hope, Love, Mercy, Peace, Truth," and the following texts of Scripture:

"Mercy and Truth are met together; Righteousness and Peace have kissed each other." Ps. lxxxv: 10.

"Blessed are the merciful; for they shall obtain mercy." Matt. v: 7.

"He that loveth not knoweth not God; for God is love." 1 John v: 8.

"Thou shalt love the Lord thy God with all thy heart, and with all thy soul, and with all thy mind, and with all thy strength; and thy neighbor as thyself." Luke x: 27.

"Love one another with a pure heart fervently." 1 Peter i: 22.

"Let love be without dissimulation." Rom. xii: 9.

"Glory to God in the highest, and on earth peace, good will toward men." Luke ii: 14.

"I am for peace; but when I speak they are for war." Ps. cxx: 7.

"Blessed are the peace-makers, for they shall be called the children of God." Matt. v: 9.

"There is no peace, saith my God, to the wicked." Isa. lvii: 21.

"Nation shall not lift up sword against nation, neither shall they learn war any more." Isa. ii: 14.

"Let us not love in word, neither in tongue; but in deed and in truth." 1 John iii: 14.

"Thy word is truth." John xvii: 17.

"Ye shall know the truth and the truth shall make you free." John viii: 32.

The leading motto of all, conspicuously displayed on the first page, was:

"Whatsoever ye would that men should do to you, do ye even so to them." "Abstain from all appearance of evil."

The dedication read: "Tendering the gratitude of our hearts to 'The Giver of all we enjoy,' 'The source from which all blessings flow,' for all our past and present blessings, we implore HIS fatherly care and protection for the future, and dedicate this little work and our whole lives to HIM." In plain type were kept standing in a conspicuous place on first page the words, "Terms actually optional with every subscriber. Absolutely free to all who are not able to pay."

The paper's greeting occupied the second page of each number. It stood as a preface, and was the same in every issue. Two sentences from that page sufficiently declare the non-combative spirit of the paper: "If, being devoid of love, you make war upon me and try to work my ruin, I shall neither defend myself nor try to injure you." Another sentence in the same paragraph was equally to the point: "I am for peace, and no word of bitterness shall ever fall from my lips, even in self-defense." In the same line an editorial note in the first number reads: "This paper possesses not the slightest belligerent proclivity—not even in a latent or dormant state. It will avoid all unpleasant discussions and personal references. One harsh, unkind or unpleasant word will be sufficient reason for consigning to the flames any article written for its pages."

These quotations sufficiently indicate the general spirit of the paper. It began with a circulation of 5,000, and reached an edition of as high as 20,000. It was continued through two volumes at a heavy financial loss; the amount of money contributed for its support not being enough to even pay postage. Its non-combative tone was not in harmony with the spirit and genius of the reformation at that time, and its heavenly benedictions read like a new departure in the style of our journalism. Our papers had always been thoroughly representative of a people decidedly argumentative in their theology, and just at that time we were trying to settle by sharp controversy through our papers several important questions of church polity. Few people cared to read a paper that did not argue against something, and this good-spirited paper was generally considered a sort of messenger without a mission, as it were. It was thoroughly Christian in spirit, whatever may be said of its financial management and literary style. It never contained an unkind word during its entire existence.

It was in 1874, he decided to undertake the publication of a paper and the founding of a university. It was hoped the contributions to the paper would more than pay all expenses of its publication, and the plan was to apply all such surplus to the building of the university. Every thing was definitely settled in his mind as early as September 17, 1874, so far as the double scheme of a monthly paper and a university was concerned. Nor did he venture to commit himself to such vast enterprises without long and careful deliberation and calculation, and full and free consultation with men of eminent ability. September 17, 1874, he wrote to a friend:

"Perhaps you deem my undertaking—the publication of a monthly pamphlet and the founding of a university—a herculean task. True it is; but '*Debemus suscipere magna dum vires suppetant;' nam vita brevis est et multa manemus faci.*" The Latin I translate, "We ought to undertake great things while opportunities are afforded; for life is short and much remains to be done."

In the next sentence he continues: "Indeed, the cause of our blessed Master demands all our powers, and it is just as easy to do great things as small ones, provided we begin aright. By the blessings of our dear father we fully expect to succeed." At another place in the same letter he says: "Our University is to be represented in the Centennial Exposition. I have just received a letter from Bro. Isaac Errett, of the *Christian Standard*, upon that subject. He is the authorized agent to attend to the matter."

The same letter speaks of "one of the trustees of the University," and makes mention of a "dining given to the trustees," at which he was present.

He fully expected to see the university building completed in 1875; but the contributions brought in by the paper were so very small that all his plans were hopelessly confused. Instead of a surplus from the paper with which to begin the building, he found himself wrestling with a heavy deficiency and very seriously embarrassed to meet the expenses of the paper. The situation at once narrowed itself down to a choice between building and operating a university without money, or abandoning the whole university scheme. As the former involved financial obligations greater than he could see his way to safely assume, he reluctantly chose the latter.

In the fall of 1875 he made a tour through Georgia, Florida, and South Alabama, returning by way of New Orleans just before the beginning of the session of 1876.

In September 1871 he held his first meeting at Lewisburg, Tennessee. This was perhaps the first meeting he had ever held with a strong and well appointed church, save the series of sermons at Memphis, Tennessee, a few years before. It was also the first time in his life that his preaching in a protracted meeting had been compared with that of other able preachers in the reformation. Lewisburg was the home of the talented T. W. Brents, and the Lewisburg church had often heard the masterly sermons of such eminent men as E. G. Sewell, David Lipscomb, T. W. Brents and Tolbert Fanning. He had preached successfully and established churches in the old school house at Collierville, Tennessee; under the spacious shelter at Cloverport, Tennessee; in the old tumble-down house at Rock Creek, Alabama; beneath the trees at Pocahontas, Tennessee; under an arbor at old Prospect, Alabama; in the grove at Antioch, Alabama; and by the wayside near Saltillo, Mississippi; but at none of these places had abler men before him presented the doctrine of the reformation. Not so at Lewisburg. Where such men as Sewell, Lipscomb, Brents and Fanning had exhausted their powers with the people, he was now to try to move them to accept the doctrine of the reformation. His first meeting there was but a week in duration, and though the number of additions was not large, he satisfied all who heard him that he could present the gospel with a power equal to the greatest men in the pulpit of the reformation in Tennessee.

In 1878 he held another meeting of one week at Lewisburg with fifty-one additions, and again in 1879 he held another meeting of one week there which resulted in thirty additions to the church. I quote, from memory, Dr. Brents estimate of him as a preacher expressed in conversation in 1883:

"I do not consider him a profound logician, nor an accomplished elocutionist; but he has by odds the finest vocabulary of any man of his age to whom I have ever listened, and in word-painting and persuasive pathos it would be difficult to find his superior."

In 1879 he held a meeting at Pinewood, Tennessee, which resulted in thirty-five additions to the church. In the summer of the same year he visited Valhermosa Springs, Morgan county, Alabama, where were a few members of the church, but in a disorganized and discouraged condition. He preached a week and received into the church by baptism thirty-nine new members, besides greatly strengthening those already in the church. That same summer he held a meeting of one week at Cathey's Creek, Maury county, Tennessee, which resulted in about twenty-five additions. This will be remembered as the place at which he preached one sermon in 1867 while traveling with R. B. Trimble.

In 1880 he was requested to preach at a country church in Lauderdale county, Alabama. We had but few members in that neighborhood, and no control over the meeting house of the neighborhood except that it was built by the people "for all denominations to preach in." "The preacher in charge," however, was a man of small soul and large prejudice, and so prevailed upon a few "leading brethren" to have the doors locked against professor Larimore. However, professor Larimore preached to the people a few times under the trees, and returned home. Mr. Stutts was a prominent citizen of that neighborhood and a Baptist. He felt that it was a disgrace to the community to suffer a few little-souled bigots to turn such a man out of a public house built by the money and labor of all the people in the neighborhood. So he headed a popular movement to build a new house much better than the old one, and in a very short time professor Larimore was invited back to formally dedicate the new house and hold a meeting in it. He went, and his meeting resulted in the establishment of a good country church there. The new house was called Bethel.

That same year he went to a Baptist church in Lauderdale county, Alabama, called Macedonia, by invitation, to preach a few sermons. The entire church decided no longer to be Baptists, but Christians, nor a Baptist church, but a church of Christ. It has since been faithful in all the appointments of apostolic worship, and to this day it is a strong and prosperous church.

The same year he was requested by a Presbyterian lady to preach in the little town of Madison, Madison county, Alabama. Brothers Herrin and Elam, two of his pupils, accompanied him to Madison, as did also his wife. We had a few members there; but no effort had ever been made to establish a church, nor had any of our brethren ever preached there. The meeting resulted in several additions to the church, and steps were immediately taken to build a house. In a few months we had a good house and a good church there.

About this time he visited Huntsville, Alabama, and delivered a series of sermons. This was the beginning of a work which resulted in the establishment of a church in that city. In later years, when it was decided to build a house of worship in Huntsville, he took the field and traveled several weeks to raise funds to help complete the house.

He visited Hot Springs, Arkansas, in 1880, to take a course of baths for nervous prostration and general debility caused from over-work. While there he filled the pulpit for the Episcopal preacher, by request, of Sundays, and during the week he visited several country churches around the city. Returning to Little Rock he delivered a series of sermons, but with no visible result. Later in the fall of that same year he made a tour to Texas and held a very successful meeting at Paris.

He is a man of marvelous power of endurance. There seems to be no limit to the amount of work he can do. For more than twenty years he has been under constant pressure of work without a single day of real recreation. The greater part of that time, those who know him best have entertained grave fears of a general break-down in his health; but he seems equal to every emergency, and in appearance, at least, gives evidence of being blessed with perpetual youth. A-part from the labor he has done, the excitement alone seems enough to have unnerved a giant. He is always under high pressure. Wherever he goes, the whole community seems wrought up to the very highest pitch of religious excitement and enthusiasm. He is never suffered to leave one place till the very last moment of time, to meet a foregone appointment at some other place. Each hour of night between appointments is carefully reckoned and highly valued as traveling time. Once when he had held an immense audience at Ripley, Mississippi, to the very last moment of time for the departure of the last train to reach his next appointment, the Superintendent of the railroad, himself an interested hearer, waited on him to say a special train would be run to take him to his next appointment if he would give Ripley the time thus gained in another sermon. He delivered the sermon, the special was sent through, and he reached his next place just in time to find an impatient audience almost disappointed. Such intense pressure has been upon him, not for a few weeks, nor even for a few months only; but for more than twenty years. It is no wonder he has done so much to establish churches throughout the South. With his magnificent talents, unlimited power of endurance, matchless perseverance and life-long application and singleness of purpose, results that would seem miraculous under other circumstances hardly assume the appearance of ordinary effects of the many causes he has brought to bear in producing them.

CHAPTER XXI.

It is hardly necessary to further continue the story of his labors in protracted meetings in the country from 1868 to 1885. From what has been said about that period of his life, it seems clear that he was widely known and universally popular as a country evangelist; but as yet he had neither experience nor reputation as a city preacher. His great success with country audiences had attracted atten-throughout the South, and his labors had often been earnestly solicited in many important cities; but with few exceptions he had declined all such invitations. It was his preference to preach in the country, and many of his close friends and confidential advisers seriously doubted his ability to succeed in cities. That he was a success as a country evangelist had been abundantly demonstrated by years of fruitful labor; but whether he could succeed as well in cities was exceedingly problematical. This question was seriously canvassed by a few confidential friends every year before his appointments for vacation were made; but it never seemed wise to those in consultation to neglect points at which every one felt confident he could do great good for the experiment of meetings in cities with the chances rather in favor of discouraging results. As for himself, his highest ambition seemed always to do the most good, in the shortest time. He was willing to try to preach in cities, if in that way he could best subserve the interests of the church; but he greatly preferred to go to the darkest corners in rural districts, if he might thereby most advance the cause of Christ. We all knew him to be a plain doctrinal preacher as well as an accomplished scholar and fascinating orator. We felt confident his eloquence and pathos would command the attention and excite the admiration of city audiences; but whether such congregations would endure his doctrinal disertations for the sake of his inimitable oratory, was an unsettled question. So, for years, calls from cities were steadily declined and his time scrupulously apportioned to country places during vacation with the view of doing the most good possible. It was a question often canvassed but never decided in his own mind before 1885, whether he could do more good by holding many short meetings, than a few long ones, during vacation. The great number of urgent appeals for his preaching which came from every part of the country, pressed greatly upon him as a seeming duty to visit as many places as possible, giving only a few days to each place; but the many good meetings closed prematurely in the midst of great interest, with every assurance of an abundant harvest of souls at hand, argued strongly in favor of longer meetings. After years of prayerful deliberation upon these matters, he decided to make the two important changes of longer meetings and preaching in cities, in the fall of 1885. R. L. Cave, who was preaching for the church in Nashville, made a long trip on horseback from the railroad to a country church where he was engaged in a meeting to appeal to him in person to hold a meeting in Nashville. He finally promised to go; but before the time came to begin the meeting he would have been relieved of a great burden if he could honorably have recalled the engagement. He feared he could not succeed, and the writer secretly entertained very grave doubts of the wisdom of the experiment just at that time. It should be remembered that Nashville was wild with admiration of Sam Jones' style of preaching about that time. It would be difficult to find a man nearer the exact opposite of Sam Jones as a preacher in every respect, than T. B. Larimore. The latter never tells frivolous anecdotes in the pulpit, never uses a slang phrase or rough expression, never approximates anything sensational or seeks notoriety in any thing bordering remotely upon levity.

The meeting began in November and continued about thirty days, resulting in about seventy-five additions to the church. This was the last meeting of that year. It closed only a few days before the beginning of the session of 1886 of Mars' Hill College. During vacation of 1886 he preached extensively among the churches of his earlier planting in the country around Mars' Hill. At Moulton, county seat of Lawrence county, Ala., he held a very successful meeting with about forty additions to the church, and at Hartselle, in Morgan county, Ala., he held another good meeting with about twenty additions to the church.

His success at Nashville in 1885 demonstrated his ability to move great cities as an evangelist. This opened to him a wider field of usefulness, and furnished an additional argument against the expediency of longer continuing Mars' Hill College. Following close upon this enlarged usefulness as an evangelist, the attendance at College in 1886 was small, and in 1887 discouragingly smaller. In the earlier part of 1887 he had a long letter from a friend and life-long correspondent whom he greatly loved and in whose judgment he had implicit confidence, strongly urging him to give up the College and devote all of his time to preaching. That letter decided him on three points, as he stated at the time, and has since reiterated on several occasions, viz.: (1) To discontinue Mars' Hill College; (2) to devote all his time to preaching; (3) to adopt the policy outlined in the letter with regard to matters of a private and business character. As that letter fully discussed the situation at that time, and dealt with the motives that have always governed him in deciding important questions of practical life, it might be of interest to the reader in this connection. Omitting names and dates, it was as follows:

"Your financial embarrassments, though burdensome, are not dangerous. By the help of friends who would esteem the extention of such a favor as a great pleasure, your debts can easily be carried any number of years you may need to pay them off. Mars' Hill College has been a heavy expense to you from the beginning. A few friends have stood with you in a liberality beyond their ability in building up and sustaining the college; but with all the help you have ever received, it has each year taken bread out of your children's mouths—bread lovingly given by the Lord's blessed poor where you have preached during vacations—to keep Mars' Hill College up. And now, with all this generous sacrifice, and with all these years of prayer and toil, Mars' Hill College is steadily falling off in attendance while your power for good in the pulpit as steadily increases. You believe in special Providence, never for one moment doubting but that God rules the affairs of men. I believe men are drifted strongly, often irresistibly, toward their proper sphere in life by the mighty current of human events. You call the tendency of such a current Providential guidance, while others give it a different name. Do you not see, and feel, and know that such a current is against your college scheme and clearly in favor of your pulpit labors? Have you not more calls to preach than pupils in college? Is there not more interest in your meetings than in your classes? Do you not feel that your preaching is appreciated more than your teaching? Then why longer struggle against the current? From your stand-point it is but stubborn resistance of Providential gudiance, while with others it is nothing less than an unwise effort to resist the current that is steadily driving you to your proper sphere in life. To longer struggle in the effort to sustain Mars' Hill College is like clinging to a theory in the face of a fact. There is an eternal fitness of things which draws every man to his proper place in this world and in the world to come. The lion and the lamb will never lie down together till by renovation they are changed in nature. The actor will never succeed in the pulpit, nor anywhere else off the stage, unless he, by a radical change, should adapt himself to other spheres. 'The cobbler should stick to his last.' Every thing in your life for years seems to have tended toward preaching the gospel as your true mission on earth. Let us reverently recognize this as the hand of God leading you, and no longer court defeat and multiply embarrassments by ignoring this heavenly guidance. Abandon Mars' Hill College and devote the balance of your life to preaching the gospel."

The letter contained also some suggestions concerning certain business matters of a private and personal nature which need not be given here. This was the letter that helped him to a final decision of a question he had long and earnestly considered. He abandoned college work and changed his general plan of preaching so far as to make but one appointment for a meeting ahead. Once in a meeting, he was not to be limited in time by any other appointment. The following description of the closing scenes at Mars' Hill College, written by Brown Godwin, who was an eye-witness of and participator in what he describes, is of interest as indicating the love pupils and teacher had for each other and for the great work in which they were engaged. Brother Godwin was on a visit at Mars' Hill at the time, having left school two years before:

"The familiar tones of the College bell called us together in early morning as of old. Teacher and pupils assembled in the chapel for the last time as a school, and possibly for the last time on earth. This thought was the great burden of every heart present, and the sorrow in every sad face. Closing scenes of previous terms had all been sad, like the parting of loving parents and affectionate children; but this was to be the last time, and it was saddest of all. Our devotional exercises that morning were like the family devotions led by the father for the last time before the final breaking up of the family circle. Above the platform the clock ticked with a sadder sound; around the walls the maps of Jerusalem, the Holy Land, Egypt and the Dead Sea seemed to speak of the garden of Gethsemane, the place Golgotha and Bethany; two mottoes, grown familiar to us all, hung, one on his right and one on his left above the platform from which he always spoke to us, bearing the words—'*No Cross, No Crown.*'

"We sang 'In The Sweet By-and-By;' but our voices were tremulous with emotion. Then he began to pray; but his heart was heavy with sorrow and his voice failed him for the first and only time in our long association with him. Pale, trembling and silent he stood for a moment with uplifted hand and wept his burden off. No one moved, no one spoke, we all wept as if our hearts were only tears, and occasionally a suppressed sigh and half sob heaved from every heart and quivered on every lip in the sorrow-burdened and grief-silent assembly. When he recovered his self-control he finished such a prayer as only he could pray under such circumstances. He drew nigh to God, and drew us all with him too, in full assurance of faith. That prayer will abide with our hearts to the day of our deaths. After the prayer he talked to us in that loving fatherly way peculiar to him, and then we sang 'Shall We Meet Beyond The River?' The last benediction was pronounced, and Mars' Hill College was a thing of the past with a rich fruitage of blessed influences for the future."

In 1887 he began a meeting in South Nashville, Tennessee, with the dedication of a new house. For six weeks crowds thronged the house, and many were turned away for want of standing room in hearing of the sermons even in the streets and grounds out-side of the house. And yet there was nothing to interest the people but the simple gospel of Christ delivered in plain language and pathetic eloquence. There were no song services by trained choirs; no sensational themes nor theatrical performances indulged in by the preacher for the sake of notoriety; no after-meetings to excite Christians to frenzy or sinners to fear; no systematic visiting from house to house, nor distributing of flashy hand bills to advertise the meeting; no instrumental music nor street harangues to draw a crowd. Day after day and night after night vast crowds assembled to find a man of youthful appearance and modest manner sitting, silent and thoughtful, beside the pulpit. At exactly the time previously announced for preaching, he would ascend the pulpit, read a short lesson, pray, preach an earnest sermon and dismiss the audience. His face was always pale, his form erect, his voice deep and strong but melodious with a burden of love and earnestness. Such was the character of his second great meeting in Nashville which continued six weeks and resulted in one hundred and twenty-six additions to the church.

His next meeting was at Fort Smith, Arkansas in the early part of 1888. The meeting continued about a month and resulted in fifty additions to the church. His sermons commanded the attention and awakened the interest of many talented men who were considered skeptical. They had not attended church for years before they heard him; but they took a deep interest in his preaching and expressed themselves as both pleased and benefitted. Some idea may be drawn, as to the great demand for his preaching, from the fact that while he was at Fort Smith telegrams were received from three prominent cities—cities in Tennessee, Kentucky and Texas—in one day urging him to set the earliest possible time to give them a meeting. Piles of letters came by every mail pleading for meetings in every part of the country. Later in the year he estimated that the calls for meetings in 1888 would certainly amount in the aggregate to over 360 and probably to 500.

His next meeting after Fort Smith was at Louisville, Kentucky. He began in April and continued about one month. He had never before preached so far North, and here for the first time his preaching was put in comparison with that of some of the ablest preachers in the reformation who had never been heard in his former fields of labor. Louisville audiences were no strangers to Hopson, Lard, Errett and Campbell in their palmiest days, as well as many others of equal merit in pulpit ability. It was with considerable misgiving, therefore, that he consented to try to preach in Louisville at all. But he fully sustained his high reputation and more than met the expectations of those who had never before heard him. Some compared him first to Hopson, then to Lard and then to Clay as an orator; and others enthusiastically pronounced him far superior to them all. His preaching created much general interest, and the meeting resulted in about seventy-five additions to the church.

His next meeting was at Sherman, Texas. It continued about a month and resulted in fifty additions to the church. While engaged in this meeting at Sherman, he delivered the commencement sermon at Whitewright College, Texas. From Sherman he returned to Mars' Hill for a short rest at home. In a few days he began a meeting at Mars' Hill and continued about two weeks with fair results. This he considered by far the happiest meeting of his life because three of his own clildren were baptized as part of the results of it. When this meeting closed he felt the inexpressible and long prayed-for joy of seeing all his children who were old enough in the church. The rest of the year 1888 was spent among the churches of Middle Tennessee, with a tour through Arkansas in November, partly on business and partly to preach.

Another question came up for settlement, as to his future course, about this time. He began to be pressed with solicitations for longer periods of labor than a single protracted meeting. It became necessary to decide whether he would continue to hold meetings as a general evangelist, or undertake longer terms of labor than a single meeting at a place. The prudent and prayerful manner in which he treated this question and the reasoning and motives which governed his final decision, will be considered in another chapter.

CHAPTER XXII.

One year of successful work as an evangelist in some of the leading cities of the South greatly extended the reputation of Professor Larimore as a preacher. Longer meetings gave him better chances to develop his powers over an audience and reap the fruits of his labors in greater numbers of additions to the church. It was now generally understood that he had abandoned college work to devote all his time to preaching. He soon found himself embarrassed by calls to such work as he had not contemplated to undertake. What to do with such calls was a troublesome question. His confidential friends had grave doubts as to whether he was adapted to a longer period of labor at a place than a protracted meeting. He had never preached except under pressure and inspiration of the excitement of a protracted meeting. In May, 1888, the writer spent several days with him at Mars' Hill, and found him deeply concerned about the course he ought to pursue. Together we looked over several letters containing official requests from different churches that he would come and labor with them for a longer time than had usually been his custom. It seemed that no church would be satisfied with a single meeting. They all wanted him for a longer time than he had been giving to an appointment. The argument that had decided him to abandon Mars' Hill College seemed to apply with equal force in favor of longer terms of labor than one continuous protracted meeting at a place. The only question with him was as to where and how he could serve God most acceptably and best advance the interests of the church at large. He saw clearly that greater works had been done by others in longer terms of labor at a place than he was doing as a general evangelist in protracted meetings. Whether he could do such works, he gravely doubted; but if he *could*, he felt that he *ought*. This conclusion was, to him, axiomatic. He has always felt it a sacred duty, as well as an exalted privilege, to do the most good in the least time he can. So long as it was possible for man to do more for Jesus than he was doing, he did not feel at liberty to refuse to try to do greater things for God. That same current of human events referred to in the memorable letter concerning the abandonment of Mars' Hill College seemed sweeping him on from the work of a general evangelist to a more permanent work in some important centers. Those who wanted him at all, wanted him for a longer time than one continuous protracted meeting. With him, this current of events was the guiding hand of his God. He did not feel at liberty to lightly consider it. He finally decided to try a period of work longer than a single meeting. He determined to live and labor at a place longer than in one meeting, and endeavor to lead the people of God in great enterprises in Christian works. Once decided to try such a course, the field was carefully surveyed, and Louisville, Ky., was selected as the place of his first experiment. There were many reasons why Louisville was selected in preference to other places asking for him; but they need not be mentioned here. His letter of acceptance was written August 20, 1888. It is a novel document, and so perfectly characteristic of the man, it will perhaps be read with interest in this connection. Following is the letter:

"MARS' HILL, NEAR FLORENCE, ALA, Aug. 20, 1888.

My Dear Brethren, Sisters—Friends: Many thanks for your patient waiting and watching and persistent pleading. May the Lord abundantly bless you all.

"Duty demands of me a definite answer to your earnest call and many blessed letters assuring me of your love, confidence, and esteem, as well as your unanimous and most earnest desire for me to live, love, and labor with you the remnant of my days; and, also, your perfect willingness and enthusiastic anxiety to do any thing and every thing reasonable and right that may be suggested by me, provided only that I will consent to come to Louisville to try to lead you on to victory in the service of the Lord.

"'The Lord willing,' I will try, if I can. By showers of letters and storms of enthusiastic—not to say extravagant—assurances received from many members of your tried, trusty, and true army (body, congregation), I am practically endowed with almost absolute power to dictate terms, specify and fix amount of salary, select a home, etc., etc., with many positive assurances that my will shall ever be your pleasure. Many, many thanks.

"This and similar cases, constituting almost a continuous and sometimes resistless stream for years have long puzzled me. At home and abroad the pressure has been bewildering. I just simply cannot understand these things—these mysterious things. They must be solved for me, if ever, beyond the deep, dark, dreaded river. For many years, considering the brevity of the time of my sojourn on the earth, I have been thus importuned, salary suggested being anywhere from—well, I must not give you the figures. They would appear embarrassingly boastful, extravagant, and unreasonable. Even now, in answer to a call on my table, I could, with much more ease than I can write this long letter, secure a salary 'during life or good behavior,' greater than any previously offered me—greater than I am willing to express. And still the calls continue to come; 'but none of these things move me, neither count I my life dear unto myself, so that I might finish my course with joy, and the ministry, which I have received of the Lord Jesus, to testify the gospel of the grace of God,' *where I can do the most good.* My financial condition, of which few are informed, is such that, while I do not *love* money, I *need* it, and worldly wisdom suggests the 'the-longest-pole-knocks-the-persimmon' policy; but I have promised to accept no call in preference to that of Louisville, and I do not regret it. Of course, the greater the salary, the greater the relief, and, probably, the greater the good I might be able to do; but I am not 'up at auction,' and shall certainly not take advantage of the suggestion—'State what salary will bring you.'

"As previously intimated, I do not know why my services are in such demand; but honestly believe I am greatly overrated. Many thousands certainly estimate me far, very far above my intrinsic worth and real merit. This may be, in part, because I love, sympathize with, and feel a deep interest in, everybody. This seems to be perfectly natural with me. Indeed, I can not understand how it can be otherwise with any one. If I know myself, I possess no wondrous ability, either natural or acquired. A certain preacher said when they voted to call me to the congregation to take the charge there, there were but two or three dissenting votes. When they voted to let me leave, there was not one.

"Now, suppose I come to Louisville, and after trying me a few weeks or months, you unanimously agree with me—your eyes being opened by experience—as to my ability. Then what? 'What shall the harvest be?' This is a very serious matter with me, and without pride, affectation or selfishness, I am writing the sincere sentiments of my anxious heart, as they present themselves, as rapidly and accurately as I conveniently can.

"'The Lord willing,' you may expect me—not my family, but me alone—to reach Louisville, ready for work—to 'do the work of an evangelist'—not later than January 1, 1889, provided you—all of you—*do*, and continue to, so desire, and Providence does not appear to point out a different path of duty for me to pursue; but you are perfectly free to make other arrangements with any one—and you will concede the same privilege to me—even to the very day mentioned—January 1, 1889. I expect to come, if at all, without any pledge or promise of salary—to do as I have always done, trust those who trust me. If you can trust me for the preaching, I can certainly trust you for the pay. With the very few exceptions, and these always under the most trying circumstances, in all my work, I have fought for truth and righteousness without money and without price, in the sense of pledge or promise. I have often said nay to a generous proposition to guarantee me a liberal salary, and 'so say I now again' to you.

"Please let it be definitely understood and never forgotten, that either party may, with perfect propriety, at any time, without explanation or previous intimation, sever our relation as evangelist and congregation — thirty days meeting all the demands of our engagement just as completely as thirty years. Let us all remember this.

Please prepare me a home—a *home*. Much, almost all, depends on this. Of course, I should have—*must* have, to succeed—a comfortable, commodious, quiet, well-lighted, well-ventilated room, properly furnished — a preacher's home and study—table, desk, book-case, and other essential helps and conveniences—in a pleasant part of the city. All my surroundings should be such as to make me feel perfectly free and easy—these things are of the greatest importance. It is neither convenient, prudent, nor proper, of course, for me to select my home. That is your province, privilege, and, I am sure, will be your pleasure. There are many among you whom it will afford the greatest pleasure to attend to all these things. I want to do, and you want me to do, my very best. To be unpleasantly situated in any respect, or to lack any thing, would necessarily, inevitably and constantly tend toward universal disappointment. However, this is not my business, but *yours*, and that assures me that the location, selection, and preparation are absolutely certain to approximate perfection.

"Well, 'what I have written I have written,' and I desire all the congregation—every member—to hear it, understand it, and fully conprehend the situation, then, if there be not perfect unanimity in an earnest and enthusiastic anxiety for me to live, love and labor with you—with, for and among you to 'do the work of an evangelist'—to 'contend earnestly for the faith which was once delivered unto the saints'—let that settle the question. I could not consistently consent to either come or stay without believing the earnest, anxious desire of the congregation for me to do so to be unanimous. Have not too high hopes. Be not too sanguine of signal success. 'Be not deceived.' I may offer you 'warmed-over' dishes, dry and dusty; hash made of state scraps, crumbs and fragments from our former feast, when I tried to spread before you about all I had in store. Bear in mind, 'blessed are they that expect little, for they shall not be disappointed.' It may be possible for me to occupy the happy home your hearts and heads and hands will prepare for me earlier than January 1, 1889; but no such promise is made. *Give the place to another at any moment if you wish.* I love you and appreciate your enthusiastic-call; but have never sought the position you tender me, nor any other. I still seriously doubt my ability to do the work you desire me to do; but, the Lord willing, I will try, and if I fail, the failure will be mine."

Gratefully, affectionately and fraternally,

T. B. LARIMORE.

Though this letter was designed to be public as to the church in Louisville, it was not written for any wider circulation than that. Every thing in it referring to finances was inserted at the request, I might say at the command, of two friends of a decidedly business turn of mind who for years had been trying to help him manage and pay off the debts he contracted while conducting Mars' Hill College. It was against his feelings to say one word about finances. It has always been his policy to determine his field of labor as a preacher without regard to money considerations. When he has made exceptions to this general course, it has been in the way of reluctant concessions to the suggestions of his business minded friends to whom he felt under weighty obligations. He greatly perfers to undertake to preach any time at any place without a definite understanding, or even approximate idea, of the amount of money he is to receive lest he should unconsciously be biased in his choice of fields of labor by money considerations. Some idea may be formed as to the pressure brought to bear on him, by the two business friends above referred to, about the money clauses in his letter, by the following extract from a letter from one of them written to him about two months before the date of his letter of acceptance:

"My idea is for you to bridge over till fall, and then dispose of your property and put it on your debts. I do not know your exact condition just now. I mean I do not know whether any debts are pressing you just at this time. I do not think they are. This is an exceedingly dull time to sell any thing. Of course I look at the business side of it more than you do. Just at this time, were I in your place, the amount of money I could receive for preaching at any place would have much to do with my course. I do not mean this in an improper sense. You are devoting your time to preaching any way—that is your life work. You did not begin it, nor are you continuing it, from a financial consideration. Your life being dedicated to that work independent of any pay, it is not improper, *especially in your present press for money,* to give attention to matters of a purely business character in connection with your preaching. I suppose you get my idea."

It should be remarked that his policy of preaching wherever he can do the most good without regard to the amount of money he is to receive for it, is a privilege he has always exercised from preference rather than a conviction of any specific doctrine of the New Testament. He does not understand that it is in violation of Scripture authority for a preacher to labor for a church for a stipulated salary. Nor does he consider preachers who adopt the business-like policy of preaching for churches on an agreed salary, inferior to himself in Scriptural information or self-sacrificing labors for the churches. Understanding that it is all a question clearly in the province of expediency and Christian liberty, he but exercises his privilege in the policy he uniformly follows from choice. It is not inconsistent, therefore, for him to deviate from his general policy in cases of emergency, though always exceedingly embarrassing for him to do it. In the case now under consideration, the most he could be induced to do, after more than two months of pursuasion similar to the above, was to make the statement found in his letter of acceptance.

His cautious reservation of the right to follow what he might consider the guidance of Providence at any time after the writing of the letter, is worthy of special note. His anxiety that all the members of the church should be consulted, and his determination neither to go, nor to remain in case he should go, if all the members of the church were not unanimously in favor of him as their preacher, lifts him high above the plane of a mere place-hunter.

In declining to select his own home, he will not fail to remind every member of the Bible classes at Mars' Hill of many a word of caution and advice he gave the young preachers who went out from there. He always taught them to be cautious as to the homes they selected, guarded as to the company they kept and doubly prudent about committing themselves on questions of discord in churches and neighborhoods. They were advised to let the best people of the churches and neighborhoods where they labored, assign them homes, to keep company with no person of questionable repute, to talk but little and that little upon subjects pertaining to the Kingdom of God and the name of Jesus Christ, and never to take part in church troubles or neighborhood wrangles.

CHAPTER XXIII.

It takes two great women to make a great man; the one is usually his mother and the other should always be his wife. Perhaps it would be better to say the natural order is for one to be his mother and the other his wife. There have been exceptions to this order in the relationship between great men and the women who helped to make them great; but a great man can hardly be found in whose development two great women have not been potent factors, whether the natural relationship of mother and son, husband and wife, can always be established or not. The presence of faults in a wife or mother, however much to be deplored, is by no means as seriously disqualifying, as the absence of great virtues. The son and husband of sound discretion will find it easy enough to pass by very grave defects in wife or mother if he can always find the noble elements of true greatness to help him in time of need. Mothers of very limited education have been known to perform well their part in shaping the character of eminently gifted sons, and wives without literary accomplishments have often been invaluable helpmates of particularly brilliant husbands. Such cases, however, should go to the credit of other superior gifts in such women, rather than to the disparagement of female education. No man will ever attain true greatness so long as he esteems the graces and accomplishments of etiquette and education in womankind in general, above the intuitions and natural instinct of a noble mother or devoted wife. It is both an evidence of a great man, and an assurance of a successful future, to see a son devoted to his mother and a husband in love with his wife.

The home-life and family circle of every great man are of paramount interest to all who desire to study his character and acquaint themselves with his labors. The home and family of T. B. Larimore, can not be otherwise than interesting to the reader. He has ever found in them abundant inspiration and encouragement for his great life-work, and in them the world will not fail to see, in turn, a splendid reflection of the many noble qualities of his great and good soul.

Julia Esther Gresham, was born July 11, 1845; baptized by Robert Usery, October 21, 1859; married to T. B. Larimore on Lord's day, August 30, 1868. In stature she is rather tall, but well proportioned—her average weight is about 145 pounds and her height is five feet ten and one-fourth inches. Four years of war just at the time she should have spent in finishing her education—war that practically closed all schools and called upon the women and girls of the country to endure such toils and hardships as a former chapter attempts to describe—left her with little more than a good common school English education. Her mother was a widow, and the large family, mostly girls, found it necessary to practice both industry and economy to "provide things honest in the sight of all men" for subsistence. Fortunately, Mrs. Larimore inherited a clear and well-balanced intellect, a courageous and affectionate heart, a deeply pious nature and a robust and healthy body. She is industrious by nature, economical but not parsimonious, by early training, and thoroughly business-like in management of affairs from life-long necessity. She is dignified in bearing, kind in manner, calm under trying circumstances, firm in her convictions, constant in her affections and patient in hope. She has the fortitude of a martyr, but she is neither fanatical nor excitable by nature. She is forever at work, and an incessant singer. She sings over the cook stove, sings while arranging the dining room, sings in the nursery, sings at the sewing machine, sings in the garden—wherever she goes she sings and works with an earnestness that defies penury and mocks despondency. "As a mother, wife, Christian, she is the equal of the best—an honor to Christ and a blessing to his cause"—is the estimate a distinguished man who knows her well has expressed of her. In formulating and carrying out practical business plans, she is an invaluable assistant of her distinguished husband. In this line she is peculiarly well adapted, both by natural gifts and early training, to be a true helpmate for him. He has said, of her, "I have never had reason to regret having followed her advice; but often have I deeply regretted going contrary to it. Such has been my experience in this respect, that, now, I always deem it safe to do as her judgment dictates, and unsafe to do otherwise, even when I see the case in an entirely different light. In every thing, little and great, she has been a safe adviser for me for twenty years; but often I have gone contrary to her advice and as often found, when it was too late, that she was correct."

She rarely becomes excited, and always makes the most of what is in sight—the best of the situation. If her house were in flames, she would first see that every member of the family was safe and then, if she could save nothing but a wash bowl or a dish rag, she would save that and go right along to work singing, as if no loss had been suffered.

She is quick to read his feelings in his face when he is despondent, and, stopping her song for a moment, she will rally him with a laugh and a "see here my boy, that'll never do. We're all alive, and able to work. If we do our best God will provide a way out of all our difficulties. Just think how much worse it might be."

She does more hard work, or did in the days when I was at Mars' Hill, than any other woman I have ever known. She never complains. And she knows how to get work out of her children too. She seems actually to love work, and she has no patience with worthlessness or idleness. She loves the cause of Christ, and she is regular in attending the Lord's day assembly of Christians whether any preacher is present or not. She delights to see many sinners converted to Christ, and would feel greatly rejoiced if the whole world should come to the knowledge of the truth as it is in Christ Jesus; but as to her own convictions and personal Christian duties, great numbers have no bearing with her. If no one else understood the Bible and Christian duty as she does, she would never for a moment think of changing her church relations or neglecting her own duty. She loves her children, and entertains high hopes of them; but deems it no dishonor for them to work. She tries hard to train them for lives of morality as citizens, independence in making a living, and usefulness in the discharge of Christian duties in the church. She teaches them to love and serve the Lord, to love and assist each other, and to *work*. There is no discount as to the work. She does not drive, but leads them. With her example of constant industry before them, they are ashamed to be idlers or sluggards. She inspires and encourages in them a wholesome rivalry in their work, and carefully cultivates their ambition to do well what they undertake to do at all.

Together they make home beautiful by all the adornments labor can provide, and at the same time effectually guard the home circle against the vices of dissipation, extravagance and idleness. When he is absent on preaching tours, she takes the management of business matters, domestic affairs, and their little farm, in hand in a way that keeps every thing fully up to time in its place. He has accomplished great good, and his praise is in all the churches for his work's sake; but who has thought to consider the magnitude of her part in his labors, or sound abroad her praise for her labors of love and prayers of faith in furthering his good works? I would not take from his crown a single star to ornament hers; but I beseech you brethren, in common justice, to remember always to make the one crown of his praise encircle both their brows; for are not the twain one flesh? And what I say of these two made one, applies to every husband and wife in every station in life.

Mary Dedie Larimore, their first born, was baptized by her father, June 4, 1883. She is a model of robust health and well-proportioned physical development. In manner, modest and diffident, pious by nature, industrious and domestic by education, her mother's companion and her father's idol, she is a worthy ornament and an important factor in this notable family.

Granville Lipscomb, their next, was baptized by his father, July 25, 1888; Theophilus Brown, their third, was baptized by his father July 25, 1888; William Herschell, their fourth, was baptized by his father July 16, 1888. Julia Esther, their fifth, and Andrew Virgil, their sixth, complete the family. The last two are not yet old enough to understand and obey the gospel. It would be difficult to find a family of uniformly better health, finer forms or stronger constitutions. There is not a moral blemish, physical defect or mental crotchet in the family. Not one of them has ever used tobacco in any form or intoxicating spirits of any kind. They all have fair educations, considering their ages, and they all respect themselves and their family honor in a way that will no doubt prove a safeguard in the future as it has in the past, against every kind of vice. They are all devoted to their father and his great work, and the four older ones know well how much depends upon them to make him and his work the success for which he so earnesty and self-sacrificingly strives. They are members of the church and devoted to the Lord. They understand fully what a reproach it is to Christianity for a preacher's family to contradict in practice the doctrine he preaches to others, and in their love for him, their anxiety for the success of his work and their devotion to the cause of Christianity, they live constantly in full consciousness of the great responsibility resting upon them. Such a feeling can not be otherwise than helpful to their highest development and education. In them is illustrated the value of his preaching and godly walk, and from them is reflected the ennobling and refining influence of the gospel of Christ. For one of them to fall away from the righteousness of Christ would cast a shadow over the light of his preaching and bring disappointment to the hearts of his brethren. It is impossible to foretell what vocations in life these promising boys will select; but it is easy to see they have the native ability and practical training which, with persistent and well-directed effort, will insure success in any ordinary calling. Surely preachers children are not always failures in life. That oft repeated misrepresentation is clearly refuted by this family.

As I write of these stalwart young men, it is difficult to

realize that they are the same I knew as rollicking boys but a few years ago. I think of one evening in early spring when, school-boy like, I fell asleep over my book in a woodland near the college. I was suddenly aroused from my nap by a sonorous voice yelling—"Run boys, run; run boys, run; run boys, run." At the same time I heard children's voices shouting and laughing in great glee, and the next moment the stalwart form of Professor Larimore came into view, his boys—Theophilus holding on to one hand, Herschell to the other and Granville swinging fast to his coat tail—all making their very best rate of speed to keep up with papa, and falling with many a ludicrous tumble over occasional stumps and over each other. Seeing me, he stopped to explain that they were out looking for the calves and having some fun along with business, as well as gaining a little wholesome recreation and exercise. That was the way Professor Larimore enjoyed himself with his boys. That was in 1878, when Granville was seven, Theophilus six and Herschell four. This little incident will illustrate his general manner of life with his family. He is jolly, playful, indulgent and affectionate. One thing worthy of special note is his uniform courtesy as well as kindness in his intercourse with his children. He never enters a room where one of his children stays without rapping at the door and removing his hat; he never commands a child to do any thing, but always expresses his wishes as requests which he would be greatly obliged if the child addressed would attend to; he always recognizes the obedience of a child by a polite "thank you darling" or "I am very much obliged, my son;" in a word he habitually observes all the forms of etiquette with his own children as carefully as with the most distinguished guests.

CHAPTER XXIV.

In an intimate personal acquaintance and close confidential friendship covering a period of over twenty years, I have had every opportunity to study the private life of T. B. Larimore. He has expressed himself to me fully and freely at divers times, and under almost every conceivable variety of circumstances. I think I know all the secret motives of his life, and all the peculiarities of his private character. He has revealed the motives that prompted him to undertake all the great enterprises of his life, as well as the plans by which he hoped to succeed. Of all I have learned of this remarkable man during these twenty years and more, this is the sum:

1. I have never known him to undertake to do a small thing. He is most emphatically a man of big ideas, big plans, big enterprises. He does not underestimate small things, nor feel himself above them. When it becomes necessary to do small things in carrying out big enterprises, he does not hesitate to give his personal attention to the most insignificant details. But he never does a small thing, in a small way, except it is in some way connected with a great and important end. When he bought a bell for Mars' Hill College, he ordered the *biggest* and *best* bell the foundry could make. When it came it weighed 1,800 pounds, and it could be distinctly heard eight miles under favorable circumstances. When he built a barn-yard gate, he planted two posts *five feet* in the ground; they extended

about *fourteen feet* above the ground, and between them he swung a gate wide enough to drive two wagons through abreast. When he started a paper, he issued 20,000 copies at his own expense without a subscriber; and when he taught school, he undertook to establish a university. He does every thing on a big plan. He could no more calculate on a small scheme than an elephant could thread a needle.

2. I have never known him to be prompted by a selfiish or unworthy motive in any enterprise. He assumes great burdens and responsibilities, and plans great enterprises, but always from the noblest of motives. He is a Christian and philanthropist, and all of his enterprises are prompted by the sincere desire of his heart to see the church prosper and mankind made happy. He is incapable of doing any thing from any other motive, because these feelings completely occupy his mind and heart.

3. I have never known him to try to succeed in any thing by resorting to unworthy means. No matter how important the *end*, it never justifies unworthy *means*, with him. It is no part of his theology to do evil that good may come of it. He never seeks to accomplish good in that way. His motives are always pure, his enterprises big, his methods above reproach.

To love everybody, and to be beloved and respected by everybody, seem to be two fixed laws of his nature. If you see him at a big fire in a city, where everybody is excited, the engines all at work, and the police scolding, threatening, commanding, and brandishing their clubs to keep the excited crowd back so the firemen can work, *he* is cool and collected, polite, and courteous, very likely with his hat in hand bowing and begging pardon of some street gammin for being jostled against the little fellow in the crush and excitement of the great crowd. Nobody speaks coarselv or impolitely to him. In a private letter he says:

"People have treated me with such marked kindness, courtesy and deference so long, with so few exceptions, that I have come to consider myself under obligations to everybody. I feel that I owe a debt of gratitude to the whole world. I have always tried to keep out of rough company; but if necessary I believe I could go into the maddest mob and reason with its maddest man and not be roughly or harshly treated."

His life certainly has some very remarkable incidents in it along this line. One night during the war he stayed in a perfect den of robbers and murderers on the Cumberland Mountain. He was in their camp, and had asked permission to spend the night, before he knew who they were, and he feared to venture to leave them then. They were all men whose heartless, bloody crimes would have chilled the heart of a Nero. He spent the night with them, and sat close beside the captain of the band whose awful, fearful, bloody name was the terror of the whole country. He was, Providence excepted, as helpless in their power as a lamb in a den of lions; yet not an unkind word did they say to him, not a rude thing did they do, not an impertinent question did they ask. Day dawned, the sun arose, and he footed it away without seeing indications that the bloody band was more cruel or impolite than angels of mercy. It is proper to remark that he has always believed firmly that God protected him that night the same as He protected Daniel in the den of lions.

Among country people in the darker corners of the rural districts, the idea that city preachers are selfish, proud, jealous, and worldly-minded, prevails to a shameful extent. Before he ever preached any in cities, or associated intimately with city preachers, well-meaning but misguided brethren had talked to him much about the worthlessness of city preachers, and had done all they could to secure his active co-operation in their unholy onslaught upon city preachers. But when he came to know these much-abused city preachers, he found them so unlike every thing they had been represented as being, he could not refrain from expressing himself in a private letter:

"With few exceptions," he wrote, "preachers have treated me with the greatest kindness always and everywhere. That there should be jealousies, or any other unpleasant feeling among preachers or Christians, is a mystery to me. We are one, and, wherever the line of battle extends against sin and worldliness, we are all soldiers of the cross, fighting for a common cause, and we should love, trust, and honor each other."

A sour-minded, bitter-spirited misanthrope once spoke to him by way of reproof concerning his love for, and confidence in, all the brethren, and warned him not to trust certain classes of them too far lest they should betray his confidence. With a smile he said:

"My abiding trust in Providence, my brethren, and the whole world, may seem to be blind ignorance and fanaticism; but I think I have done right well in life considering my start, and I propose to go through this way."

It has often been remarked by those who know him well, that he never seems to consider any person, place, or thing under the slightest obligations to him. He seems to consider himself under obligations to everybody; but never to realize that any thing he does can possibly place anybody under obligations to him. Hence he is never heard complaining of mistreatment. Whether he feels thus because people uniformly treat him so well, or everybody treats him well because he so feels and acts, it is difficult to determine. While he has no equal in loving and trusting all men, he is also without a rival in the courtesy and kindness which all men universally lavish upon him. Possibly we have here an illustration of the meaning of the text, "For with what measure you mete it shall be measured to you again." There may be, also, a valuable lesson for those whom the world and the church have so grievously mistreated. Would it not be well for such to start a needed reformation by setting the world and the church a good example of kind treatment? Who knows but that "Whatsoever a man soweth, that shall he also reap" is a principle that applies in these things as perfectly as in the harvest-field? Brethren, try it. Love more and complain less.

All efforts to draw him into controversy with brethren concerning questions of church polity have been unavailing. He has never committed himself in any thing like a church difficulty, nor taken any part in the discussion of questions of church polity with brethren. In a private letter he once wrote, on these questions:

"I do not pitch into my brethren who do not do exactly as I do, or understand every thing just as I do, for two reasons: 1. I can understand how it is possible for them to act correctly and still not always do exactly as I do. 2. I love my brethren, and, long, long ago solemnly resolved to never go to war with them, or, rather, *against* them. It seems to suit some good brethren to dispute with each other; but it does not suit me. They may be able to do much good in that way, but I believe I would do great harm and no good if I should attempt it. I love some of my brethren better than others, and admire the ways of some more than others; but I *hate* none of them. I love them all, and am unchanged and unchangeable in my determination to never dispute with any of them, or basely suspect any of them of evil motives and designs."

The steadfastness with which he has kept this resolution is rather remarkable, when all the circumstances are considered. He has been stabbed in the back more than once by brethren when his face was to the common enemy and he was battling manfully for our common cause while carrying a heavy cross; but he has never turned upon such brethren, even in his own defense, against their misguided but perhaps well-meant attack. In such cases he has always felt sorry and sad, but never revengeful. On this point, the following, from one of his private letters is clear:

"I propose to keep my face to the common foe as long as life lasts, but to never try to down a brother. If falsely accused and harshly assailed, publicly or privately, I propose to undertake neither explanation, retaliation, nor defense. I am determined to follow our Savior's example as nearly as I can, and I think he never tried to avenge himself. If I live as I should live, my life will sufficiently vindicate me; if not, I ought not to be vindicated. So then, in any event, it is both useless and sinful for me to undertake to vindicate or avenge myself. This is settled, in my mind, and, as a necessary and natural result, many other things are settled too."

He made strong appeals to the boys in school to quit themselves honorably for the sake of their friends. He never missed a chance to remind them what a great disappointment it would be to those who loved them and had high hopes of them, if they should turn out badly. Few men understand as well as he how to bolster a man up with the love and confidence of friends till he can not fall, because he is so compassed about by moral support. I fancy I can hear him now talking to the boys in his earnest manner about these things. In a private letter to one of them he said:

"Nothing encourages and helps me more than the devotion of friends, and for such friends' sake, if for nothing else, I would die rather than disgrace myself and the cause, and disappoint those who love me and have confidence in me. Devotion of friends braces me."

He brings the full power of the principle to his aid in saving men. He trusts them, believes in them, and makes them feel that if they fail he will be sadly disappointed. He never gives a man any chance at all to retreat when once he makes a start for reformation. He will not for one moment entertain a fear that the man may fall.

His devotion to his mother and his love of home are two of the noblest traits of his estimable character. He makes no disgusting parade of these things in public; but, while he is judiciously and cautiously reticent concerning such feelings in his public work, his sensitive and loving heart delights to commune with confidential friends concerning home and mother. In a private letter addressed to the writer from Louisville, he said:

"I am just a little homesick to-day, and it does seem to me that Mars' Hill beats Louisville ten to one. We are strange beings. Rock Creek and Mars' Hill are second to no spots on this old earth. You have never been happier, I think, than when the dinner-horn called you from hard toil to the noon refreshments in your humble home; I, than when, at sunset Saturday, I was permitted by my masters to run home to my mother and spend Sunday with her. Happy day! While I write, I feel momentarily, as I felt then, and then a feeling of indescribable sadness comes over me as I remember those dark days are all in the sweet—bitter-sweet—long ago. No boy, I think, ever loved his mother more ardently, tenderly, and devotedly than I. This world can never give me sweeter bliss than filled my bounding heart as I wended my weary way home from the dusty fields miles away at the close of the week, to be with my mother till called to the toils of another week. Sometimes I could carry home some unexpected delicacy for her; but if we had nothing but corn bread, which was often the case, even that was better to me than a marriage feast without my mother."

He was greatly moved by a paragraph which went the rounds of the papers to the effect that arrangements were made for the boy-king, Alexander, to meet his mother, Queen Natilie, on the Servian frontier. Referring to this paragraph he said:

"Alexander, it is said, longs to see his mother. He is worthy of being king. I shall watch his course with interest. Exiled and divorced by the brute who promised to be her husband, she yet has a noble boy who is true to his mother. I am never afraid to trust a boy who loves his mother, and is really true to her. I try, wherever I go, to encourage boys to love, honor and protect their mothers."

When at home he enters into domestic affairs with a relish as charming as it is novel. Imagine a preacher of national reputation and universal popularity writing to a friend:

"I am spending the first twenty days of December at home. I get up at 5:20, make fire in our room, pump water, put pan of water on hearth for Mrs. L., make fire in the kitchen, fill kettle and buckets with water, make fire in dining-room, help a little about breakfast, or churn, make fire in the study, and then comes breakfast."

When he is away from home he never forgets loved ones left behind in the enjoyment of the delicacies specially prepared for him by loving friends. He never speaks of these things except very rarely to close confidential friends; but he greatly prefers to live during his meetings, as nearly as possible, just as his loved ones at home live. Without any explanation at all, he often declines some choice delicacy prepared for him, because he knows the home-folks are living on different diet. Of his home, in one of his great meetings, he wrote to a friend: "I am delightfully situated; only one trouble—my loved ones at home are not so well situated." At another time he wrote:

"A feeling comes over me to-day that revives similar feelings of the sweet long ago. Strawberries are in market—25 cents to $1.25 per quart, according to quality. Of course I can get the best of every thing where I am now; but that makes me think of loved ones at home, and makes the best berries, richest repasts, and finest feasts comparatively tasteless, unattractive, and commonplace. It has always been thus with me. From the earliest recollection of my childhood up to mature manhood, a ginger-cake to take to my mother was far more to me than the richest repast ever set before me while I remembered that my mother fed on rougher fare."

In such feelings may be clearly seen unmistakable evidences of a noble, generous, unselfish nature.

He loves babies, and is always deeply moved by orphans. The matron of an orphan school marched her little band of motherless children into the crowded auditorium at one of his meetings just as he was ready to begin the sermon. Room was scarce and seats were all occupied. As the little ones looked hopelessly around for a place to sit, he arose and approached them with the pent-up emotions of his loving nature beaming in his face. He tenderly seated them all at his feet on the edge of the pulpit, and then, giving free expression to his aroused feelings in a sermon of unusual pathos, he made an impression upon every one present that *time* will never efface. In one of his letters are the words: "Whenever I see a clean baby, I want to get hold of it. If I see seven at once, I want all of them I would rather nurse babies than to eat."

This is a short route to every mother's heart, and many a time has it opened the way to sow the seed of the Kingdom of God in a good and honest heart.

He is continually longing and praying for a perfectly pure heart and a right spirit. He does not often speak freely about himself; but when he does express his heart-secrets, the burden of his soul seems to be an earnest desire for a purer heart and a closer walk with God. Every ambition to be great, distinguished, learned, or popular, he seems to utterly forget or else bitterly despise, while from his humble heart there comes a perfect wail of anxiety to be *pure* and *good* that is really distressing in its earnestness. "I must get out of debt," he writes to a friend, "stay out and do all the good I can for the cause of Christ. Oh! how short my time is! *I must hurry to be good and do good!*"

Every enterprise he is asked to undertake must be commended by *some good* to be accomplished. When I first conceived the idea of preparing this book, I wrote him, giving the general outlines of the scheme, and asking his consent and co-operation. In reply he wrote:

"As to a book about my life and labors, I never thought of such a thing till your letter suggested it. I hardly know what to say about it. I have always shrunk from publicity and avoided notoriety, unless some good could be accomplished by such things. What you suggest is simply to reveal what I have tried all my life to conceal. I do not glory in myself, nor would I have the world glory in me, but in the cross of Christ. However, I am willing for my life to be made an open book, if thereby good may be accomplished. All that I am, and all that I have, belong to the Lord, and I am ready, willing, and anxious to lay *all* upon the altar of His blessed cause in whatever way and at whatever time duty may demand."

He believes in vows, and often meditates deeply upon

questions of duty and then solemnly writes out vows which he performs with the exactness and conscientiousness of religious ceremonies. He usually apprises one confidential friend of the nature of such vows, whom he calls to witness their performance. He claims Scripture authority for such meditation and vows, and feels such things obligatory as matters of religious duty. At the close of the year is a favorite time with him for such vows, and on the first day of almost every year since I have known him he has written me a long letter, giving the subject of his meditation and the nature of his vows. Take this as a sample, written January 1, 1889:

"The year 1888 is between us and the cradle; no longer between us and the grave. Another year has passed away with all its sunshine and shadaws, joys and sorrows, trials and triumphs; its temptations, troubles, tribulations, and tears; its pain and anguish; its wondrous blessings, precious opportunities, and almost infinite possibilities—gone to be a witness to approve or condemn at the judgment of Jehovah, where every soul of every age, country and clime shall stand before the rightcous Judge. The year 1889 is here, demanding the faithful discharge of the duties of life. What shall we do? How shall we live? Let us do whatever duty demands, and live as becometh children of the heavenly King. My home is a delightful one, my surroundings are all pleasant, my prospects are good. I ought to be thankful and happy; but above all, *I ought to be good.* How strange that mortals here below should ever be thoughtless, careless or unkind! I know not what others may do, but as for me, whether my remaining days be many or few, I have cherished my last unkind thought, spoken my last unkind word, performed my last unkind deed. Sad as I am now, I *rejoice* to record this solemn, blessed vow."

A few days later he wrote again: "Vows recorded when I was so sad at the beginning of the new year are never to be broken. That is just as I please, and, God helping me, I will never break them."

At another time his meditations and vows were:

"Well, the foot-prints are on the sands of time; I have done the best I could. Mars' Hill school lived seventeen years, and the amount spent here during that time to advance the cause of Christ—it was all spent for that—was not less than $30,000. At times fully sixty per cent. of the school was charity work—every thing furnished free. Seventeen years of incessant toil, with no compensation but the good we have done. We have laid up nothing. I am sorry for the many mistakes I can now see I have made, but thankful for the compensation. The deep, dark, dreaded river divides the Mars' Hill family now. Many are on the other side; but that river will not divide us long. A few more days and we will all be on the other side. Let us be ready. We can not afford to run any risk. We may risk health, wealth, body—all but the soul. This we must not trifle with. 'My soul, be on thy guard.' One thing is settled; I am determined to do my very best in all respects as long as life lasts—to do as much good and as little evil as possible while the days are going by. If I fall, I shall fall trying to stand. I love my friends, love to be loved, and I am determined to do and to dare and to die in defense of truth and right. When my hand is still, my tongue silent, my eyes closed; and when friends look through tears upon my pale face, I want them, at least, to be able to say, He did the best he could. They may not say, He was great; but I pray they may say, He was good. Whether my days be many or few, I am determined to never again do, say, or think, intentionally, one thing that my friends may regret, angels disapprove, or God condemn. The loving Lord being my helper, I am immovably and unchangeably determined to live a life of as nearly absolute perfection as it is possible for me to live."

CHAPTER XXV.

He believes in special Providence. He has not a doubt but that God continually guards and protects every true Christian. There are many remarkable incidents in his own life, which, to him, are so many infallible proofs that God has ever been with him to deliver him out of dangers both seen and unseen. That God leads him day by day, and so directs his ways as to make his life blessed and a blessing, he no more doubts than that spring time and autumn succeed each other in the unchangeable cycle of years. On this subject he wrote to a friend:

"One of the sweetest night's sleep in my recollection was enjoyed in the midst of the greatest dangers that ever surrounded me in this world. In all such dangers, I believe I was just as safe as Daniel in the den of lions, Elijah in the holy chariot, or the Hebrew children in the furnace of fire. The Lord Almighty protected me."

At another time, reflecting upon his labors at Mars' Hill, he exclaimed:

"Did ever such a man train such a band of blessed boys for such a grand work with such meagre facilities—he and they all alike from the cornfield in the backwoods—without money, without fame, without a support, without a library, encyclopedia, commentary—with no books but God's eternal book of truth? Mars' Hill is a mystery, and her blessed boys a wonder! The wisdom and power of God were there."

Some very remarkable incidents in his life, which *he*

considers cases of special Providence, have come under my observation. They are certainly worth considering.

One very dark night he was returning home from Memphis, Tennessee. A cyclone had carried away the railroad bridge at Tuscumbia, Alabama, and well nigh destroyed the town. Many houses were swept away, several people were killed and a great many others were seriously injured. The train he was on, not knowing of the destruction, plunged into the swollen stream where the bridge was blown away, while running at full speed. He went under the raging current, from which he emerged, and by some means unknown to him, *crossed the stream.* He was thoroughly wet, and wholly unconscious as to how he got out of the wreck and across the creek. When he came to himself, he was leaning against a telegraph pole on the bank of the stream. Some one, he never knew who, kindly pulled off his boots, drained the water out of them and put them on again for him. He walked to Florence, five miles, through the darkness and the mud.

At another time, he was in a carriage on his way to an appointment in Middle Tennessee, in company with one of the school boys. Passing around the base of a mountain, the horses took fright, wheeled suddenly to the right and leaped over a precipice twenty feet high into a creek. The school-boy escaped the fall by quickly leaping out of the carriage; but *he* went over into the creek with the horses and carriage. He was entangled among the horses, harness, and shattered carriage, *and his feet were fastened by something at the bottom of the creek.* Suddenly his feet were released, he knew not how, and he swam to the bank; but his boots were left in the wreck. The school-boy who was with him went into the creek and succeeded in getting the boots; but they were completely torn to pieces and utterly worthless. The carriage was entirely ruined; the horses reached the opposite bank of the creek with a piece of it as large as an ordinary door shutter across their backs! How he ever escaped unhurt was a mystery. He was in the water, under the horses, his feet fast at the bottom of the creek, when *somehow* his boots were torn to pieces and his feet released. *He* says—"*The Lord delivered me.*"

He loves to preach from such texts as: "I will bless thee and make thy name great; and thou shalt be a blessing. And I will bless them that bless thee, and curse him that curseth thee." "Fear not Abraham; I am thy shield and thy exceeding great reward." "The angel of the Lord encampeth round about them that fear Him, and delivereth them." On such passages he remarks:

"God did not protect Abraham because He said He would; *but He said He would because He would.* The law of divine love guaranteeing protection, made it proper for the promise to be made. Had the promise never been made, the protection had been just the same. I believe, with all my heart, that Providence protects all who put their trust in God and lovingly obey Him, just as surely, clearly, constantly, and obviously, as the same character of protection was ever thrown around Abraham, David or Paul. I have not a doubt of it."

To a friend in trouble he wrote:

"God blesses you when you trust in Him and do good. Can you not see it? Look at your own life. Have you not prospered, as never before, since you so heroically threw yourself and all you possessed into that dangerous breach, to save a friend and godly man and crown with signal success his noble work? You know you have. God is doing that for you. Providence is paving your way through life with the fulfillment of unwritten, but sacred and precious promises of success, joy, peace and prosperity—glory, honor and immortality. You are safe. The Almighty is doing it all. Providence points out the way and protects you, while the Spirit of Jehovah blesses your labors of love. I have seen and learned enough, to forever settle these questions in my mind. *Think on these things.*"

As to the expression—"I will curse him that curseth thee," he believes that those who wickedly oppose true Christians and do them harm will as certainly come to grief as effect follows cause. His confidence in this unfailing principle of divine government, causes him to feel sorry and alarmed for any man who tries to injure one of God's children. He believes it would be better for such one if a mill stone were hung about his neck and he cast into the depths of the sea. This causes him to be exceedingly cautious not to make an enemy. While he never speaks of himself in illustration of his faith on this question, I have observed some incidents in his life which he no doubt considers cases of the fulfillment of the text. There was one man, a preacher, I will not say what church he belonged to, who always seemed to take special pains to try to injure Larimore. He was healthy, talented, highly educated, universally popular and a recognized leader in his church. Larimore was young, a stranger in a strange land, unknown, diffident and easily discouraged. By all human calculations and philosophy it seemed certain that the gifted man would crush out the unknown stripling. But the great man grew steadily less while the small one as steadily grew greater; till the former ended a declining career, which had already proved a hopeless failure, in a premature death as tragic as his latter days had been gloomy.

In one of his greatest financial pressures, a post-office order for fifty dollars came to him from a friend and brother, with a brief note asking him to use it as he deemed best for the cause of Christianity. Since then a similar note with a like sum of money has come each year from the same source. He scrupulously and religiously applies each remittance in the way he thinks will accomplish most good. These sums of money have been the means of establishing several churches, all of which he watches over and helps on with special interest and care. While many a man would simply regard these sums as the contributions of the good man who sends them to the good work they are intended to aid, *he* regards the dear good brother as but an agent in God's hands for the accomplishment of this noble work. While he duly appreciates the brother for the good work he is doing, he looks beyond the *human* agent and, by faith, recognizes the hand of God in the work. By request of the good brother, his name has never been revealed to any one. But few people know any thing at all about these annual contributions, and no one knows the name of him who sends them save the one to whom they are sent.

He believes in prayer; believes "The effectual fervent prayer of a righteous man availeth much." He believes "The eyes of the Lord are over the righteous and his ears are open unto their prayers." It is difficult to state facts without arguing a theory; but as this is a record of events and not a treatise on prayer, the reader must be content with a few incidents that have come under the observation of the writer in the life of this man touching the efficacy of prayer.

One Sunday morning we were called to see sister Moore, who lived at Mars' Hill, and had long been in feeble health. The writer and a few other boys went with him, and at the yard gate we met the family physician who assured us she was dying and would perhaps be dead before we could get into the house. Her brother met us at the door, sobbing, and said, "she is almost gone." We went in, she was conscious, but apparently about dead. He seated himself by the bed, took her hand, looked troubled, but said nothing. We all knelt while he prayed. When we arose she was still alive, and he continued to hold her hand. In a few moments we knelt down and he prayed again. Then we sang a few songs, and I returned to the college. He remained a short time after I left, and also returned. When I left, I thought she would die in a few moments. When he left, she seemed to be recovering. Sister Moore is alive at this writing, and perhaps in better health than she has been for many years. When told, next day, that she was alive and decidedly better, the family physician exclaimed, "Impossible! As well tell me she was alive after I had seen her buried. I tell you she was undoubtedly dying when I left. I went away, to keep from witnessing the shock to the family when the end came."

I have never heard him express an opinion as to whether he thought his prayers had any thing to do with her recovery or not, neither have I ever heard an opinion from sister Moore or any of her people. As for myself, I have never attached any such power to prayer as seems to have accompanied it in this case. But, as I was an eye witness of this, I give the facts for what they are worth.

To reason against such things is very much like arguing against Scripture and facts both; but most men have their theory concerning prayer, and if facts come in conflict with it, so much the worse for the facts!

About the same time a young lady was at the point of death in Florence, and he was called in by her mother, to pray for her recovery. I knew the family well, in fact was related to them by marriage. When he went to the house he met the physicians who had been in consultation on the case. Five of as able physicians as lived in Florence, examined her and pronounced her "*In articulo mortis.*" That was the phrase. He went in and prayed for her. She recovered, and is in excellent health at this writing. I never heard him express an opinion as to whether his prayers caused her to recover; but I know her mother believed to the day of her death, that his prayers saved her daughter's life after five eminent physicians had pronounced her "*In articulo mortis.*"

While I have never heard him express an opinion as to whether his prayers saved the lives of these two women, I have heard him express his convictions as to the efficacy of prayer in words of no uncertain meaning. That God hears and answers the prayers of his faithful servants, does not admit of argument with him.

He has a keen appreciation of good humor, and he makes a jolly companion whenever he thinks it prudent to indulge a spirit of social levity.

He tells, with great relish, the story of an old janitor in a city church who said: "I have heard every sermon that has been preached in this church for forty years, and thank God I am a Christian still!"

He also enjoys the story of the preacher who wrote a prayer and read it on a special occasion by way of opening a railroad meeting. An old negro who was present was heard to soliloquize: "Well, I lay dat's de firs' time de Lawd bin writ' to 'bout de railroad!"

His old teacher, President Fanning, used to tell a story about General Jackson's old servant, which he specially enjoys. Mr. Fanning, after hearing the old negro tell the wonderful things "old Mass' Jackson did when he fit de

Britishers at New 'rleans," gravely asked: "Do you think your old master Jackson will go to heaven uncle?" The old darkey aptly expressed his faith in General Jackson's strongest point when he quickly answered: "I doan know sah! But if he set 'is head to go, I guess he be mighty ap' to git dah."

In giving some suggestions to a friend in feeble health, he closed his letter by saying: "Josh Billings said the Scripture which says 'It is more blessed to give than to receive,' has reference to advice and medicine. I propose to give you both; take or not, just as you please."

After returning from a trip to Cincinnati, to the exposition, he wrote:

"Well, we have been away up toward the North Pole—where they wear store clothes every day, work late into the *night* which *they* call *evening*, and sleep late into the next *day* which *they* call *morning*—to Cincinnati. I brought back a troubled conscience, which I have tried to shake off; but it will not shake—at least it will not off. I have been working with all my might in the church of Christ twenty-five years, never stopping to go to a circus, 'shindig'—(shindig is the word for dance in the country where he grew up—Ed.) exposition or 'blow-out' of any kind, till October, 1888, when I went to Cincinnati, while hundreds were crying come over and help us. I am disposed to say I will never do so any more. Now I am ready for another twenty-five years work in the church, or such part of it as I may live."

After trying to conduct a protracted meeting in a church at war in itself and weakened by factions and dissensions, he wrote good humoredly:

"Three parties in that congregation, one party for the preacher they now have, one party against him and one party for the peace and prosperity of the church above every thing else. Big *I* and little *u* figure extensively.

Of course our meeting was not a success. All things considered, a successful meeting there would be a miracle. Some are determined to keep the preacher they now have or destroy the church, others to dismiss him or destroy it; and nearly all of them have decided to *boss* it or *bust* it!"

Hon. M. H. Meeks, of Nashville, Tenn., an old pupil and life-long confidential friend of his, wrote him a letter soon after he went to Louisville, in which he confessed to considerable embarrassment in addressing a city pastor of such eminent ability, one who could not appreciate the short comings of an illiterate country-bred attorney at law. Of course the whole letter was a farce and written in pleasantry. In reply came the following humorous document:

"You apologize for poor writing and express the fear that your rough expressións will sound harshly to me since my promotion to a Louisville pastorate. Of course backwood's phraseology is painfully grating on the cultivated tympanum of a Louisville divine of exquisite taste and rare culture; especially one who has always been so fortunate as to never come in contact with rustic roughs and rural roughness. Nevertheless, even if you do not understand and cannot comprehend, my elegant diction, polished language and pointed paragraphs, you should always write me without embarrassment. I can, at least, understand you, having in my very early childhood, (I was a remarkable child) caught a few commonplace phrases from my dear old Grandmother, who, in her childhood, was so unfortunate as to be compelled to live, for a very short time, in the country—a painful experience which she never forgot, a misfortune from the effects of which she never fully recovered. Moreover, I inherited that rare but invaluable faculty peculiar to the truly great, which enables me to dispassionately consider the source and make due allowance for the mistakes of illiterate but well-meaning men like you. Relative to your chirography, space forbids my writing at length. That is to say, I have not sufficient space to fully express my sympathy for you. If you will write me, the best you can, enclosing stamps, I will write you, I, myself, individually, in person, a few simple copies, to give you a start in learning to write. That is a favor never bestowed on me; but, still, there are few men known to me who can write exactly such a hand as mine. This is the more remarkable as it is generally conceded comparatively few truly great men write a good hand."

On the death of an old family horse he wrote:

"Old Douglas died on the 27th, ult., of cholera infantum or some other disease common to white horses, in the twenty-ninth year of his age. He was a dead expense for years; but, having been a faithful servant in his eariler life, he was cared for tenderly in old age. This is as it should be; but old preachers are sometimes turned out of the pasture to graze where grass never grows. This is a shame. My time to graze on the bare ground has not come yet, but how soon it may come none can tell. I prefer to die in the zenith of my usefulness. I do not want to live to feel myself slighted because my day of usefulness has given place to the weight of age.

By way of advice to a young preacher he wrote:

"Some one has said, and it is certainly good advice—When thou knowest not what to say, do not say thou knowest not what."

CHAPTER XXVI.

Professor Larimore's methods of preparing sermons are peculiar. He uses but few books, very rarely quotes poetry, never writes a sermon, and seldom quotes any authority but the Bible in the pulpit. His preaching is largely a matter of present inspiration from his environments while delivering a sermon, hence his efforts, under unfavorable circumstances, are labored, commonplace, monotonous. He makes notes of every sermon before he goes into the pulpit, but such notes are lifeless forms which his environments in the pulpit must furnish inspiration to vitalize. He can not preach without the sympathy of the congregation. His pulpit oratory, which has carried the truth to so many hearts with such good effect, is but a reflection of the eloquence which comes from the congregation. In cases of pressing emergency, it is but the work of a very few moments for him to prepare notes, or outline, of a sermon, and, if circumstances are favorable, he will enter the pulpit immediately after thus sketching the course of thought and deliver a splendid sermon. Under pressure, his mind acts very rapidly, and with proper inspiration as to his theme, and the sympathy of his audience, he finds ready and happy expression for his rapidly-collected and classified ideas in a perfect torrent of eloquence. He has a way of rubbing his forehead and looking bewildered when he is thinking intensely in an effort to formulate his ideas for a sermon on an untried text at short notice. Many a time

I have seen him rub his head, apparently in deep perplexity, when requested to preach on a new text fifteen to thirty minutes before time for preaching, while the congregation was singing, till suddenly his face would clear up and his eyes brighten in a way that showed he had caught the raveling end of an interesting train of thought. Then he would go into the pulpit and plunge recklessly into the brightening subject, which would develop before him as much to his own astonishment and admiration as to the interest and edification of the audience, while the sympathy and enthusiasm of an admiring congregation would inspire him with moving eloquence in a ready and felicitous expression of his ideas.

As to books, he uses but few. I have often heard him say that if he had to be confined to three books—no more—in getting up all his sermons, he would take *two Bibles and a Webster's Unabridged Dictionary!* He finds pleasure and profit in reading commentaries, sermons, and skeletons; but such books are never quoted in his sermons. He has often said that a skeleton is as dry as a bundle of bones to him; and commentaries and other men's written sermons are just about as dry as skeletons. In his own sermons he finds no place for extracts or quotations from such books. During a part of his life as a preacher, he has enjoyed access to a perfect wilderness of books in an extensive public library—books of sermons, commentaries, sketches, and skeletons; but after long and patient research through such books for something to preach, he always turns, with painful disappointment, to his Bible, picking up a few dates and definitions from Webster, and soon he has material enough for a good sermon.

Owing to peculiar fertility of mind, it is impossible for him to confine his attention to a sermon or lecture while it is read or delivered before him. When he tries to give attention, the first thing he knows, like a fish catching a crumb as it strikes the surface, and diving into the depths with it, he has caught a fruitful thought, and is far away, taking it to pieces and making a sermon out of it; or, perhaps it is a beautiful gem of an idea, and he is trying to frame it in language worthy of such a thought. Sometimes, listening to one whom he appreciates in conversation, he will catch a thought, run right off with it, see a bit of wit or fun in it, and, entirely forgetful of where he is, be just ready to laugh right out when the confusion on the face of the speaker calls him back to himself. I have observed these peculiarities of his mind on many occasions, and we have often talked them over together. He seems to regret that he has not the power to control his thoughts better; but, try as he will, his mind *will* work away on every suggestive idea it gets hold of whether he wishes it to or not.

His mind holds the general outline of a sermon clearly and steadily before it while he is preaching, and at the same time gathers readily every good thought and beautiful expression along the way that may be naturally associated with the main idea in the sermon. He can see the way clearly through a sermon from beginning to end if it is two hours long. At the same time many of his happiest thoughts and finest figures flash upon his mind as suddenly as lightning while he is in the very midst of animated discourse. Sometimes he unconsciously steps to one side of the pulpit, as if to let a broad, deep current of thought rush by; then again he seems entirely swept away, helplessly drifted by the waves and the winds in a perfect tornado of thoughts and words and emotions. When he preaches at his best, it is always under high pressure. Unless his mind acts well and rapidly in the midst of a discourse, his sermons are flat and unsatisfactory. He can not gather material enough for a satisfactory sermon before he goes into the pulpit. He can map out the road he is to travel in a sermon before he begins to deliver it, but he can not carry his provisions with him when he starts. He must forage along the road, or his sermon will be lean and famished.

It is said Marshal Ney invariably weakened, trembled, and had to dismount, on account of nervousness, as he went into a fight; but once the fight was fairly begun, his brave, warrior spirit aroused within him and asserted itself in a way that made him a perfect thunderbolt of destruction, and won for him the enviable title, "*Bravest of the brave.*" I have observed a similar weakening in Professor Larimore before beginning a sermon. In fact, he always trembles, turns pale, and dreads to begin a sermon, no matter whether it is a special occasion before an immense assembly in a city, or an ordinary appointment under the trees before a handful of country people at a cross-roads. But, once he is well-started in a sermon, he seems to utterly forget himself and his surroundings, and to speak with earnestness of *faith unfailing* and enthusiasm ungovernable. As the time drew near for him to begin his work in Louisville, he wrote in a private letter:

"The nearer the time comes for me to go to Louisville, the more I weaken and dread it. It seems utterly impossible for me to fill that place passably well for three months. Well, I have never sought the place—never, directly or indirectly, sought any place. They have begged and persuaded me into it, and if I fail they can not blame me. I expect to go trusting in Israel's God, and to do my best. I am dreading, especially the first Sunday. Ah, well! it will all be a thing of the past in a few more years. Fifty years from now, nor you nor I will worry over it. We will be dust then. . . . I have simply resigned myself to a higher power, and expect all my days to drift as I am driven by the unseen power that thus far has guided me."

A few days later he wrote:

"Possibly you may think, as I am to begin my work in Louisville in a few days, I am now preparing my introductory sermon, especially as a reporter may be there to take it down; but I am not. That would be reason, but it is not my way. As at South Nashville, at dedication of the church, my text and subject were both suggested to me by the scripture Brother David Lipscomb read immediately before I went into the pulpit, so some such suggestion may decide that question for me at Louisville. This looks almost idiotic; but it is my way, and I can not help it."

A few days later he wrote again:

"I am determined to face the difficulties and battle for the right. That my barque is driven by 'the storm breath of Omnipotence,' while the hand of Providence is ever steadily on the helm, is not a debatable question with me. My whole life proves it. The plotting of foes has as certainly tended to bless me as the love and devotion of friends. My heavenly Father leadeth me, and, relying upon Him for help, I go to Louisville to do the best I can."

As a business man, he seems far more successful in commanding money than judicious in investing it. He never uses money to make money. As a preacher, he has been well sustained, even liberally paid, all his life. In personal expenses he has been economical. His whole family has always been industrious and cautious as to expenditures. There has been no extravagance, not even comfortable liberality, in the use of money at home for himself or his family. Still he has used all that has come into his hands. He uses it in various plans and enterprises to do good. "Florence is booming," he wrote to a friend, "and real estate is selling at fabulous prices. Men are making immense fortunes, speculating, in a single day. I am content. Though poor, I am rich. Friends are greater riches than gold. Riches that never take wings are best."

At another time he wrote:

"Fortunately, I have every thing of a business nature satisfactorily arranged for some time yet to come, and I am now putting every thing in shape as rapidly as possible, to abandon, forever, all business entanglements so that I may devote the remnant of my days to the work of an evangelist. I want to take the wide, wide world as my field, and try to do the work of an evangelist till I die. What use have I for money, save to meet the demands of duty, justice, right, love, and conscience? Why should I wish to hoard it up? What good could it do me to die rich? My shadow now falls toward the east. It is true, those who love me tell me I grow young instead of old; that I am younger to-day than I was twenty years ago; and some of them go into ecstacies over my perpetual youth; but while I *feel* like a child, and have never been able to realize that I am a grown man, I know I am growing old. I am going down the hill, and I propose to live the balance of my days for eternity. So far as the eternal results are concerned, I dread death no more than I dread the kiss of the sweetest flower, and I hope to live so as to always feel just that way. *I am ready.*

Brothers R. Lin Cave and David Lipscomb deserve mention as entitled to the credit of first inducing him to preach in cities. He had declined all solicitations to preach in cities for years, when Brother Cave determined to make a personal appeal to him to hold a meeting at the church for which he was preaching in Nashville, Tenn., in November, 1885. Taking the train at Nashville, Brother Cave went to the nearest point on the railroad to where he was engaged in a meeting, and rode out into the country on horseback to where he was. He stayed there until he secured a promise for a meeting in Nashville, to begin the first Sunday in November. The promise was reluctantly given, and it darkened his life from the moment it was made till the meeting was proved to be a success. He feared he could not meet the expectations of the people or do any good. Having great confidence in Brother David Lipscomb, he decided to consult him, and if possible get released from the engagement. Brother Lipscomb gave no countenance to the idea of abandoning the meeting, but encouraged him to trust God, do the best he could, and leave the results with God and the people. He also assured him his preaching would be eminently satisfactory to the church, and, he felt sure, would result in much good. In a letter to the writer he spoke in the strongest terms of the love and kindness of these two brethren, and to them he attributed, very largely, the success of the meeting.

With but few exceptions, he has held all his meetings without any understanding or agreement as to the amount of money he is to receive as remuneration. He usually goes and preaches wherever he thinks he can do the most good, relying entirely upon the liberality of the people where he preaches to support him by voluntary contributions. In a few instances he has labored a definite time for a stipulated salary; but such cases have been very rare. There have been instances enough, however, of stipulated salary for a certain amount of labor, during his life as a preacher, to show that he does not consider such an arrangement as a violation of the teachings of the New Testament. He pursues the course of leaving the question of his remuneration entirely to the liberality of the people where he labors, as a matter of choice, and does *not* ride that theory as a hobby. He never censures preachers who take a different course, and make contracts for stipulated salaries, as being inferior to himself in loyalty to God or devotion to the church. He claims that he has a right to preach where he thinks he can do the most good without a stipulated salary, and it suits his taste and feelings to preach that way.

He does not always, even when in special financial embarrassment, preach where he can get most money. In fact, so far as I can determine, he has always gone where he thought he could do most good regardless of financial considerations. I submit one incident that came under my observation while I was with him, and was familiar with his business and correspondence.

He was called to a place in Texas and offered $250 cash, above traveling expenses, for two weeks' preaching. At the same time he received a letter from a Presbyterian lady, who had heard him preach a few times, asking him come and hold a meeting at her town, *where we had not a member*, and expressing regret that the work, if he did it, would be wholly without remuneration. Just at that time he was so seriously embarrassed financially that he was compelled to borrow a small sum of money for a short time. Yet he declined the Texas call and sent an appointment to the Presbyterian lady. He went and preached two weeks, received nothing of consequence, paid his own expenses with borrowed money, but established a church there, soon afterward a meeting-house was built, and to this day a small but zealous membership worship regularly there, and the church is steadily building up.

While this is his choice, and while he acts this way from preference, he makes no unseemly boasts about it, neither does he consider himself more sacrificing than many others who labor for stipulated salaries. In fact, he has been more liberally paid than most preachers who labor for stipulated salaries.

He has some strange superstition about "*lucky numbers*," as he terms them. His favorite numbers are 3, 5, 7, 10, 17, 20, 25, 27, 30, 77, 100. Of these numbers, 7, 17, 27, and 77 are his special favorites. Once when we were traveling together we stopped at a strange hotel, and were told by the clerk that he had only three vacant rooms—21, 22, and 17. Without a moment's hesitation he said he would take 17. He always prefers to write an important letter on the 1st, 3d, 7th, 10th, 17th, or 30th day of the month. He once remarked:

"If I were to purchase a lottery ticket with one of my favorite numbers on it, especially 7, 17, or 77, I should fully expect to draw a big prize."

In a private letter to the writer, he said:

"This is an important letter, and I want to give it the advantage of my favorite number, 17; but as this is the 17th of the month, it is not necessay for me to write seventeen pages to get the charm."

He had some very decided convictions on the subject of funerals and funeral-preaching. He thinks the usual funeral ceremonies are lacking in appropriateness and misleading as to the true character of the deceased.

"I have just been to a funeral," he wrote in a private letter, "and if the preacher stumbled on the truth once, I failed to detect it. Deceased lived fifty years in the community, and yet the people who had known him all that time had never learned of a single one of the many good qualities attributed to him by the preacher in the funeral sermon. The entire sermon was a new revelation. Deceased was a big, rough, thrifty, shifty hog, living many years where mast was abundant, crops good, and fences low, weak and rotten—never trying to bite any one, but rooting anywhere and everywhere, throwing fences over his back and eating every thing a hog can eat. The preacher's picture of him was John, Mary, and Martha combined, purified, and refined. I mean no disrespect to any one; but really such things trouble me. After the sermon they tried to sing. They squealed, squeaked and strained through a long, inconsistent, unscriptural and inappropriate song. Why this? Strange time to sing."

As to his own funeral, he wrote as follows in the same letter:

"Not the future prospects of my spirit trouble me—not one doubt on that subject troubles me; but I do shudder when I think of the body. I want no singing, eloquent eulogies, or any thing of the kind over my dead body. My choice is the sensible old Roman burial—burn the body to dust and ashes immediately after death. If that decent disposition cannot be made of my body—I would be happy if I knew my wish would be granted in this—then, as soon as my feet touch the other shore, bury me on some high hill in a plain plank coffin, and there let me return to dust. No noise, ceremony, reading, singing, praying, preaching—nothing. Just cover me and let me alone. The idea of a slow decay of the body, loathsome stench, sickening sight, corruption, is revolting to me. That may be silly, but I can not help it. I can no more get away from it than away from my own shadow. I can not rid myself of the idea that even my own decaying body will be ever conscious of its repulsiveness. This may be derangement; I may be crazy on this subject; but no burial save the decent old Roman kind is endurable to me, and I hope to go that way. Never bury me in a metallic coffin, never, never—rather none."

In another letter I find this language:

"I long for but three things: 1. My race to be righteously run. 2. My body to be burned. 3. My soul to be saved. May the Lord grant me these three earnest desires."

He has a passion for the English language, and loves pure words as he loves little children. He has the greatest aversion to foreign phrases and words, and would never tolerate their use in school. As to a slovenly use of English words, I find this paragraph in one of his letters:

"Feelings I can not express come over me when I hear one whom I love, especially one of education, say aren't, weren't, worn't, or any other one of a long list of dime-novel abominations with which the pure, beautiful, helpless, unoffending, long-suffering English language is outraged. I know better persons than I am, and better educated, use these—I was about to call them words, in deference to those who use them; but as I can not consistently or conscientiously do that, I will make a liberal compromise and call them *things*. I came from way back, came slowly, over a rough, rocky, slippery road, with a heavy load and a sorry team, barefooted, bareheaded, and on short rations, and I am still pulling, but I have never been far enough back or hard enough pressed to say aren't, wern't or worn't."

In regard to health, he is a great dieter. He has perfect control of his appetite, and he never eats any thing he does not consider good for his health. In a private letter he says:

"Many a sermon is a failure because the preacher lacks piety and has too much pie-eat-y."

In another letter he says:

"Appetite has no control over me. I can eat three times a day, or I can eat once in three days. I can eat the coarsest diet at a wedding feast, and enjoy it just the same as the most palatable food. Really, I am never hungry nor thirsty. My taste is not deficient; my appetite is not impaired. I simply have my appetite under such perfect control that it ups and downs at my bidding without murmur or complaint. There would be no excuse for my being either a drunkard or a glutton. Which is the more disgusting or the worse, I do not pretend to say. God classes them together. Deut. xxi: 18–21; Prov. xxiii: 21. My knowledge is what is deficient. If I always knew what, when, and how much, I would be perfect in respect to diet."

This is not the place to argue questions of hygiene; but I give the following in answer to this letter, so that the reader may have both sides of the question: "Allow me to suggest that the appetite was probably given as a guide in these important matters of '*what, when and how much.*' Of course the appetite is often abnormal, and then it needs governing; but to set aside a normal appetite and presume to determine what and how much to eat by intellect, is about as reasonable, to me, as to try to determine the color and odor of a rose by a mathematical calculation. If the appetite was not designed to guide us in matters of diet, I am curious to know what it was given for. Gormandizing is sinful and should be carefully avoided; but there is probably another extreme to be guarded against in the direction of excessive abstemiousness."

On the question of physic, he expresses himself thus:

"I am anti-medicine, anti-narcotic, anti-stimulant, anti-hog-meat, anti-gluttony. If I could go back to the cradle and come through life again, having my present convictions relative to these things, I would avoid all of them. Of course, a case may occasionally be found which demands medicine, but as a rule we do not need it."

In the field where he has labored, great and good men have differed concerning certain questions of polity. Among these questions may be mentioned Missionary Societies and instrumental music in church. Some good brethren, in their zeal, have carried these questions almost to the extent of causing a division in the church. He has never taken any active part in the discussion of such questions; and extreme partisans on both sides have vainly endeavored to enlist him actively in their cause; but he has kept entirely free from such questions. Referring to these tendencies to division in the church, he wrote in a private letter:

"If I know what and where I am, I belong to the church of Christ; not a branch or wing of it, or a party in it; but to the church itself. I propose to never stand identified with one special wing, branch, or party of the church. My aim is to preach the gospel, do the work of an evangelist, teach God's children how to live, and, as long as I do live, to live as nearly an absolutely perfect life as possible. To this end, I am ready to go wherever and when ever duty calls, always using myself and all that I possess in the cause of Christ in the way that I think will accomplish most good."

CHAPTER XXVII.

He has now been in Louisville more than half a year preaching regularly for the same congregation. He entered upon the work there in fear and trembling lest he should not be able to give satisfaction; but he has more than fulfilled the high expectations of his people there He has grown steadily in favor and popularity as a man and preacher throughout the city with the world and the church. His audiences have been measured by the capacity of the house where he preaches, and his sermons have given satisfaction both in depth of thought and variety and beauty of expression. He has enjoyed the love, confidence and co-operation of the entire church, and those who were entrusted with the selection and arrangement of his home have spared neither pains nor expense to make his surroundings pleasant and helpful to him in his work. Every thing is exactly to his liking. The whole congregation seems to be in deep sympathy and perfect *rapport* with him, and each one who has heard his preaching has imbibed something of his gentle spirit and loving nature. In a private letter to a friend he recently said: "In all my mingling with the members, I have never heard any one member say one word against any other member—have never heard any member of the congregation say an unkind word of any person, place or thing. This, I consider remarkable. It certainly speaks well for the congregation." Much of this is no doubt due to the teaching and influence of the gentle-spirited Broadhurst who went in and out among that people as their beloved minister in word and doctrine for so many years before the day of Larimore's labors; but his own tender feelings and loving manners have done much to further perfect the work so well inaugurated by his predecessor. And in this good work both of these noble men of God have been ably seconded by prudent and consecrated officers of the church, and a thoroughly consecrated membership as well as by the valuable labors of other able ministers before them.

There is a gentleness in his nature that impresses itself upon the churches he builds up, the pupils he teaches and the converts he makes. Just as William Penn impressed himself upon an entire religious community so indelibly that his leading characteristics are plain to be seen in his followers to this day, so does this man impress his tender, loving and humble spirit upon converts, pupils and churches. These admirable principles of Christianity, so difficult to reduce to practice when abstractly considered, seem easy enough to follow when once they are seen and admired in his lovable nature. And herein is the great power, as well as the immeasurable value, of his preaching. Wherever he labors, he not only instructs people in the doctrine of Christ, but teaches and shows them how to receive, retain and cultivate the *Spirit* of Christ as well.

During the last twenty years the religious people with whom Larimore and his boys are identified have been almost continuously engaged in discussions and controversies among themselves over questions of church polity. Such discussions have not always been conducted in a spirit of tolerance and love. We have not always kept ourselves free from jealousies, suspicions and bickerings unbecoming Christians. It is no small merit in Mars' Hill boys, or ordinary compliment to their distinguished teacher, that they have not fallen into such things to any great extent. Of all the boys educated at Mars' Hill, very few, if any, have taken any part in these discussions and wrangles. The boys all have convictions on these subjects, and they maintain them too; but never in an undignified manner or wrangling spirit. If any boy from Mars' Hill has ever used unkind words, manifested an unchristian spirit or resorted to unfair means, to maintain his convictions or carry his point, he has departed from the precept and example of his illustrious teacher. It is a pleasure to be able to say no such case has come under my observation. Our church papers are not marred by articles from Mars' Hill boys, on any subject, containing expressions calculated to stir up strife or wound the feelings of the most sensitive Christians. And yet, it would be difficult, if not impossible, to find preachers more uncompromising than Mars' Hill boys on every question pertaining to their sincere convictions. They preach their convictions with a directness and an earnestness which offer no compromise with error; but at the same time they treat those who differ from them with the courtesy and kindness becoming Christians and due to all men. What is true of Mars' Hill boys in these respects, is also true of the converts he has made and the churches he has built up. They are all remarkably free from unseemly wrangling or bitter personalities, firm in their convictions, yet abounding in love for each other and for all mankind.

As a preacher, he has a special gift for word-painting or vivid description. This peculiarity has been alluded to more than once; but no effort has yet been made to describe it. Any effort we may make can not be more than a partial success at best. His power in this respect is hard to describe. Nothing short of a gift equal to his own can do it justice. The writer claims no such gift. One must hear him to appreciate him. I heard a Methodist preacher say he listened to Larimore's description of a spring of clear water with its rippling little brooklet till he became so thirsty he could hardly keep from leaving his seat to get a drink of water.

On one occasion he was describing, in one of his sermons, the lonely parents, aged and feeble, talking together, at eventide, about the loved ones scattered abroad in distant lands. An observer noticed him lean upon the pulpit, as if for support, in the midst of the description. When his attention was called to it afterwards he said: "I can not explain it; but for a moment I felt my strength give way, my knees trembled and my form tottered exactly as if I had been too old and infirm to support my own weight. I believe I would have sunk down from sheer weakness and exhaustion if I had not leaned upon the pulpit for support." Some idea may be formed from this as to the earnestness with which he enters into the spirit of those descriptions which so powerfully effect his audiences.

Referring to his power of description, Mrs. Cooper, of Nashville, Tennessee, who is quoted at length in the first chapter of this book, says:

"His descriptions are not the cold and lifeless things which so many speakers force upon indifferent listeners; but they glitter with the 'white light' of his own glowing imagination. His hearers respond with rapt attention and seem to see and enjoy the scenes so vividly wrought before them. Especially did this seem to be the case as he described, in one of his sermons, the 'baptism in Jordan.' There were the 'circling dove;' the bowed head of the 'Holy One;' the strong, stalwart, rough-clad form of the Baptist; the awe-struck hills and waters; the watchful multitude; then the opening heavens and the voice of the 'Father' falling as it had never fallen before upon the ears of man in the wondrous declaration, 'This is my beloved Son.' The spell he placed upon the audience in the description of the baptismal scene was not lost or weakened when he, immediately afterwards, described, with equal vividness, the 'temptation' in the wilderness. Each one present seemed to hear for himself the interviews between the tempter and the tempted. There was a sigh of general relief in the audience when the tempter left him, and all present seemed to feel the blessed presence of the celestial messengers when 'angels came and strengthened him.' With the congregation now completely under his magic influence, he wended his way from the wilderness of trial to the mountain of 'transfiguration.' With matchless skill he pictured that memorable scene till each one seemed to feel something of the glory that enshrouded the Lord's chosen few on that ever sacred spot. In almost breathless interest the congregation followed him next to the 'stilling of the tempest.' The strong blasts came sweeping down from the heights of the Hermon, 'bowing the 'palms of Manasseh' in their might and sending the wild mad waves of the darkling waters in breakers loud and surges deep against the struggling barque of the helpless mariners. The lowly disciples sat weeping and praying in the frail little boat on the bosom of an angry sea. Then the ever 'watchful Preserver' came hastening to save over the turbulent waters, as the flashing lightnings and the rolling thunders added to the terrors of the situation. The low 'God-spoken' 'peace be still,' at once relieved the anxiety of the audience, quieted the troubled waves of the raging sea and rejoiced the hearts of the terror-stricken mariners. In a moment all was quiet and restful, the audience breathed easy and the blue depths of the lovely sea were all smiling and calm. With the audience still under perfect control, he wandered aimlessly on through the scenes in the life of Christ till, with bowed head, he stood at the gate of the 'garden of Gethsemane.' All seemed to hear the stir of leaf and bough above the 'sleep-shrouded disciples' as the suffering Savior knelt alone in that gloomy spot at midnight's solemn hour. Borne on the wings of the gentle midnight zephyr, that loving; tender voice in humble supplication to the 'Father' seemed faintly heard by each one present. In painful suspense the audience seemed to witness the last battle between the human and divine nature in an agony intensified by the Savior's vain appeal to his sleeping disciples for human love and human sympathy. Then he wandered on through the deeper stillness of that other 'garden' while the mournful sighing of the night-winds added to the gloom that hung over the angel-guarded tomb where the Savior slept through the long dark night of his death. Then his style suddenly changed, his countenance beamed with a new light and his voice thrilled with a great joy as he stooped over and peered into the empty sepulcher and lifted on high the cast-off grave-clothes. Each one present felt that the Lord was risen indeed. The world's life-boat seemed wafted over summer seas or driven triumphantly before the 'storm breath of Omnipotence' while the tender hand of Providence was ever firmly on the helm."

It is easy to imagine the effect of the appeals he makes to sinners after such descriptions of scenes in the life of Christ as the above. They come by scores, crowding to confess their faith in Jesus and vow their submission to His commandments. He has the power of talking about

Jesus and His sufferings so as to make men feel themselves in the very presence of the Holy One. After all Christ has done for the world, the hardest-hearted sinner feels, under the influence of such vivid descriptions, that it is really mean and contemptible for any one to turn a deaf ear to His tender appeals to burdened sinners to come to Him.

While all this is well said as to the way he preaches, there are many, no doubt, who are curious to know *what* he preaches. What church does he belong to, and what doctrine does he preach? For twenty years and more he has been preaching through the South, and the greater part of that time he has been at the head of a school for preachers. He and his boys have made themselves felt in the religion of this country. It is but fair that the world know what they believe and teach. To understand this, the reader should know the state of things in religion in this country when he began to preach. These questions will be considered in another chapter.

CHAPTER XXVIII.

It is difficult to clearly understand the doctrine of any religious body without first carefully considering the peculiar doctrines and prevailing customs of other contemporaneous religious orders. Hence, to understand the religious faith and practice of Larimore and his boys, some attention must be given to the general status and trend of religious thought in that locality and at that time. These men stood out as dissenters from much of the commonly-received religious teaching of that age and country. They were considered setters-forth of new and strange doctrine, which the popular religious denominations thought it not lawful to receive. They rejected *in toto* many things which the dominant religious organizations deemed of vital importance in religion. They were violently opposed and fearfully misrepresented. They were falsely accused of teaching many absurd and dangerous things—all of which caused no small stir among the people of that country. The light in which they were viewed by the dominant religious organizations of that time and country, and the peculiarities of the religious faith and customs which prevailed among the people who so violently opposed them, may be inferred from a few incidents which it has been deemed proper to give in this chapter.

A man who had heard one of the boys in a series of sermons, became greatly interested in the subject of salvation. He felt himself a sinner without hope in the world, and resolved to have a private conference with the preacher on the subject. He had heard many things about "these people," and he determined not to commit himself to this doctrine till he knew whether "those things" were true. So he took the preacher a long walk into a dense forest hard by the meeting-house, and, seating himself on a log, looked the young theologue squarely in the face as he inquired:

"Well, parson, can a man *jine* your church without quitting the Democratic party?"

A member of one of the religious denominations heard him preach, and, by-and-by, became somewhat confused in his theology. He could not read, but the preacher understood all mysteries, so to the preacher he went, who, having heard his case, patiently said:

"Them folks don't b'lieve in repentance a-tall; but the Bible says, 'Bring forth, therefore, fruits meet for repentance.' You give 'em that text, and I guess it'll settle 'em."

The next time he met one of them he said:

"I don't b'lieve in such *doctering* as you preach. The Bible says—er—ah—it says—lemme see what it says—er—well, it says something 'bout 'Fruits, meats, 'pentance'! What yer goin' to do with *that?*"

A preacher in one of the religious denominations heard some of the boys preach on the second chapter of Acts, and afterwards became greatly troubled because he could not harmonize the doctrine and practice of his church with Peter's language, "Repent ye, and be baptized every one of you in the name of Jesus Christ for the remission of sins, and ye shall receive the gift of the Holy Ghost." He began to talk rather seriously about leaving his church and going with the boys, when "the powers that be" in his church called him before a regularly constituted tribunal to answer for his heresy. He came with a leaf turned down in his Bible at the well-thumbed passage. He read the verse with great solemnity and said:

"Brethering, these air posictive terms, and how *can you get over them?*"

One of the "brethering" said:

"Never you mind 'bout Scriptur. These people you air a followin' off don't b'lieve in the Holy Ghost *a-tall.* How can *you* get over *that?*"

"I aint talkin' 'bout ther Holy Ghost, but a readin' *Scriptur!*"

"Well, we aint here to listen to you a readin' Scriptur; but to see what you air goin' to do 'bout followin' these folks that don't b'lieve in ther Holy Ghost."

"Brethering, I am a goin' to stand on these posictive terms. *What did Peter say?*"

"We don't care *what Peter said*; we want to know what *you* got ter say 'bout goin' off after these folks that don't b'lieve in the Holy Ghost."

On one occasion a brother took the confession of several people and announced time and place of their baptism; whereupon an old negro, far back in the audience, unable longer to restrain his feelings of protest against such unprecedented departure from the custom of his religious fathers, exclaimed aloud:

"My God, white man! You aint goin' to baptize all dem folks 'fo' dey get 'ligion, is ye?"

These and other similar incidents of almost daily occurrence among the common people of that country will indicate the general misunderstanding as to what Larimore and his boys believed and preached. It was no unusual thing to hear it gravely asserted, even from pulpits, that they were only baptized infidels; that they did not believe in a change of heart; that they denied the work of the Holy Ghost in regeneration; that they had nothing but head religion; that they believed the Bible was the Holy Ghost; that they did not believe in repentance at all; that they believed man could work his way to heaven without faith, conversion or divine assistance; that they did not believe in prayer; that they knew nothing at all about regeneration or saving faith; and that all they taught people to do was to be baptized. It is difficult to understand how such erroneous ideas ever started. It is strange, too, with what tenacity the people clung to such idle reports in the face of repeated denials and explanations from those concerned.

In justice to those who believed and circulated such groundless charges, it is proper to plead the paliating circumstance of the general ignorance of the times and country. Illiterate people are always bitterly prejudiced against every thing that does not exactly conform to their standards of orthodoxy. How men can differ in faith and opinions and yet treat each other fairly, courteously, and even kindly, is an idea too big for the diminutive heads of religious bigots. We had just grounds of complaint against those partisans for the unfair way they persistently misrepresented and opposed us; and yet the poor misguided souls acted, perhaps, from the very best of motives. Like Paul in his blind prejudice and consuming zeal while murdering Christians, they, no doubt, thought they were doing God's service in the way they opposed us. That we would all be damned, was as absolutely certain, with them, as that our doctrine was wrong. And the prospect of our damnation seemed to give them pleasure enough to fully compensate for the annoyance they suffered at the progress of our doctrine. It is astonishing how much solid comfort a narrow-minded, little-souled religious bigot can get out of the conviction that those who differ from him in doctrine will be damned. Verily, there is more joy, with such men, over one soul that departs from their creed and is *damned*, than over ninety-and-nine faithful brethren who never renounce their creed.

The people of that country were not worse than the average citizens of other countries; and yet any effort to reason with them about their religious faith aroused at once their bitterest feelings of hatred and resentment. This is one of the strange things in human nature. Such intolerance is an essential element of man's nature in all ages and on all subjects. Education and a higher civilization may subdue it, and teach man how to control it; but it has never yet been entirely eradicated from his nature. It does not manifest itself in religion alone; but in politics, science, society—every thing and at all times where man is at all concerned. It is an enemy to all progress and a barrier to all education. Hence those poor misguided people, in opposing, abusing, and misrepresenting us, were but doing what all ages before them had done. It was an unfortunate state of affairs which called louder for *pity* than *censure*.

They were not harder with us than upon each other. They had differences among themselves, and in those differences they used offensive epithets and base misrepresentations as unsparingly as in their treatment of us. It is worthy of note, however, that we were held as the common enemy of all factions; and when it came to the tug of war with us they shook hands over the bloody chasm of their disagreements and came up to the help of their common religion against the mighty with singular unanimity.

But as soon as the fight was off with us, they gave attention again to their own disagreements.

One of the largest churches in that country divided on the subject of Free Masonry. One of the leading preachers became a member of a lodge of Free Masons, and another preacher denounced his heresy in no mincing words, declaring he would worship God in caves and dens in the earth before he would fellowship any man who would corrupt the faith in any such manner. On that question the church formally divided. Later, there arose a question in one wing of this divided church concerning "washing the saints' feet." This had long been practiced as a sort of church ordinance twice a year in connection with the Lord's Supper; but some of the brethren, led by a prominent preacher, began to argue that, to save time, each member of the church should have only one foot washed. This idea was vigorously opposed by many in the church, and the result was another formal division. A little later the question was raised in one of these subdivisions of the original church as to whether members should be received from the other subdivisions without requiring them to be baptized again. On this question there was disagreement which caused another division in this handful of the original worshipers. The way they opposed, misrepresented, and devoured each other must be imagined—it can not be described.

Nor is it any wonder the religious people of that time and country could neither clearly understand or fairly represent one who differed from them on religious subjects. They had not been brought up to use ordinary mental faculties in *studying* and *understanding* religious subjects. The prevailing ignorance and superstition concerning the whole subject of religion, even among the better-informed classes of society, were absolutely appalling.

One of the leading merchants of that country, a man of fair education and good business qualifications, dreamed he swallowed a wagon—a common ox-wagon, with four wheels and tongue complete—and this remarkable dream he took as evidence that he was regenerated, and that God had forgiven all his past sins. And to have told him such a dream was no evidence at all that God had pardoned his sins would have been to offer him a grave insult.

A favorite text with the preachers of that time and country was, "Every tub shall set on its own bottom — ah!" Certainly that is a very proper thing for tubs to do, nor can we see how they could conveniently do any thing else; but for any one to have suggested to those preachers that such language was not in the Bible at all, would have aroused a perfect furor of prejudice and opposition.

They did not stop to think on the subject of religion as they would think about other things. With them, religion was all mystery, feeling, and blind fanaticism, without a single ray of ordinary intelligence in it. In their revivals, they would work themselves into perfect paroxysms of nervous excitement, and then give place to the wildest freaks of the imagination and the most excessive follies of conduct. They would whoop, jump, clap their hands, shout, and, clasping each other in close embrace, roll on the floor in the altar, in a perfect ecstasy of delight for hours in succession. Mourners under conviction frequently went into a trance, or comatose state, and remained for hours as completely oblivious to every thing around them as Lazarus in the grave. Out of this death-like trance they would often come suddenly and unexpectedly with a spring and a bound, at the same time cleaving the air with an ear-splitting yell that would awaken the echos for half a mile around. As to *what they said* that first glad shout, it seemed wholly unpremeditated. Sometimes it was a beautiful sentiment vociferously expressed, sometimes a silly jingle of words without any meaning at all, and sometimes a familiar, but inappropriate expression, as ludicrous as it was unexpected.

One man, after a long struggle in deep conviction, received the Spirit's quickening power when his friends least expected it. With a bound which carried him over several rude seats and landed him fairly in the midst of a circle of rejoicing friends, he yelled, "*Christmas gift!*" in a voice like a fog-whistle.

People under the influence of the Holy Ghost would go into "the jerks"; at other times they would have "the holy laugh," or the "holy dance."

"The jerks" can not be described easily. Those whom the Holy Ghost operated upon would begin, at first, to be shaken at regular intervals by slight twiching of the muscles, which would increase in power till the whole body would be convulsed by periodic "jerks" perfectly fearful to see. Strong men would be completely lifted off their seats, and would bounce around like India-rubber balls. Women's hair would be disheveled and made to crack like coach-whips by the sudden and violent "jerks" of their heads and bodies. Frail girls would "jerk" with such violence and astonishing power that strong men could not hold them during the convulsions. The whole congregation would often "jerk" this way for hours at a time under the influence of the Holy Ghost. At the close of one of these services a man undertook to mount his horse while yet in the "jerks." Just as he put his foot in the stirrup and made the effort to mount, he was seized by a paroxysm of the "jerks" which hoisted him entirely over the horse. This he repeated three times, and each time jumped clear over the horse in the effort to mount. Some idea can be formed from this as to the nature and power of "the jerks." Those who were under such influences had no power at all to control themselves or prevent the paroxysms.

The "*holy dance*" was a very common manifestation of the Holy Ghost in those early days. Under the dispensation of the dance, those whom the Spirit operated upon would dance over the house with a recklessness and soulfulness that defied imitation. They would continue to dance till completely exhausted, and then they would go into a trance. This dance seemed to be caused by a nervous excitement. It was evidently not subject to the volition of the dancer. In some instances it was, no doubt, hypocritically feigned; but in all genuine cases of "the holy dance," the dancers were as powerless to control their movements as in the cases of "St. Vitus's dance."

The writer once witnessed a remarkable "out-pouring" of the Holy Ghost which convulsed a congregation of perhaps three hundred people with side-splitting paroxysms of "holy laughter." To the uninitated, it seemed to be a genuine article of unsanctified fun. The meeting was conducted under a bush arbor in the woods, and the altar was well covered with straw. The congregation would kneel in the altar for prayer; in death-like solemnity some old brother would begin to preface an earnest petition by reminding the Lord that we were all weak and sinful creatures, and, whether prepared or unprepared, must all soon appear before the righteous Judge, to give an account of the deeds done in the body—about that time the Holy Ghost would strike some brother and he would go off into a guf-faw of laughter so hearty and natural that the congregation could not refrain from joining in the holy fun. Every body would say "*Praise God*," seeminly in one voice, and then they would all fall over in the straw and roll and laugh as though the Holy Ghost had gotten off a good joke! Women would laugh till they were completely exhausted and then lie perfectly helpless for hours.

During all these exercises, the entire congregation kept up a loud shouting, the preachers exhorted vociferously and the singers made things lively with song. Many of the songs they sang on such occasions have never been seen in print. They sang without books, and relied almost entirely upon memory for the songs. Sometimes the preacher had a hymn-book and would "line the hymns" for the congregation; but this process was entirely too slow for the exigencies of the occasion when things began to "warm up." Books would be laid aside and a few select singers would climb up into the high pulpit and throw themselves vociferously into such songs as:

"O mourners aint you happy and don't you want to go
"To leave this world of sorrow and trouble here below?"

When things began to cool off, the singers would stir them up with a lively rendering of

"Lord I want more religion, yes I want more religion
"Lord I want more religion, to help me on to thee."

Then when one of the mourners would profess religion the singers would move out lively with:

"The devil is mad and I am glad, oh glory hallelujah!
He's lost the soul he thought he had, oh glory hallelujah."

When the whole congregation began to take an interest in the proceedings, and the shouting became somewhat general, the singers would show their keen appreciation of the eternal fitness of things by starting in a lively tune and a brisk movement:

"Shout, shout, we're gaining ground,
"For the love of God is a coming down," etc.

One who has never witnessed such things can scarcely imagine the extent to which they were carried. Only among the colored people of the South can any thing approximating such exercises be found at this day. And it may as well be said here, once for all, that such absurdities in the name of religion were not confined to a little back-woods spot in the hills of North Alabama. While such things continued to a later day down in the mountains of Alabama, perhaps, than in any other part of the country, if the reader will take the trouble to talk with very old people, he will be surprised to learn that such things as are here described prevailed all over the United States within the present century. What Larimore and his boys had to meet in the hills of North Alabama, men of like faith had to combat in every part of the country at an earlier day. All these things were gravely attributed to the Holy Ghost, working in the hearts of the people. Those who could not accept such absurdities as the work of God, were at once denounced as preachers of a dangerous doctrine. It was to no purpose to tell them such things were wholly unknown in the Bible. They knew it was the work of the Spirit, they said, because they had *felt* it, and the work of the Holy Ghost shed abroad in their hearts was good enough for them, no matter what the Bible said. It was time wasted to remind them that the Bible does not give any account of such things attending the meetings held by the apostles. They knew but little, and cared less about what the Bible said. They had felt that wonderful and indescribable ecstacy, and any effort to reason with them about it, or to try to show them that such effects might be produced by something entirely different from the Holy Spirit, they considered as either a reflection upon their honesty or a base scheme to rob them of the only thing that made life enjoyable or heaven attainable. From that moment they looked upon you as their spiritual enemy, a religious fraud and a dangerous character. As well try to reason with a stark lunatic against his favorite hobby, as to try to reason with them against their fanaticism.

It is plain enough to see now why they so bitterly opposed those who denied that the Holy Ghost did all these absurd things in their religious exercises. These absurdities and excesses constituted the whole of their religion. Such trances and frantic capers as have been described, they referred to as religion. To go wildly and blindly into such things was, in the language of the times, to "get religion." How any man could have saving faith and not engage in such tricks before high heaven, was beyond their comprehension. For a man to claim that he believed in a change of heart, but repudiated such fanaticism was, with them, an incomprehensible contradiction of terms. They understoood those things to be a change of heart. It was no use to say you believed in repentance if you could not approve such exercises. To go through such performances was the only repentance they knew any thing about. To put the case clearly, this thing they called "getting religion" was faith, change of heart, repentance, conversion, regeneration, the work of the Holy Ghost and the new birth. Hence, when a man rejected this, he was but a baptized infidel who rejected faith, repentance, prayer, conversion, change of heart, regeneration and the Holy Ghost. They had drifted away from the Bible and had followed the guidance of excited and superstitious imaginations till the whole subject of religion had become one confused and dreamy mass of fuss and feelings without a scintillation of Scripture to support it. If the reader fully comprehends the situation, it will take but few words to explain what Larimore and his boys believed and taught.

Against all those vague fancies and wild theories, they urged the Bible as the only authoritative guide in matters of religion. They insisted that preachers should follow closely the plain teaching of the word of God in the management of all religious exercises. If such things as were being practiced were not taught in the New Testament, then they ought to be abandoned. And what Larimore and his boys did in Alabama, other men of like convictions have done all over the United States since the beginning of the present century. We look back to those days now and smile to think people could ever have so far drifted from the plain teaching of the New Testament as to seriously believe and practice such absurdities. A mighty revolution has been produced in all religious denominations. There are no preachers now in any denomination to champion such follies. The intelligence of all churches speaks now with one voice against such absurdities, and exalts the Bible as the only authoritative guide in the whole process of conversion and Christian development. The change is marvelous, the victory complete; but the fight was fierce and bitter. Those who first assailed such follies, and claimed that the Bible taught nothing like them, drew down upon their devoted heads such a storm of bitter persecution and fierce denunciation as modern times have never witnessed. The whole religious world was against them. And in the darker corners of the country, there are still small minds and narrow souls who harbor bitter feelings against the people who made this fight, gained the victory, and restored the word of God to its place as an authoritative guide in all matters of religion.

But, while such people still oppose us, and not unfrequently misrepresent us, their opposition has dwindled down to a mere inconsistent theoretical distinction on this question where there is no longer a practical difference. Of those who are brought into the various churches at the present day, not one in every hundred—hardly one in every thousand—"*gets religion*" in the old fashioned way.

When we took the New Testament as our only authoritative guide in religion, we found it necessary to oppose, not only the extreme fanaticism so prevalent in all parts of the country, upon the whole question of religion; but to reject, as unscriptural, the whole of the altar exercises in the process of conversion. It appeared from the word of God that the whole process of conversion was clear and simple, and that it consisted of certain well-defined steps which every sinner might take without a moment's confusion or uncertain delay. These steps seemed to be:

(1) To believe in God with all the heart, and to believe in Jesus Christ, the only begotten Son of God. This faith was produced by *testimony*, and included perfect trust in Christ for Salvation. "So then faith comes by hearing, and hearing by the word of God." (Rom. x: 17.) "And many other signs truly did Jesus in the presence of his disciples which are not written in this book; but these are written that you might believe that Jesus is the Christ, the Son of God, and that believing ye might have life through his name." (John xx: 30, 31.)

(2) Such faith touched and changed the heart. "Now when they heard this, they were pricked in their heart, and said unto Peter and to the rest of the apostles, 'Men and brethren, what shall we do?'" (Acts ii: 37.) "And God which knoweth the hearts bare them witness, giving them the Holy Ghost even as he did unto us, and put no dif-

ference between us and them purifying their hearts by faith." (Acts xv: 8, 9.)

(3) The word of God, thus believed, not only touched and purified the heart; but quickened the soul into new and spiritual life. The Spirit of God in conversion thus acted upon the sinners heart *through the word of God.* "It is the Spirit that quickeneth, the flesh profiteth nothing. *The words that I speak unto you, they are spirit, and they are life.*" (John vi: 63.) "For the word of God is quick and powerful, sharper than any two-edged sword, piercing even to the dividing asunder of soul and spirit, and of the joints and marrow, and is a discerner of the thoughts and intents of the heart." (Heb. iv: 12.) "Whosoever believeth that Jesus is the Christ is born of God." (1 John v: 1.) "For though you have ten thousand instructors in Christ, yet have ye not many fathers; for in Christ Jesus I have begotten you *through the gospel.*" (1 Cor. iv: 15.) "Being born again, not of corruptible seed, but of incorruptible, *by the word of God*, which liveth and abideth for ever." (1 Peter i: 23.)

(4) Thus quickened, they were commanded to "Repent and be baptized every one of you in the name of Jesus Christ, for the remission of sins, and ye shall receive the gift of the Holy Ghost." (Acts ii: 38.) They were taught that "Repentance and remission of sins should be preached in his name among all nations, beginning at Jerusalem." (Luke xxiv: 47.) "For with the heart man believeth unto righteousness and with the mouth confession is made unto salvation." (Rom. x: 10.)

With these and many other similar passages of God's word, did they instruct sinners in the way of life. Without frantic excitement or unnecessary delay, sinners were led to believe on the Lord Jesus Christ, repent of their sins, confess their faith in Christ and be baptized. They were buried with Christ "by baptism into death, and like as Christ was raised up from the dead by the glory of the Father" even so they also were taught to walk in newness of life. (Rom. vi: 4.) This, they understood, made men Christians, or disciples of Christ, not Baptists, Methodists, or Presbyterians. Why a Christian should become a Baptist, Methodist, Presbyterian, or any thing else in the way of a religious denomination, Larimore and his boys could not understand. On this point, as on the question of conversion, they insisted that the word of God should be closely followed. It was easy to see that a Christian could do every thing required of him by the word of God and yet not become a Methodist, Baptist, Presbyterian or any thing else in the way of religious denominations. Moreover, no man could become a member of any denomination without doing something the New Testament never required. For this reason they declined to join any denomination. This led them to oppose all denominations as unwarranted by the word of God. To do what God, in the New Testament has required, will make a Christian—will constitute one a member of the church of Christ. Beyond this we can not go if we follow closely the word of God as our guide in all matters of religion.

CHAPTER XXIX.

Several paragraphs of the last chapter, as well as other parts of this book, are in dialect, and they indicate rather a low degree of Bible information and general education. Well, the picture is not overdrawn; still these facts are not brought out simply to amuse the reader, much less to ridicule those dear good people. They were honest of heart and earnest in religion, but it seems necessary to describe things *just as they were*, in order to trace clearly the great changes that have been going on in religious faith and practice during the present century. Let no one mistake the purpose of the author in giving such passages, or lose the lesson he intended to teach by them.

It is well enough to remember, too, that the hill country of North Alabama, which seems so far behind the times, from the passages alluded to, has managed to take care of itself, with all of its disadvantages, and that from its humble homes and illiterate society have come not a few of the brilliant men who have honored the country and distinguished themselves as leaders at the bar, in politics, in commerce, on the battle-field in defense of their homes, and, in fact, in all vocations. And notwithstanding the poverty of the country as regards agriculture, those hills abound in mineral wealth inestimable; and in the development of its resources, this same country now leads all other parts of the State—yea, the whole South—in enterprising industries and material prosperity. Since the time described in these dialect paragraphs, railroads have been built, towns have grown up as if by magic, vast manufacturing industries have been started, and the whole country has been revolutionized. True, much of this has been done by an influx of capital and immigration from other States; but the mountaineers have not been left behind. They are not the sort of people to walk behind anybody's triumphal procession. They have mind and muscle, and they are neither too backward nor too lazy to use both. They have kept their heads above the rapidly rising current, and most of them are still on top with enlarged ideas and sharpened wits, ready for any sort of a tussel future emergencies may precipitate.

Now that the question of "getting religion" is up, it may as well be considered in all its bearings. Those wonderful "bodily exercises" under the "operation of the Holy Ghost" were not confined to the hill country of North Alabama, but they prevailed all over the United States within the present century. In the biography of George Donnell, T. C. Anderson gives some graphic descriptions of revival scenes in North Carolina, Kentucky, and Tennessee early in the present century. It is proper to explain that George Donnell was a Cumberland Presbyterian preacher, and that T. C. Anderson was also a preacher of the same church, and for several years President of the Cumberland University, Lebanon, Tenn. Donnell and Anderson labored together in some of the revivals described in the book. The book was written in 1858, and only ten years before Larimore began to preach in North Alabama. President Anderson firmly believed in every thing described in the book at the time he wrote, and to the day of his death. So this does not leave Alabama so very far behind Tennessee, Kentucky, and North Carolina in abandoning such absurdities, after all. If any reader inclines to think what has been said about revival absurdities in North Alabama is in the least degree exaggerated, they should give careful attention to what President Anderson, a believer in, and practicer of, such things, says about what occurred in Kentucky, Tennessee, and North Carolina under the influence of the "Holy Spirit."

President Anderson traces the history of a people who settled in Ireland from Scotland while Ireland was yet dominated entirely by the Catholic church, and very far sunk in barbarism and gross immorality. These Scotch immigrants in Ireland were called Scotch-Irish, and from them came the famous Scotch-Irish race. They were all Protestants, and principally Presbyterians. They had a hard time to maintain their Protestantism in Catholic Ireland; but by great sacrifices and consuming zeal they held out firmly, and by-and-by began to make great headway converting the Irish Catholics. The Government and the established church interfered, many Scotch-Irish preachers were silenced, some were arrested, and a few executed. This caused the Scotch-Irish to emigrate from there to America, where they settled colonies in North Carolina, Tennessee, and Kentucky. These Scotch-Irish Presbyterians were the leaders in the great camp-meeting revivals in the States named during the first half of the present century. The greatest excitement in these camp-meeting revivals was in the first decade of the present century. After the first decade, such excitement began to decline; but not till within the last twenty years did revival excitements entirely give place to intelligent faith and orderly piety in all parts of the country. In fact, the colored people of the South have not sobered down entirely yet.

President Anderson shows that "the bodily exercises," as he terms them, prevailed under the influence of the Holy Spirit in the revivals held by the Scotch-Irish Presbyterians in Ireland more than a hundred years before any thing of the kind was ever witnessed in America, and from this he argues, I think correctly, that such "bodily exercises" were imported from Ireland to America by the Scotch-Irish Presbyterians who began to establish churches in North Carolina, Tennessee, and Kentucky the latter part of the eighteenth century. He gives the following facts and comments concerning the Scotch-Irish revivals in Ireland:

"To use the language of a quaint historian, 'They fell into such anxiety and terror of conscience that they looked upon themselves as altogether lost and damned.' 'I have seen them myself,' says he, 'struck into a swoon with a word; yea, a dozen in a day carried out of doors as dead—so marvelous was the power of God, smiting their hearts for sin. And these were none of the weaker sex or spirits, but, indeed, some of the boldest spirits, who formerly feared not, with their swords, to put a whole market-town in a fray.' . . . . It is added that this revival was accompanied by 'new and strange bodily exercises. The subjects were violently affected with hard breathing, and convulsions of the body.' The young converts gave the usual manifestations of joy and transport. . . . . Thus was Mr. Glendenning, though a weak man, made the honored instrument in exciting one of those powerful and widely-extended revivals, which, in different ages and countries, have waked the church to life and activity—such as have been witnessed among the *same race* in America. And, like those in our own country, it was attended by certain bodily exercises, the mention of which will not fail to arrest the attention of those who witnessed the great revival of 1800 in Kentucky and Tennessee, and that of 1802 in North Carolina. Those under conviction swooned, fell down, were carried out as dead, had '**convulsions**'—the jerks—lay in a swoon for hours, waked to newness of life, and praised God aloud! How like a Western revival! But they had lay preachers who *rode the circuit*, and preached in private houses. They held anxious-meetings, and gave the mourners *personal* instructions, and thousands were converted, and the whole face of society was changed—just as it was in 1800. How striking the coincidence! Religion, when freed from the trammels of dull formality, is the same in every age and clime."

It is well enough to exclaim, "How like a Western revival!" Strange it did not occur to him to add, "And how *un*like any thing we have read about in the New Testament!" President Anderson succeeds well in tracing the absurdities practiced in American revivals half a century ago and more, to benighted Catholic Ireland something like a century earlier; but this leaves him eighteen hundred years this side of apostolic authority, and not in the best of company either. He takes pains to tell us these same Irish Catholics were well-nigh destitute of morality or civilization—not an astonishing thing after all to find such "bodily exercises" among such a people. The only wonder is that such authority for such astonishing absurdities in relgion should have been satisfactory to the president of a great university only thirty years ago. And when he remarks that "Religion, when freed from the trammels of dull formality, is the same in every age and clime," one can but pity such formalists in religion as Paul, Peter, John, and Christ! If their religion had only been "freed from the trammels of dull formality," we might have had an account of such "bodily exercises" in the New Testament.

Passing from Ireland to America, President Anderson gives the following description of "bodily exercises" under the influence of the Holy Spirit in Kentucky:

As early as the summer of 1797, Mr. McGready began to witness the first fruits of his labors at Gasper, and in 1799 the three churches of his charge were blessed with reviving influences. But these seasons of refreshing were not signalized by any remarkable displays of Divine power until 1798, when the influence of the Spirit became so overwhelming that men of stout hearts and iron will fell down as dead, and, after lying speechless and powerless for hours, would wake to newness of life in Christ. As the practice of calling out the anxious, and conversing and praying with them, had not been introduced, those who were laboring under conviction generally suppressed their feelings until they were overpowered and fell to the ground. And while some lay silent and motionless, others rolled and tossed as one in great agony, uttering the most distressing groans and piteous moanings. The muscles of the face were contracted, as when one is suffering intense pain, and in some cases the whole frame was convulsed with spasmodic action, while the mind was agonized with convictions of sin and awful apprehensions of hell. But when a consciousness of pardon was realized, the muscles relaxed, a heavenly radiance lighted up the countenance, and the tongue became vocal with praise and adoration."

This great meeting was held in Kentucky in June, 1800. Many people attended in wagons from Tennessee, and as the sparsely settled country where the meeting was held could not provide entertainment for all who came from a distance, many who came in wagons camped on the ground. This suggested the idea of a *camp-meeting*. President Anderson says, on this subject:

"Having noticed that those families who camped on the ground, were peculiarly blessed, and foreseeing that it would be impracticable to furnish lodgings for the growing multitudes that congregated to the sacramental-meetings, Mr. McGready conceived the idea of a *camp-meeting*. He therefore made proclamation that at the next meeting, to be held in July, all who were disposed should come in their wagons, furnished with provisions, and prepared to camp on the ground during the meeting."

In another paragraph, referring to this meeting, President Anderson says:

"Much has been written, in latter days, respecting the origin of camp-meetings. The meeting held at Gasper, in Logan county, Ky., July 1800, ... was the 'FIRST CAMP-MEETING EVER HELD IN CHRISTENDOM.'"

As this question of camp-meeting revivals is of historic interest and philosophic importance to those who wish to understand the religious revolution of modern times, President Anderson will be heard in a few paragraphs concerning them:

"The news that there was to be a *camp-meeting* at Gasper, Ky., was circulated in Tennessee. McGee and Hodge, accompanied by many of their congregations, attended this meeting. A vast multitude congregated, the most of whom remained encamped during the meeting. The excitement was intense; many fell prostrate, and some of them lay all night. About forty-five gave evidence of having passed from death in sin to newness of life in Christ. Such, after lying prostrate for hours, would arise with the most brilliant and heavenly expression of countenance, glorifying God for his pardoning mercy. Many left the meeting under the most pungent convictions, some of whom professed on the road, and others after they reached home."

The excitement in these camp-meetings so far surpassed any thing ever before witnessed, that religious people who believed in such bodily exercises began to look upon all their former religious experience as a delusion. Many who had been faithful and consistent members of the church for years lost faith in the genuineness of their conversion and fell into great despondency over their deplorable condition. They renounced all their former experiences, and began again to seek the pardon of their sins and the converting power of the Holy Ghost. On this point President Anderson says:

"It was a remarkable feature of this great revival, from first to last, that convictions for sin, and professions of faith in Christ, were not limited to those beyond the pale of the church. Many who had maintained for years a fair standing in the church, and had never seriously doubted their interest in Christ until they witnessed the displays of Divine power manifested in the progress of this strange work, abandoned their hope, and publicly proclaimed their destitution of spiritual religion; and after days of angnish and despondency, they experienced regeneration and 'joy in the Holy Ghost.' Five of the members of the Shiloh (Tenn.) church professed at the meeting at Gasper (Ky.), and many others at other meetings. When the Shiloh (Tenn.) people returned, they brought the revival with them, and the evening they reached home a revival commenced in the congregation. Samuel King was one of the five church-members that had professed at Gasper, Ky. Solemnly impressed with the conviction that many of the members of the church were resting upon a false hope, content with the outward form of piety while they were destitute of spiritual life in the soul, on his arrival at home he began to warn his friends of the necessity of a radical change of heart, assuring them that religion is a conscious experience of spiritual illumination, revealing the glory of the Savior, and filling the heart with peace and joy. The fervor of his exhortations soon brought some of his associates to their knees, and before the morning light dawned the Sun of righteousness shined into their hearts, revealing the glory of God; and they too were enabled to testify that religion is not a 'dead faith,' but a living principle in the soul. The next day the neighborhood came together for prayer, and some fell prostrate, and were unable to rise until they were regenerated and raised to newness of life in Christ. The revival became general, and by the next Sabbath about twenty had experienced a change of heart, most of whom had been for years orderly and acceptable members of the church. Among the converts within the pale of the church was Richard King, the elder brother of Samuel, and an intelligent and influential man, in the prime of life. His wife, a sister of Dr. James Blythe, and an acceptable member of the church, became deeply concerned about her soul, and after a season of prayer, she fell into despair, and for weeks believed herself doomed to perdition. Her friends induced her to attend one of Mr. McGready's meetings in Kentucky. She seemed indisposed, for a time, to engage in the exercises of the meeting. But her mind became so impressed with a sense of her hopeless condition, that, under the agony of her feelings, she mounted a bench, and began, in a most impressive manner, to exhort the unregenerate to repentance while there was hope, lest despair should overtake them. A crowd gathered around, while she admonished with a fervor and solemnity that carried conviction to the heart. Many inquired, 'Who is that speaking so much like Dr. Blythe?' She exhorted sinners, till, overcome with exhaustion, she sank down, and remained prostrate till she experienced pardon, and then she rose to proclaim a Savior's wondrous love."

According to President Anderson's statement, the first camp-meeting ever held in Christendom was at Gasper, Logan county, Ky., in July, 1790. During the fall of 1800 camp-meetings were held at three points in Sumner county, Tenn., and one in Davidson county, Tenn. At one point in Sumner county three Presbyterian preachers and one Methodist preacher were in attendance. The congregation was the largest that had ever been assembled in the country on any occasion, and the excitement exceeded all that had been witnessed before. President Anderson thus describes it:

"On Sabbath evening more than a hundred fell prostrate. The exercises of singing, prayer, exhortation, and personal conversation were kept up through the night. Monday morning witnessed 'a glorious resurrection.' More than one hundred were translated from the bondage of sin to the light and liberty of the sons of God. During the preceding night the whole encampment resembled a battle-field, resounding with the groans and piteous wailings of the dying; in the morning it became vocal with shouts of joy and rapturous songs of praise."

That is a sample of the way they did at camp-meetings in Tennessee. It will be noted that these camp-meetings originated with the Presbyterians in the year 1800. It was not long, however, till they were adopted by other denominations.

"So admirably adapted were they to the wants of a sparsely-settled country," says President Anderson, "that they were at once adopted by all the principal denominations in the Cumberland Valley; and for many years they were the chief reliance for the promotion of revivals. In the towns and densely populated districts protracted meetings have, of late years, superseded in part, the camp-meetings, but in sparsely settled sections they are, to this day (1858), the favorite meetings with Cumberland Presbyterians."

These camp-meetings, with the wonderful excitement and "bodily exercises" attending them, originated in Kentucky, passed into Tennessee, and, moving on through East Tennessee, reached North Carolina and South Carolina.

"And everywhere," says President Anderson, "they were distinguished by universal displays of Divine power. In East Tennessee and in the Carolinas, it was the same strange, awful, and gracious work of God, attended by the same peculiar manifestations. The jerks, falling down, swooning, trances and transports of rapturous joy, were as common in Carolina, as in the Cumberland, and as they had been a century before in Ireland."

Of camp-meetings and "bodily exercises" in the Carolinas, President Anderson says:

"When the pastor rose to dismiss the service, greatly distressed that the meeting was about to close without any special interest, he essayed to give utterance to his feelings but, overcome with emotion, he sat down without uttering a word. It was a solemn moment—manifest emotion pervaded the congregation. He rose again, but still, unable to speak, he stood silent, struggling with his feelings. At that moment a young man from Tennessee, who had been in the great revival, raising both hands, with a loud voice exclaimed: 'Stand still and see the salvation of God!' In an instant intense excitement thrilled the entire congregation, 'and, as if by an electric shock, a large number, in every direction, fell down.' 'Mingled groans, sobs, and cries for mercy, arose from every part of the house.' 'All thought of dismissing the congregation vanished.' The remainder of the day was spent in prayer, exhortation, singing and personal conversation, and midnight came before the congregation could be persuaded to retire. The excitement continued for a length of time, aud many were hopefully converted to God."

Of another meeting he says:

"Though it was midwinter, multitudes came. The ministers and many of their flocks, reached the encampment on Friday evening, but those of Dr. Hall's congregation who came in wagons, stopped five miles short of the encampment. At evening prayers, a man thirty years of age, who had long been a member of the church, became deeply concerned about his soul, and in a short time almost all the young people in the company were in distress, and the most of the night was spent in prayer, singing, and personal conversations with those under conviction. Next day, when they arrived at the meeting, the excitement soon spread over the whole assembly. That afternoon, towards the close of the public services, a large number fell, in great mental agony. Many obtained comfort, but some lay prostrate all night. On Sabbath morning a number of the anxious retired to the woods for prayer, where many of them 'were struck down,' and lay prostrate all day and all night, and until nine o'clock Monday morning. As it was midwinter, their friends had to furnish them with fire and bedding in the woods."

That some idea may be formed concerning the magnitude of this camp-meeting business, President Anderson remarks:

"Dr. Hall says, 'The number of wagons which came to the ground, was about 180; the number of persons who attended on Sabbath was about 4,000. As an evidence of the intensity of the excitement, it is stated that 'on Saturday a heavy sleet began to fall about nine o'clock, then snow, which turned into rain; this lasted till four in the afternoon; and the day was, without exception, the most unpleasant of any during the whole winter. Notwithstanding this, the people collected at ten, in two assemblies and all ages and sexes stood there exposed until sunset.' 'The work went on, gradually increasing, until Tuesday morning, except a few hours before day on Monday morning, when the camp was chiefly silent.'"

Of another meeting he says:

"The number of wagons present, 262; the number of persons in attendance 8,000 to 10,000. The multitude was divided into four assemblies, in all of which services were conducted simultaneously * * * * Great excitement prevailed. 'Many hundreds were constrained to cry aloud for mercy, of whom many went home rejoicing.'"

Of another meeting he says:

"Six or seven thousand were supposed to have been in attendance. Services were conducted simultaneously in five different places. Religious exercises were kept up day and night, at the stand, in the tents, and in the woods, from Friday till Tuesday. On Monday the excitement was most intense. At the close of the sermon six ministers prayed in succession, and during these prayers many more than a hundred sank down in less than half an hour. At one time there was scarcely a cry to be heard, but shortly afterwards one minister rose to address the assembly, when the excitement was so great that he failed to arrest the attention of more than twenty persons, and he sat down."

Many other meetings were held during the summer and fall of 1802, all of which, were much the same as those already described. The revival is represented as covering a scope of country in North Carolina, that year about one hundred miles wide, by two hundred miles long, and the next year it is said to have prevailed over a large portion of South Carolina.

It may be of interest to the reader to know that "the practice of inviting mourners to present themselves before the pulpit, for prayer and personal instruction had not as yet been introduced, and as to anxious seats, they were not thought of till twenty years afterwards. No means whatever were adopted to induce the serious to distinguish themselves. They were left free to struggle with their convictions, till, overcome by conflicting emotions, they fell prostrate; then they were recognized as fit subjects for prayer and personal instructions. This seems to have been almost the only mark of distinction between those under conviction and the careless. Hence the custom of estimating the success of a meeting by the number that were stricken down, instead of the number of professions," as at a later day.

The meetings in the Carolinas seem to have been fully up to the standard of those of Kentncky and Tennessee, in point of excitement. President Anderson says:

"As in the West, so also in Carolina, intelligent, strong minded men fell as suddenly, and lay many hours as powerless, as if stricken by lightning. Those thus effected did not always receive comfort before they rose, but they generally persevered till they were comforted. These meetings were also attended by those bodily exercises which were so common in the Cumberland country, such as jerks, swooning, falling into a trance, audible groans, and shouting. Of all these affections, the jerks are the most unaccountable."

An effort was made to describe the jerks in a preceding chapter, but as the writer is known to be no believer in the divine origin of such bodily exercises, some may think the description he attempted is an exaggeration. President Anderson, who was a firm believer in such things, and never doubted, but that they were the awful work of God, gives the following description of the jerks:

"A venerable clergyman, returning from a meeting, stopped for the night with a friend. During the evening, his mind was deeply impressed with a sense of the presence, holiness and majesty of God. After family worship, a sense of the presence of a pure and holy God overawed him; it seemed to him he should sink under it. He walked out to get by himself, and started to go across a little piece of corn, towards a small retired valley. Before he could reach the retirement, he was seized in a most surprising manner. Suddenly he began leaping about, first forward, then sidewise, and sometimes, standing still, he would swing backward and forward, see-saw fashion. This motion of the body was both involuntary and irresistible at the commencement; afterwards there was scarcely a disposition to resist it, and in itself the motion was neither painful nor unpleasant. The people in the house, hearing the noise, came to his relief, and carried him to the dwelling. The paroxysm lasted about an hour, during which, if the attendants let go their hold, he would jerk about the room as he had done in the field. Gradually it passed away, and he retired to rest, humbled at the exhibition he had made. The next day, while calmly conversing with a friend about the meeting, he was suddenly seized again and jerked across the room, and continued under the influence of the exercise about fifteen minutes."

Of the jerks in East Tennessee at a later date President Anderson says:

"Great excitement prevailed; some shouted, and others were affected with the jerks. One man was jerked under the benches, and continued jerking while under them, till he was extricated by his friends. This strange affection was common in East Tennesse, as elsewhere, during the prevalence of the great revival of 1801, till 1818. It is said that Dr. Samuel Doak, who was much prejudiced against the exercise, was subject to it; and that on one occasion, while in the pulpit, he was seized with a paroxysm, and jerked so violently as to throw his wig from his head into the congregation."

These strange bodily exercises were carried to such extremes that many of the more sober minded religious people protested against such absurdities. It never occurred to any of them that such things were purely nervous excitements, and that God operates in an entirely different manner upon the hearts of sinners. They all believed in what is now termed the abstract operation of the Spirit of God upon the hearts of sinners; but some of them protested against these excesses on the ground of disorderly conduct in the worshipers. A sharp controversy arose, of which Preident Anderson gives the following samples of argument in support of the revival methods:

"They call themselves friends to the work of God; but the uncommon bodily exercises they term the excressences of it, and wish to suppress them. Alas! shall crawling worms of the dust pretend to direct Almighty, or lay down plans for infinite, unerring wisdom to carry on his work? I am often shocked and terrified, when I hear ministers and sober professors speaking of jerks, falling down, loud outcries, dancing, shouting,, etc., with contempt and ridicule; and wishing to see a revival of religion carried on in another form. But they say these things are not religion, nor essential to it. I say the same. But it is evident that an infinite God, for wise purposes, has permitted falling down, loud outcries, jerking, dancing, shouting, laughing, etc., to attend this mighty revival of his work, in every part of our country where it has prevailed, and though these exercises and bodily agitations are not essential to the work, yet Jehovah has thought it proper that they should be attached to it. Therefore is it not fit and proper that such creatures as we are should submit to his sovereign will, and rejoice to see the Lord's work going on in whatever form Eternal Wisdom thinks best? Is it not daring presumption for the potsherds of the earth to call the Almighty to order, to direct the operations of his Spirit, or to demand of him why or what he does? * * * Tell my Christian friends and brethren, to let the Lord choose his own way of working; to bid the Spirit of God welcome, even though he should choose to work among them (Presbyterians) as he works among the Methodists."

In another paragraph, he speaks of the prejudice against these revival methods on this wise:

"But when he saw people falling down by the hundred, and heard their dismal groans and loud cries for mercy, mingled with prayers, exhortations, songs of praise, and shouts of joy, the scene was so strange, so different from any thing he had ever witnessed before, that he was utterly confounded. Said he: 'This, to me, perfectly new and sudden sight, I viewed with horror, and, in spite of all my previous reasoning upon revivals, with some degree of disgust. Is it possible, said I, that this scene of seeming confusion can come from the Spirit of God? Can He who called light from darkness, and order from confusion, educe light, and order from such a dark mental and moral chaos?' But despite the prejudices of Dr. McCorkle, he found, amid this confusion and chaos, an angel, in the person of a little girl, about seven years old, reclining, with her eyes closed, in the arms of a female friend. And O, what a serene, angelic smile was on her face! If ever heaven was enjoyed in any little creature's heart, it was enjoyed in hers. * * * * But so strong were his prejudices, that he debarred this little angel from communion, because he found her deficient in doctrinal knowledge. * * * While praying over his son, he became so deeply interested, not only for his conversion, but for the conversion of the world, and so overwhelmed with a sense of the goodness and ineffable glory of God, that all doubt was dispelled, and ever after he engaged cordially and zealously in the promotion of the gracious work."

This is a fair sample of the arguments, if indeed it be lawful to call such things arguments, by which such revival methods and bodily exercises were maintained. As this controversy over revival methods caused the division in the Presbyterian church which led to the establishment of the Cumberland Presbyterian Church, and as the writer of the book quoted from was a Cumberland Presbyterian, and a believer in the revival methods, it is safe to say he selects for this book the *strongest arguments* ever offered in support of such methods. Yet it is a remarkable fact that in all the arguments he gives, *not one passage of Scripture is quoted or cited in support of such things.* Dr. McCorkle gravely doubted such things, and was converted to them by the looks of a seven-year-old girl with her eyes shut, and too ignorant of the teaching of the Bible to be deemed worthy to commune! This was pretty much the state of things in North Alabama, when Larimore and his boys began to preach through that country. The excitement had somewhat abated, but Scripture intelligence had not perceptibly increased. Revivalists had succeeded in "calling God to order," to some extent, but no progress had been made or attempted in teaching the people the Scriptures. People had ceased to jerk and dance, but they still shouted, clapped their hands, mourned, and, occasionally laughed the holy laugh.

Larimore and his boys undertook to change the procedure; but they did not "call God to order." They boldly took the ground that God did not work in that way. They claimed that God's Spirit reached man's heart, not through an excited imagination or unstrung nervous organization; *but through the understanding.* They took the position that the Holy Spirit in conversion operates through the word of God, and effects man's heart through his understanding. This is the issue that has been sharply contended for these many years.

In a discussion of this question with a Methodist preacher in West Tennessee in 1879, the inimitable John S. Sweeney described the scenes familiar to him in younger days—scenes similar to those described in this chapter—and then said:

"That is the thing I began to oppose many years ago. That is the thing my brethren have been opposing all over the United States for fifty years and more. In the beginning of this reformation, we said that sort of thing was not the work of God at all, and for saying that we have been denounced, misrepresented and persecuted as no other religious people have been in this country during all these years. And yet I venture to say my opponent in this discussion will not undertake to defend such absurdities as we started out to oppose fifty years ago. No body believes in or practices such things now. My brethren may never receive the credit due them in this great reformation; but they have essentially modified and well nigh corrected entirely, the absurdities that prevailed all over the country in the memory of people yet living on this question of the operation of the Spirit on the hearts of men in conversion."

CHAPTER XXX.

What I have written in this book is not, exclusively, history, nor biography, nor theology; but something of all these combined. I have tried to describe *things as they were*, within the memory of people yet living. Many pages in this book are but descriptions of scenes and incidents to which I have been an eye-witness, and every thing that is related as truth or described as fact can be substantiated by creditable witnesses, upon whose testimony I have written. I have not tried to follow any chronological order of events. The design of the book is to show that there has been a marked change in this country within the present century, especially in religious doctrine and customs. To bring out this change in the clearest manner, it is not necessary—perhaps not best—to try to follow chronological order too closely, or attempt to determine the exact day and hour when we put away the crude ideas and traditions of our religious fathers and began to follow more closely the plain teaching of the word of God in religious matters. The better plan is to note carefully the peculiarities of the prevailing religious doctrine and customs twenty to eighty years ago, and leave the reader to contrast those things with what he knows to be the teaching and practice of religious people now. It would be difficult, perhaps impossible, to tell just when this great change occurred; but that it *has* occurred no one can doubt. The fact is, it never occurred at any particular time any more than an acorn can become an oak at any specific moment of time. This great change is a process which has been going on over a period of time reaching back toward the beginning of the present century. It has been so gradual that those who have lived through it hardly appreciate its full proportions. It is not easy to tell the exact day and hour when, in the natural order of development, a pig becomes a hog, a colt a horse, or a boy a man. But if we observe carefully the peculiarity of pigs, colts, and boys, it is easy to see the wide difference between them and hogs, horses, and men. And in no other way can we so well understand the magnitude of the change wrought in the process of development.

In referring to those absurdities in the religious doctrine and practices of early days, no particular church has been mentioned. They were peculiar to no church, but common to all churches. In organization and written creeds, the *churches then* were much the same as *now*. The great change is in that common religion which lies outside of all churches, and which everybody must partake of as an essential qualification to membership in any church. One could not have a choice between joining a church that believed and practiced such things, and joining one which rejected them entirely, in the early days before the men of like faith with Larimore and his boys protested against those things. Until such men began an earnest fight against such excesses and absurdities, they were everywhere recognized as an essential part—almost the whole process and substance—of religion. One could accept them and be religious, or reject them and be irreligious. It was not till the beginning of the second quarter of this century that any considerable number of people grasped the idea that one might reject all these absurdities and yet be religious. Those who first caught the idea that such excesses were abuses of religion and not essential parts of it, saw also, as clearly in the sunbeams, that they had a different origin from religion. Religion, or Christianity, with them came from God by revelation, and is taught in the inspired book as a system of moral and spiritual regeneration and government; while these excesses and absurdities sprang from excited, benighted and superstitious imaginations, and were taught by tradition. The whole question hinged upon the origin of man's religious ideas, and the manner in which they are received. Those who believed and practiced the absurdities described, understood man received his religion by miracle and through immediate inspiration, and that he should follow the guidance of a light within him—his feelings, intuitions, and imaginations—in matters of religion. Those who rejected such things contended that man received his religion from God, *but not by miracle now, neither by immediate inspiration.* They contended that the day of miracles was past, and that God made his last revelation by inspiration and miracle *through the writers of the New Testament.* Man, therefore, receives his religion *by inspiration through the New Testament*, and in all matters of religion he must follow the guidance of that holy book. This narrowed the whole controversy down to a well-defined issue concerning our authoritative guide in religious matters. Shall we follow our *feelings*, or the *word of God?* That was the issue, and upon that issue the battle was fought and won. The religious world was asked to leave off following dreams, superstitions, intuitions, feelings, and traditions in religious matters, and to be governed by the teaching of the New Testament. Conversion, regeneration, the new birth, and the whole process of Christian development were divested of every thing miraculous and mysterious, and taught as great moral and spiritual changes wrought by the power of the Most High upon and in the spirit of man *through the inspired word.* Spiritual birth and the development of Christian character were understood to be results wrought out in the plainest manner through instrumentalities adapted to such ends, and no more mysterious or miraculous than natural birth and the growth of a physical body. Divine ideas, communicated to New Testament writers by inspiration, are conveyed to the spirit of man now *through the words of the New Testament.* These ideas quicken man's spirit into a new and spiritual life when he believes and obeys the teaching of the New Testament. This is what it is to be born again. Hence it is said, "Whosoever believeth that Jesus is the Christ is born of God"—"For in Christ Jesus I have begotten you through the gospel"—"Being born again, not of corruptible seed, but of incorruptible, by the word of God, which liveth and abideth forever," etc., etc. Spiritual life, thus inaugurated by believing and putting into practice spiritual ideas communicated from God to the writers of the New Testament by inspiration, and conveyed to man by the words used by New Testament writers, was to be developed—made to grow to the stature of a perfect man in Christ Jesus—by continuing to receive and practice spiritual ideas from the same source. Hence such Scripture as, "As new-born babes, desire the sincere milk of the word, that you may grow thereby." 1 Peter ii: 2. "But grow in grace and in the knowledge of our Lord and Savior Jesus Christ." 2 Peter iii: 18. "Till we all come in the unity of the faith, and of the knowledge of the Son of God, unto a perfect man, unto the measure of the stature of the fullness of Christ." Eph. iv: 13. "And now, brethren, I commend you to God, *and to the word of His grace,* which is able to build you up, and to give you an inheritance among all them which are sanctified." Acts xx: 32.

As no one church was more responsible than others for the state of things referred to, so all churches have been affected to the same extent and in the same way by the change. It was a change in the process of preparing persons for membership in all churches, rather than a modification of the distinctive creed of any particular church. Hence all churches were committed against it, and united in opposing it. When the change came against the protest and active opposition of all churches, it had to be accepted by all alike. Experiences of grace; the tedious process of the old-time altar exercises in "getting religion;" dreams and trances; "the jerks," and the "holy laugh;" the "holy dance," and vague visions; wild excitement and vociferous "shouting;" mysterious impressions and ecstatic feelings; miraculous regeneration and darkened imaginations—all these things went together and in the same way. They all gave place to the plain teaching of the New Testament as an authoritative guide in religious matters. All churches accepted the change and adapted their methods in conversion to the new order of things. The change came first in cities and towns, then gradually extended over rural districts. It came slowly, but it came surely and to stay.

In speaking of Larimore and his boys in connection with this great religious revolution in certain regions in Alabama, it is not to be understood that no part of the work was done by men in no way connected with Mars' Hill College. There were great and godly men who labored extensively and with splendid results in helping on the great religious revolution in that country, but who were in no way connected with Mars Hill College. I am not unmindful of the value of the labors of such men, or unappreciative of the sacrifices they made. Jesse Wood, J. M. Pickens, A. C. Henry, J. M. Barnes, and many others whom I either never knew personally or do not now call to mind, rendered invaluable service in the good work. I speak more particularly of Larimore and his boys because, (1) they perhaps did more than any other one body or collection of workers in that particular locality; (2) they fairly represented the revolutionary idea, and collectively attracted more attention than any other one body of workmen; (3) I knew them, and therefore could speak more fully as to the obstacles they met and overcame, and the results they accomplished. The truth is, this great change, or revolution, was not effected by Larimore and his boys, or any other man or body of men; *but by an idea.* Larimore and his boys believed and advocated that idea, but they did not originate it. Long before any of them were born, hundreds of great and good men all over the United States were making a determined fight against the vagaries and absurdities of popular religion with the watch-word and battle-cry of "WHERE THE SCRIPTURES SPEAK WE WILL SPEAK, AND WHERE THE SCRIPTURES ARE SILENT WE WILL BE SILENT." Larimore and his boys, with others who cooperated with them, caught the spirit of the contest and carried the revolution into Alabama. This idea of exalting the Scriptures as the only authoritative guide and the all-sufficient rule of faith and practice in religious matters, was what did the work. To the extent men accepted this idea they modified their excesses and turned away from their superstitious dreams and vague fancies in religion. This idea was fundamental to all religion and revolutionary in its tendency. It permeated all churches, and affected, more or less, all society outside of the churches. Those who grasped its full import saw at once that it could never be harmonized with existing religious creeds and denominations, and therefore they carried it to its logical and inevitable consequences at once, in rejecting all creeds and declining to unite with any denomination. They stood aloof from all denominational organizations, preached the gospel, baptized believers, assembled every Lord's day for prayers, exhortations, reading the Scriptures and breaking bread in holy communion. They were not Baptists, Presbyterians, or Methodists; but Christians—disciples of Christ—brethren in Christ. They did not belong to any church in the denominational sense, and yet they constituted churches of Christ all over the country, wherever they assembled, to observe the appointments of the New Testament, there they constituted a church of Christ in the New Testament sense. They never formed any general or ecclesiastic or denominational organization. They never acknowledged any names or individuals or churches, save such undenominational titles as are applied by New Testament writers to disciples of Christ and churches of Christ. They formulated no creed, neither did they concede to any ecclesiasticism, convention, council, or constituted authority in the church the right to formulate a creed for individuals in the church. They held that the New Testament was not simply a revelation from God to an ecclesiastic council to be interpreted and delivered to lay members as a religious guide in the form of a denominational creed; but rather a revelation from God through inspired men to individual sinners and disciples of Christ, to be interpreted and followed by each individual for himself, without dictation or interference of ecclesiastic courts or councils. Religion was individualized; men walked by faith, in the new order, or rather in the return to the apostolic order, the same as in the the numerous churches;

but each man was presumed to walk by his own faith, and was considered competent to study the New Testament for himself, and formulate his own faith according to its teaching. It needed not a council of the wise men of the church to tell what members of the church believed. Each man was supposed to be able to believe for himself from the teaching of the New Testament, and was left perfectly free to form his faith—and express it too, for that matter—in accordance with his understanding of God's word. "So then faith cometh by hearing, and hearing by the word of God." (Rom. x: 17.) This was widely different from the ordinary way of formulating the faith of a whole denomination by a constituted council of a few wise men in the denomination. Men no longer waited for the assembly of a few wise men in the church to determine what they believed; but each man threw all such formulated creeds to the winds, and studied the New Testament for himself, that he might formulate his own faith according to his understanding of the teaching of that book. This greatly stimulated individual investigation, and wonderfully increased the general knowledge of the Scriptures among the people. It also liberated individual consciences, and broke the fetters of creeds and ecclesiastic dictation off the individual intellects of religious people. Men began to understand that God had spoken to each individual in the New Testament, and not merely to councils and ecclesiasticisms, and they began to assert their right to think for themselves and to form their faith for themselves from their own investigations and understanding of the New Testament. As this idea gradually permeated the religious denominations, a still more serious revolution than that concerning the process of conversion was inaugurated. When lay members began to study the New Testament for themselves and to form their own faith from the teaching of the Scriptures, they found that their denominational councils had not fairly represented them in formulating their faith in church creeds. It began to be clearly understood that no councils or ecclesiastic committees can possibly state fairly and clearly what whole denominations, consisting of hundreds of thousands of members, believe. The fact forced itself upon them that no man can possibly formulate clearly, and fairly state, what another man believes. The most any man can do, no matter how great and good he may be, is to formulate his own faith and tell what he himself believes. When the lay members found their creeds did not fairly represent them as an expression of their faith, it began to be a grave question as to whose faith the creeds really did represent and fairly express. It required no very tedious investigation to discover that at most, no creed could safely be assumed to express the faith of any one except those who made it. Those who had no voice in formulating a creed might believe it all, it is true, and it might, moreover, fairly and fully express all they did believe; but this fact could not be *known* nor fairly *assumed.* But a closer investigation called attention to the fact that, as several men engaged in the formation of each creed, no two of whom, perhaps, believed exactly the same things on all the questions which the creed proposed to settle authoritatively, every such creed derived its existence from *liberal compromises* as to individual convictions, or faith, and hence represented nobody fairly and fully. It is very probable that no creed ever fully and fairly represented the faith of any living soul on every question it presumed to settle authoritatively.

The denominational world was brought to face a very serious problem on this question of creeds. No body seemed to believe them. It became an imperative necessity, therefore, to either abandon creeds altogether, or modify very materially the use made of them. It was quite evident that they could no longer be used as dictations of faith to which church members must subscribe without mental reservation or individual liberty of conscience, or intellect to think and believe for themselves regardless of the dictum of such creeds. Referring to this stage in the great change or religious revolution wrought by this return to the New Testament as authoritative guide in religious matters, Dr. Kelley, a leading, and talented preacher of the Methodist church, in May 1889, in a speech at Columbia, Tennessee, before the Scotch-Irish congress, aptly expressed the situation by saying, creeds had to be used simply as *mile-posts* and not as *anchors*. Their authoritative reign was ended; but they were permitted to occupy a sort of honorary position as giving a general idea, in condensed form of the peculiarities of denominations. Men were no longer compelled to believe every thing in them, or prohibited from speaking openly against anything they contained, in order to maintain membership in denominations under them. It is among the unheard-of things now-a-days, for a man to be excluded from membership in any denomination because he does not believe every thing taught in the creed of such denomination. It is now deemed quite the proper thing for members in all denominations to boldly express dissent from the formulated doctrines of such denominations as found in the creeds. All this is but the working of the great idea of appealing directly to the word of God as the authoritative guide in all questions of religion. Thus has a single revolutionary idea completely changed the whole process of conversion, and effectually broken the dominance of denominational creeds in religion, within the memory of people yet living.

When once men found themselves free from, and superior to, creeds in matters of religious faith, and each one began to formulate his own faith from his study, and understanding of the New Testament, denominational fences began to give way. Men often found themselves at issue with each other in the same denomination, in the formula of their own individual faith—a faith each had thought out and formed for himself from his own study and understanding of the New Testament—while at the same time agreements were unexpectedly discovered between individuals across denominational lines. While Methodists with Methodists were not always agreed, sometimes a strange harmony of faith or convictions would be discovered between an individual Methodist and a certain Presbyterian.

It therefore became necessary to relax denominational barriers and limitations after the same manner the authority of creeds had been modified. It was clear enough that denominations could no longer hold absolute monopoly and uncircumscribed authority over their members. The example of tolerance in matters of faith and fellowship, notwithstanding material differences of convictions, had been set in the solution of the creed question, and the precedent soon prevailed to a wider extent in a free and general interdenominational co-operation and fellowship. Men retained their formal connection with denominations, but reserved the right to carry their Christian co-operation and fellowship beyond their denominational limits without hindrance or interference of ecclesiastic authorities. This feeling in favor of Christian union and general co-operation in the broad field of religious endeavor without regard to denominational lines, grew rapidly and soon became so great that "union meetings" were the rule instead of the exception, and the most successful evangelists conducted their work entirely upon an undenominational basis. That the abandonment of human creeds; a complete change in the whole process of conversion and Christian development; the destruction of all denominations and the union of all Christians—that all these would inevitably result from a return to the New Testament as the only authoritative guide in matters of religion, the great leaders in this revolution firmly believed and boldly preached from the very beginning. The changes that have everywhere followed the adoption of this idea, make the sermons of those grand old leaders of fifty years ago and more read like prophecy. This great change or revolution has been slow and gradual and the many factors in it have, perhaps, not always been conscious of the part they performed or the full meaning of the principles they proclaimed. A greater tolerance and a broader liberty in religious doctrine and practice have kept pace with the idea of returning to the New Testament as the only authoritative guide and all-sufficient rule of faith and practice in religion. There have been those who tried to follow the New Testament with very narrow denominational ideas, and others whose undenominational ideas and feelings were commendably liberal while their knowledge of the New Testament was shamefully defective; but both of these classes were dwarfs. They were one-ideaed, lop-sided misrepresentatives of the true spirit of the age. The real revolutionary idea is fidelity to the New Testament in doctrine and practice, and liberty of individual consciences and intellects in all matters of religious opinions. As we come up to this idea, the process of conversion and Christian development conforms to the plain teaching of the New Testament; Christian love takes the place of denominational excommunication; conventions and councils, to formulate creeds, give place to general individual study of, and faith in, the word of God; faith comes from original study of the New Testament to each individual member, rather than from the edicts of ecclesiastic councils to whole denominations *en-masse*; men forget they are Methodists, Baptists and Presbyterians in their love for each other as Christians; and faith in the Lord Jesus Christ and obedience to His commandments are universally recognized as the only tests of Christian fellowship and conditions of eternal salvation.

It remains to notice the one fundamental and comprehensive article of faith in the Christian's creed. "Thou art the Christ, the Son of the living God." (Matt. xvi: 16.) This is the one proposition fundamental to the whole Christian religion. The whole superstructure of Christianity is founded upon the assumption that Jesus is divine in nature and supreme in power. Our whole dependence for salvation is in Him, and upon Him do all our faith and hopes rest. If He is the Christ, the Son of the living God, our faith is well founded and all our hopes may be realized; if not, our faith is a myth, and our hopes are delusions. This proposition underlies the whole fabric of the Christian religion, "Thou art Peter, and upon this rock I will build my church and the gates of hell shall not prevail against it." At this, we may draw the line of Christian fellowship and Christian communion. Those who do not believe it are not of us, and should not be with us. Those who do believe it in sincerity and in truth will not renounce His authority or neglect to obey His commandments. Does any one ask for our fellowship in Christ, we can only say: "If thou believest with all thine heart thou mayest." (Acts viii: 37.) Does any one confess: "I belive that Jesus Christ is the Son of God?" (Acts viii: 37.) Then by what authority can we refuse to baptize him into the fellowship of the saints and full participation of all the blessings of the church of God? Our faith is not in a dogma, or doctrine; but in a divine *person.* Christ becomes the model of our lives and the hope of our souls. Faith in him and conformity of our lives to the example He left us in His own faultless character, will save us from sin, perfect us in Christian virtues and secure for us all spiritual blessings in heavenly places in Him, here and hereafter. The whole sum and substance of Christianity may thus be reduced to faith in Christ and obedience to His commandments. Beyond this, men should not be restricted in opinions or circumscribed in investigations. When we believe in Christ and obey His commandments, we are Christians. Having done this, if we differ, we should differ as Christians—as brethren in the Lord—and not make our differences, denominational barriers which interdict Christian love, destroy brotherly fellowship, prevent successful co-operation, and promote party strife and ugly contentions.

Perhaps we may claim too much for Larimore and his boys and men of like faith in the great religious revolution of this century; but certainly we can not claim too much for the principle on which the revolution has proceeded. To what extent that principle has prevailed through the advocacy of those who, from the first, have stood aloof from all denominational organizations and have fully comprehended all the logical tendencies and results of its adoption, it is difficult to determine. The general disposition and determination to leave off following such absurd fancies and superstitions as have been described, and to return to the teaching of the New Testament as the authoritative and all-sufficient guide on all religious questions, must be recognized by all who reflect, as the cause of this great revolution. But how much of that determination resulted from the advocacy of the men referred to, and how much of it sprang from the manifest absurdities of popular religion and the wide-spread dissatisfaction with prevailing superstitions—these are questions not so easily settled. It seems that the religious world followed *feelings*, *dreams*, *impressions* and *superstitions* till there was general dissatisfaction with the result. The theory demonstrated its own folly by *reductio ad absurdum*, and broke down completely of its own inherent weakness. There was a universal and almost simultaneous revolt against such a system. Without consultation or concert of action, great and good men in different countries and in all denominations called a halt and began to preach a change, about the same time. Every body seemed more or less dissatisfied with things as they were, and the times were ripe for the revolution. But, whether or not we can tell how much of the change was due to Larimore and his boys and men of like faith, and how much was due to the readiness of men to receive such an idea, this one thing we do know, viz: those who receive the New Testament as the only authoritative and all-sufficient guide in religious matters, have the principle that has saved the Christian religion from the absurdities described in this book, broken the authority of uninspired creeds; crushed the narrow spirit of religious bigotry; established a broad Christian liberty in defiance of ecclesiastic restraints; weakened the denominational fences; inaugurated Christian union and co-operation across denominational limits—in a word, *revolutionized* religious doctrine and practice within the memory of people yet living. A principle that has done all this is not a bad thing in the way of a theological tool. It is a good thing to take along, and there is much more good service in it yet. If wisely used it will accomplish yet greater things than these. "*Where the Scriptures speak we speak, and where the Scriptures are silent we will be silent.*" A simple little thing is that; but my, what a weapon against religious error of every sort! It never goes off prematurely, hangs fire, or misses the mark! It is serviceable anywhere, and a sure dependence in every emergency. It will be a dark day for the Christian religion when preachers grow tired of using it.

www.ingramcontent.com/pod-product-compliance
Lightning Source LLC
LaVergne TN
LVHW091023080826
845145LV00002B/334

* 9 7 8 1 5 8 4 2 7 1 6 4 2 *